Persuasion in Advertising

Effective adve
tising seeks to
most likely to
advertising su
adopt and illu

Offering no
Persuasion in
incorporated
difficulties of
techniques an

To illumin
as diverse as
as recent adve

A genuinel
book is essent

John O'Shaugh
Senior Associate
Cambridge. He is a
is Professor of Ma
published in many E
marketing.

Persuasion in Advertising

John O'Shaughnessy and Nicholas Jackson O'Shaughnessy

Routledge
Taylor & Francis Group

LONDON AND NEW YORK

First published 2004
by Routledge
11 New Fetter Lane, London EC4P 4EE

Simultaneously published in the USA and Canada
by Routledge
29 West 35th Street, New York, NY 10001

Routledge is an imprint of the Taylor & Francis Group

© 2004 John O'Shaughnessy and Nicholas Jackson O'Shaughnessy

Typeset in Bell Gothic and Perpetua by
Florence Production Ltd, Stoodleigh, Devon

Printed and bound in Great Britain by
The Cromwell Press, Trowbridge, Wiltshire

British Library Cataloguing in Publication Data
A catalogue record for this book is available from the British Library

Library of Congress Cataloging in Publication Data
O'Shaughnessy, John.
    Persuasion in advertising/by J. O'Shaughnessy & N.J. O'Shaughnessy.
    – 1st ed.
        p. cm.
    Includes bibliographical references and index.
    1. Advertising – Psychological aspects.   2. Persuasion (Psychology)
    I. O'Shaughnessy, Nicholas J.   II. Title
    HF5822.084 2003
    659.1'01'9–dc21   2003011531

ISBN 0–415–32223–5 (hbk)
ISBN 0–415–32224–3 (pbk)

Contents

List of case studies   vii
List of advertisement examples   viii
Preface   ix
Acknowledgements   xi

1   What facilitates persuasion and what inhibits it?   **1**

2   Rationality, symbolism and emotion in persuasion   **25**

3   Persuasive advertising appeals, 1   **55**

     Association with social norms, values and valued images 64
     Solidarity with others 80
     Status and prestige 83

4   Persuasive advertising appeals, 2   **93**

     Associations tied to the mental modes of seeking excitement
       and experiencing relaxation (reversal theory) 93
     Associations tied to positive or negative reinforcements
       (behaviourism/conditioning) 99

5   Persuasive advertising appeals, 3: cognitive approaches   **121**

     Hierarchy of effects models 123
     The elaboration likelihood model 126
     The persuasive communication approach 130
     Consistency theory 150

6   **Persuasive advertising appeals, 4**   **165**

   Psychoanalytic psychology 166
   Zaltman Metaphor Elicitation Technique (ZMET) 171
   Psychology of the adaptive unconscious 173

   Notes   197
   Index   209

Case studies

Stella Artois   48

The Oxo Family   86

Mecca Cola   88

Death Cigarettes   114

Renault Clio   155

Gold Blend   160

Advertisement examples

1.1   Getting attention: Oliver Sweeney   2

1.2   Managing our perspectives: McDonald's   22

2.1   Symbolizing the brand: Silk Cut   26

2.2   Rational argument: Pilkington Glass   46–7

3.1   The call to solidarity: Bombardier   56

3.2   Celebrity sophistication: Omega   84

3.3   Nostalgia: Panerai   85

4.1   Excitement – the paratelic mode: Oliver Sweeney   94

5.1   Creating metaphor: Ford Focus   122–3

5.2   Reconciling cognitive dissonance: BMW   154–5

Preface

Effective advertising is, almost always, persuasive advertising; and advertising that does not seek to persuade (relying, for example, on attention getting or repeated exposure effects alone) is really missing an opportunity. In a competitive situation those who persuade best are those most likely to win. Persuasion is always important, even where the competition is inept. This book seeks to explain how advertising persuades, and sets out the strategies for advertisers to adopt. Its specific contribution is to draw out the implications for marketing managers of research on persuasion done outside the field of marketing academe (for example, in social psychology, linguistics and sociology) but highly relevant to it and, as yet, almost invisible in the extant marketing literature.

This literature tends not to suggest an explanation of how advertising works, providing rules without a bedrock of understanding and offering nothing by way of explanatory theory. It does not make persuasion the main focus but concentrates on, for example, the management of advertising. Our argument is that persuasion is the most neglected area in advertising texts. We seek to remedy that literary deficiency with a more conceptual and theory-based approach. We draw on empirical research that is here, for the first time, incorporated in a marketing text.

The extant literature of advertising seems to focus almost exclusively on the functional areas, such as the construction of a campaign, media buying, budgeting, testing and measurement, analysis of famous campaigns and the ideas of eminent copywriters. It is, abundantly, a technical-professional literature, possibly discussing some psychological concepts at the margin – e.g. the Petty/Cacioppo model (see p. 127) – but remaining at the applied level. Thus there are no books on persuasion that are tied specifically to advertising. Most texts on marketing deal implicitly with effective (read 'persuasive') advertising, but permeating many accounts is a general belief that we are not sure how advertising works. This book explains how, by analysing persuasion in detail and then discussing strategies tied to these analyses.

Thus we seek to advance a framework that ties the findings of modern scholarship on persuasion together in a way suited to solving marketing problems. For instance, we claim that *perspectives* are a critical paradigm, and we discuss what persuasion strategies might be enlisted in order to exploit them. We maintain that persuasive messages must 'resonate' with their target audience; logic alone may fail, since meaning must cohere with perspective (beliefs, desires). This is true of every kind of argument, whether statistical, anecdotal or even visual. Thus perspective remains the parameter within which persuasion ought to function, and assertions are manipulated to fit it (but if the target audiences do not have the 'right' perspective, this can be changed – not by logic but by the offer of a more appealing perspective, by emotional appeal to their values or by indirect persuasion via rhetoric, in particular, the branch of rhetoric called metaphor (to defamiliarize the familiar), by redefining the situation or by asking questions).

This may be a book informed by theory, but it is no arid text. Abstract concepts are grounded and made relevant in two principal ways. First, the implications of the theory for practical managers are given in considerable detail at the end of each chapter; this clarifies and refreshes the text, and anchors it in everyday application. Second, ideas are enlivened and made vivid with a very broad spectrum of cultural examples from the media, literature, politics and history as well as from business and marketing. Original case studies illuminate the text and further ground abstractions in real-life examples; in addition, we suggest a few of the numerous possible theoretical perspectives on these cases. The theories, experimental evidence and thinking from the social sciences are summarized in plain language, in a simple but not simplistic tone, and their relevance to companies seeking to advertise is clarified. Implications for advertising norms, standards, strategies and tactics are emphasized.

This book is not, however, for every student at every business school, but is a niche product. It can function either as a supplement to standard or advanced courses in advertising, or as a self-standing course focusing on the role, meaning and explanation of persuasion in this area. At a more restricted level, this book is essential intellectual background for most marketing Ph.D.s and all marketing academics, whether or not they have a direct interest in advertising.

If accepted, these new approaches may radically challenge our thought, custom and practice in this most critical area for every kind of business in every kind of market. Through history, views on the nature of the power of advertising have ranged from the abusive ('Caliban emerging from his slimy cavern', Lord Hailsham) to the lyrical ('Promise, large Promise, is the Soul of an Advertisement', Dr Samuel Johnson), to the slick ('We don't sell cosmetics, we sell Hope', Charles Revson). Less speculative and more informed judgement would locate the study of advertising effectiveness in the study of persuasion and, from this new theoretic realm, generate practical solutions for practical people.

Acknowledgements

The authors would like to thank the following for their kind cooperation in allowing the reproduction of images used in their advertising campaigns:

BMW
Bombardier
Charles Wells and Team Saatchi
Ford Motor Company and Ogilvy and Mather
Gallaher plc and M. and C. Saatchi
McDonald's
Oliver Sweeney
Omega
Panerai
Pilkington Glass
Silk Cut
Tif Hunter

Chapter 1

What facilitates persuasion and what inhibits it?

INTRODUCTION

Persuasion is becoming more important in advertising. A major reason is that competition is finding it easier to erode any functional or price advantage attached to a product. A firm may still have the advantage of a well-established system of distribution that is not easily copied but the goodwill and preferences of distributors can be destabilized by changes in their buying policies or a decline in consumer insistence for the product. In recognition of all this, companies are scrambling to reactivate long-neglected methods of reaching the consumer, like sports sponsorship, billboards and videos wherever there are people waiting, whether at airports or in doctors' waiting rooms. *American Idol* came to the screen in 2003 in the United States, and signalled the aggressive way in which advertisers are embedding products in TV shows and films. According to *The Economist,* product placement has been taken to a whole new level in the James Bond movie *Die Another Day*, promoting everything from 'Heineken beer to Omega watches and (invisible) Aston Martin cars. BMW cars are even starring in Internet mini-movies.'[1] The article also mentions the threats to TV advertising from ad-evading systems such as TiVo and the proliferation of other media. (Interestingly, TiVo is no longer selling its digital video recorders in the UK – the result of a failure to put across its advantages persuasively?) Attempts are also being made to create useful websites to attract viewers by offering them a free service.[2] Thus a Lexus site is predominantly concerned with offering lifestyle information on subjects such as luxury hotels, high-technology homes and so on, while playing appropriate soothing music; it is hoped this will induce a sense of obligation to click the ad, as well as creating a positive attitude towards the company. This tactic changes a push to a pull strategy in that consumers are pulled to receive something and then to respond favourably. Advertisers on the web recognize that giving something for free motivates the viewer to give something in exchange, namely to look at the ad a click away. This is the *principle of reciprocity* ('You scratch my back and I'll scratch yours') which is all-pervasive in social life. Kraft

Plate 1.1 *Getting attention: Oliver Sweeney*

Source: Courtesy of Oliver Sweeney, © Oliver Sweeney Ltd

now offers recipes on the web that use its products, and so, at least, it has stopped annoying people with pop-ups. A good deal of zipping and zapping results from the poor quality of commercials. In a survey of users, TiVo found that most did in fact watch the best commercials.[3]

Some attempts to surmount the problems of reaching the target audience are controversial, as indeed are the current attempts to target teenagers by offering money to income-starved schools to buy privileged access to students or by hiring teen trendsetters to influence their peer group.[4] All this pressure is because TV advertising is being hurt, with the many channels now available encouraging zipping and zapping during the commercials. Many firms are claiming that TV advertising is no longer profitable. Thus Amazon.com which in 2002 spent $50 million on its TV campaign has dismantled its five-member advertising department on the ground that TV advertising is not worth the expense. It has decided instead to lower prices by offering free shipping for orders over $25. But how will Amazon convey the new strategy of lower prices and remind prospective customers that it is still in business?

Reaching the target audience and establishing visibility with them is a necessary condition for success. However, it is not a sufficient condition since much depends on the persuasiveness of what is conveyed. Yet, achieving visibility is crucial and much creativity is being exercised on doing so. Medtronic in the United States has promoted its device for relieving incontinence by prominently displaying its slogan in restrooms 'Bladder control problems shouldn't control your life. You should.'

Making advertising credible is a more difficult problem. With many consumer ads amounting to little more than puffery, cynicism about advertising abounds while the TV companies, in order to make up for a shortfall in profit, associate ads with punishment: constant interruptions of favourite programmes make viewers take their revenge by zipping, zapping and muting. If advertisers envisage an implicit contract whereby the viewer agrees to watch an advertisement in exchange for being able to watch a programme, viewers have no sense of this obligation.

For many advertisers, attention getting has become the focus of importance, so persuasive content is hardly considered, on the assumption that visibility via the repeated exposure effect is all that is needed. While it is true that with repeated exposure comes familiarity, and with familiarity usually comes increased liking, this level of advertising expenditure assumes deep pockets, and also that the increased liking is sufficient in itself to trigger a preference. On occasion the need to get attention leads to the adoption of 'shock' advertising. An example is Miller Brewing's 'Catfight' ad during the National Football League playoffs and on late-night TV in the United States which certainly got visibility and was talked about. It was a commercial showing two big-breasted women fighting about whether Miller Lite just tastes great or is less filling; in the end they rip each

3

other's clothes off. Such 'shock' ads have a novelty that encourages their being talked about. Whether the effect on the target audience is positive or negative depends on their attitudes. The male target audience for beer may have found the ad attractively titillating even if this attitude was not representative of the community at large, which found it outrageous. Miller itself did not regret this, since it then 'fast-tracked' four similar shock ads. An ad for Egg Banking, a British financial group, marketing their credit card in France, set out to overturn the received wisdom on the sexes, race, household pets, etc. One ad, for instance, in autumn 2002, showed a dark-skinned man wearing an orange string bikini that reveals an outline of his small sex organ with the caption: 'Black men are well endowed.' These ads evoked a storm of protest but also a lot of free publicity about the firm's offer to pay users of its card 1 per cent on their purchases.

Advertising in market growth

To put advertising in context, we can sketch what commonly occurs if a market develops, without restating the somewhat simplistic story of the product life cycle. Whenever a new-to-the-world product enters the market, it needs to establish visibility with its target audience. What facilitates this visibility is a novel (but not too complex) product since consumers aim 'always to find out what is new, then passing on quickly to what is newer still'.[5] The novelty should prefer-ably be central to the function for which the product is being bought, yet unique to the company. Such a *critical advantage* encourages word-of-mouth, increasing the number of people buying the product, with still more buying it when they see others doing so.[6] The innovating firm and other early market entrants tend to focus on beating competition by performing better in the core-use function (design function). This situation can be described as *product parallelism* in that competitors are all going in the same direction, seeking a competitive advantage through enhancing performance in the core-use function. This can be the road to disaster for many companies. Foster of McKinsey, the consulting firm, provides the explanation of why this might be so.[7] He points out that increases in tech-nological performance depend on how quickly the underlying technology can be exploited, which in turn depends on the level of expenditure on R&D. The rela-tionship between expenditure on R&D and progress in increasing performance follows an S-shaped curve: progress is slow at first, then there is rapid progress and finally a plateau is reached as the technology matures. Thus the firms with the most R&D resources are likely to attain technological leadership, with tech-nological laggards dropping out of the market. This explains the early fall-out of competitors at the growth stage: they had wrongly believed that they could compete on technical performance in the core-use function when they were ill-equipped to do so. If the remaining competitors continue to be exclusively concerned with performance in the core-use function, what might be termed *product convergence* will ultimately be reached, as the technology matures and all competitors become technologically mature and equal. The result is a market of undifferentiated products. It is the situation we commonly find today. If product convergence occurs in conditions where price, promotion and distribution are all comparable in appeal, consumers will choose on the basis of habit, picking on whim or just gut liking. In picking, consumers have a reason for buying the product class but no particular reason for their specific choice. What all this means is that since every firm cannot be a technological leader, those that cannot be leaders must compete in some other way from the very start. They may try product *radiation*, modifying the product by adding ancillary-use functions (e.g. an answering device for a telephone) and/or convenience-in-use functions (e.g. making the phone portable) that meet the desires of specific segments. Thus for toothpaste, the added ancillary function in the 1940s was ammonia; in the 1950s it was chlorophyll; in the 1960s it was fluoride; in the 1970s it was gels; since then have come plaque fighters, tartar fighters and whiteners. The convenience-in-use functions added comprised packaging to facilitate accessibility to the toothpaste and to make the tube less bulky and easier to handle. Where the focus is on the product itself, a good deal of competition alternates between product parallelism, product convergence and product radiation. But if *product* competition were the only type of competition open to a firm, many of the leaders in consumer markets would now be out of business. An obvious point is that many consumers are willing to trade off high technical performance for a lower price. But, most significantly, technical and economic criteria are not the only basis of a competitive advantage.[8] The consumer buys not just a product *per se*, but a product under a description. How a product comes across in that description determines how it is envisaged and how attractive a buy it is likely to be. Persuasion appeals can provide a new perspective on a brand and create a whole new aura for it. Persuasive advertising can imbue a brand with symbolic meanings (e.g. as to status) which are just as much a real part of it as its substantive properties: consumer satisfaction does not separate the tangible from the symbolic images with which the product is indissolubly linked.

PERSUASION AND INFLUENCE

If we define persuasion as the process of trying to alter, modify or change the saliency of the values, wants, beliefs and actions of others, social life is dominated by conscious or unconscious, forceful or tangential, attempts at persuasion. This is because a commonality of beliefs and values facilitates getting along with others and there is pressure for this end. Wilhelm Dilthey (1833–1911), the German philosopher, once said that if we all understood everything in the same way, there would be no point in communicating at all. In fact, as soon as we move beyond the reaffirmation of our shared existence by greeting each other,

5

we are in the realm of persuasion. Even when we are promising or complaining about something, apologizing or guaranteeing, we are still aiming to persuade in that we are implicitly soliciting the trust of others in the truth or sincerity of our words.

Persuasion differs from 'influence'. Although persuasion is a way of influencing, all ways of influencing are not persuasion. People can influence the beliefs, values, wants or actions of others without making any deliberate attempt to do so. Thus a celebrity influences others by acting as a role model without consciously being aware of doing so. We can even influence others to act in ways that are detrimental to our interests as when we cause them to hate us. Persuasion, in contrast, deliberately aims to mould beliefs, values and actions in a direction favoured by the persuader. The word 'influence', on the other hand, does not carry the notion of intended effort directed at changing others.

There is another respect in which persuasion differs from influence in the general sense. We can influence others and they can influence us without any trust being involved. On the other hand, no form of persuasion gets off the ground without some degree of trust. Trust allows give and take in dealings with others and, when added to sentiment, creates loyalty. Loyalty means the consumer cares and may even care for a brand which does not play an important function for him or her. When there is loyalty or trust, lapses in service become more tolerable as there is a measure of goodwill to cushion the damage. Trust presupposes, as a minimum, that the other party is not out to deceive and is sincere. This is not the tall order it appears since deception succeeds only when non-deception is the rule.

Advertising, like personal selling, must engender trust to be effective. This is because a necessary condition for any cooperative activity is trust that the other party will meet obligations, and behave in an acceptable way. In particular, advertising is expected to fulfil its promise since, at its core, advertising always involves a promise even if one recognized by all concerned as something less than the puffery containing it would suggest. Consumers learn to trust and, with trust comes greater tolerance of slips in performance, in the knowledge that things will even out in the long term. Trust develops most quickly when sellers/ advertisers are perceived as sincere with openness as if revealing all and a willingness to declare what one stands for (one of the reasons why some 'shock' ads have gained a loyal following is that they openly declare their values or where they stand). A sincere proposal cannot be one which the seller does not believe: advertisers cannot expect others to believe what they do not believe themselves. Deceit involves manipulating the beliefs of the target audience, and may be successful with an audience ignorant of the true facts. But trying to distort the truth is how advertisers arouse most anger and indignation. An advertiser who has the reputation for getting the key facts right (accuracy) will always add to his reputational capital.

People are social animals, constantly interacting with each other and, in the process, persuading and being persuaded. While all communication takes certain things for granted (e.g. that certain things exist or that both persuader and audience have the same reference for a certain word), what can be taken for granted is not the major problem in communicating with others. In practice, communication is full of evaluative phrases about what is good or bad. Even if the evaluative adjective is missing it is implied, as when we greet others by saying it is a sunny day, tacitly sharing with them the idea of the weather being good. We constantly reveal opinions to which we seek agreement, and in doing so we seek to persuade. Persuasion is an essential skill for getting on in life. It is, as Frank says in the opening paragraph of his book *Persuasion and Healing*, the common denominator of all psychotherapeutic methods: 'despite their diversity . . . all are attempts to heal through persuasion.'[9]

Whenever we use evaluative language ('I think the company's advertising is deceptive'; 'I thought the movie was good'; 'This is the best sports car on the market'), there is implicit persuasion. Similarly, if we say 'You ought to do this or that', it is an attempt at persuasion. The same is true for all descriptions, explanations, predictions and prescriptions. Thus any particular description is a selection from all the possible descriptions of a given thing, and may or may not be the best for inducing agreement. We can never know whether someone could be persuaded to buy in the absence of the most persuasive appeal, part of which will be some description of the product. Similarly, explanations may not ring true unless they are put across in the most persuasive way. Again, predictions only appear convincing if their basis is persuasive. Finally, recommending a course of action means persuasively showing why it is desirable, feasible and likely to be viable.

If a description, an explanation, a prediction, an evaluation or a prescription is put to friends, and its truth is of no concern to them, we anticipate agreement. If this is not forthcoming, yet is of concern to us, we feel hurt, as it suggests a friendship less secure than we thought. It is because friends expect support that we go along with their strongly expressed opinions, other things remaining equal. When others endorse our views, we tend to conclude that everyone is of like mind on the issue. This is what commonly misleads politicians concerned with national or local opinion, as only properly conducted research is capable of discovering anything approaching the true position.

The process of persuasion is distinct from that of seeking compliance through coercion or material reward. With coercion there is no voluntary compliance, the result being only minimal compliance. In the case of material reward, compliance is voluntary but only because allegiance is rented; when the material reward ceases, so does the allegiance. Persuasion is different from coercion or material reward in that, when successful, it cultivates bonding through commonality of judgements. And judgements are what are important for, as Epictetus, the Greek

7

Stoic philosopher, recognized, it is not things themselves that disturb men, but their judgements about these things. Persuasion implies an agent whose intent, implicitly or explicitly, is to persuade. On the surface, persuasion seems the natural way to resolve disputes but force comes more easily to the mind of a party with coercive power, like the military, while material reward with its direct appeal to self-interest is something everyone understands.

THE TASK OF PERSUASION

As social animals, we all try to get on with others and implicitly accept that this means trying to understand the views of those whose support, friendship and companionship we seek. Similarly, the creative people who produce ads need to understand their target audience. And just as people value the comfort of being accepted and so value group affirmation of their beliefs and actions, advertising that associates a product with such acceptance and peer group affirmation is more effective. And just as some individuals' views receive more attention and endorsement, some ads receive more attention and acceptance. In both cases, this success relates to source visibility, credibility and attractiveness. Credibility is tied to projected expertise and trustworthiness while attractiveness is tied to values projected that evoke a sense of sharing.

Yet this picture is too simplistic if it suggests members of a target audience are tokens of each other, equally open to persuasion, and forgets that consumers often confront an ad with firm beliefs, rival loyalties and established preferences. It is important to appreciate how these differences influence interpretations and reactions. In fact, every person reading or viewing an advertisement is armed with a lot of 'shields' that may be raised during persuasive overtures. However, it is also true that people want to agree with a credible and attractive source because this brings with it a sense of sharing, avoids the emotion evoked by disagreement and saves on cognitive energy. The potential shields are external and internal (see Figure 1.1):

1 *external*: people's social attachments to culture, reference groups, social class and emotionally grounded experiences;
2 *internal*: people's overall perspective or view of the world, tied to some constellation of interrelated beliefs, values, emotions and expectancies about themselves and their social world.

The external shields derive from the influences to which the target has been exposed, structuring his or her viewpoint and giving content to the beliefs and values characterizing his or her perspective. The internal shields consisting of current beliefs and values are the result of learning within the context of social attachments. Beliefs are important as they tell us how the world is while values are important as they point to what we want from that world.

External: social attachments	*Internal: overall perspective*
Culture	Current beliefs
Reference groups	Values
Social class	
Emotionally grounded experiences	

Figure 1.1 *Shields against persuasive overtures*

We need information on our target audiences, on their social attachments and overall perspective, since these can facilitate or inhibit persuasive communication. This is not to suggest that collecting this information makes the selection of persuasive appeals a routine matter. Information on the target audience is like headlights to the night driver; they illuminate the road ahead but do not eliminate the need for good judgement.

External shields: social attachments

Culture

Apart from the artefacts and institutions of a country, its culture is reflected in its values and beliefs. Values are determined mainly by consumers' social and cultural histories, and act as criteria in determining what trade-offs they will make. Values are tied to the emotions, so knowing what upsets people is a guide to their values. Beliefs, in contrast, aim at truth and they cannot just be taken on board for reasons of expediency. We cannot coerce someone into believing something though this is sometimes forgotten. For example, the Augsburg Treaty (a religious settlement) in Europe (1555) set out the principle of 'cuius regio eius religio'; that is, the ruler was to determine the religion of his subjects as if this was as simple as insisting on a common dress code. 'Convert or die' may have been a slogan of the Inquisition but coercion only results in public, not private, commitment to a belief; we are not free to believe at will. Yet beliefs may be influenced by a preceding change in behaviour, particularly beliefs on matters of taste or what is socially appropriate. In other words, if people are made to adopt a certain type of behaviour, they may come to change their minds and approve of that behaviour even if this runs contrary to their former position. Thus if President Bush senior had been obliged to eat broccoli (he claimed to hate it), he might have come to like it. It was once common to argue that the

9

legal system cannot be effective in uprooting racial discrimination but in fact laws have made racial discrimination something disapproved of and in the process, both in the United States and in the UK, have brought about a sea change in attitudes and behaviour compared with the 1950s. Advertising that induces consumers to try a product may result, not only in removing doubts but also in changing beliefs about the potential of the product to enrich their lives.

Where the evidence is equivocal, we choose whatever most promotes our concerns. Beliefs are typically part of a system of beliefs, so attacking one belief may not undermine the whole set of beliefs. Thus the consumer's belief that genetically modified food is inherently harmful will be part of a whole host of beliefs about genetic modification and environmental dangers. Although people may do things which are contrary to their beliefs and may be persuaded that their beliefs are wrong, in general advertising finds it easier to present its appeals in a way that is supportive of beliefs or at least does not undermine them.

To live in a culture is to absorb certain perspectives, certain ways of looking at the world and certain ways of behaving which may be in conflict with new ideas which are being promoted. A culture's social norms, tied to its social values, act as rules for judging what is socially appropriate and acceptable; as such, they influence reactions to persuasive communications. Socrates followed Greek societal norms when he chose death rather than dishonour.

Within any culture, there are, of course, subcultures based on, say, age, gender, social class, religion, ethnicity or geographical location. Although subcultures are influenced by the broader culture, they may be so distinct as to require different persuasive appeals. Even where there is no need to modify a product, the advertising may have to be changed to suit the 'foreign' culture. This is because the persuasive job to be done may have to be tailored to the beliefs and/or values of the culture while various persuasive appeals vary in cultural appropriateness. Even the famous Marlboro cigarette advertisement (shown throughout the world) is changed in certain regions. In Hong Kong, the cowboy rides a white horse because this is a symbol of esteem and counter-balances the cowboy association with low-class manual labour.

Reference groups

A *reference group* consists of those whose behaviour an individual uses to guide his or her own behaviour. Reference groups tie in with culture since in the aggregate they can be viewed as approximating a person's actual culture. A consumer need not belong to each of her reference groups since some may be those which she aspires to join. In any case, reference groups can be powerful influences since attachment to them is part of a person's social identity.

The family is generally the first of many reference groups and perhaps is always the one that most of us use as a background check. But reference groups serve both *comparative* and *normative* functions. A group is a 'normative reference group' if the consumer uses it to establish behavioural standards, for example in dress or in opinions about products. A group is a 'comparative reference group' if it is used by the consumer as a basis for comparing personal qualities and different behaviours. Not surprisingly, there are 'positive' and 'negative' reference groups for every consumer: *positive reference groups* are those with which the individual identifies, accepts and wants to join or remain in, while *negative reference groups* are those privately rejected, used to define what we do not want to be. Used without qualification, the term 'reference group' is intended positively.

The influence of negative reference groups in any market is very under-researched, as if only positive reference groups influenced behaviour. This cannot be so since people know what they hate better than what they love. Anything associated with a negative reference group makes the task of persuasion more difficult. In contrast, positive reference groups help in persuasion: consider the use of celebrities in advertising.

The more attractive the reference group, the greater the motivation to adhere to its norms and submit to its persuasive endeavours. 'Group norms' are the accepted ways of thinking, feeling or behaving that are shared by members. They come about through social interaction, for example over what is fashionable. Group norms are both *descriptive* of behaviour (i.e. reflect similarities in behaviour among members) and *prescriptive* of behaviour (i.e. reflect shared beliefs about what are appropriate opinions and behaviour).

One way to persuade people to change is to show that what they believe or the way they act is not in line with reference group norms. A person who arrives at some conclusion (for example, which car is the best buy) which no one else in his or her social milieu accepts will have little confidence in its validity. By acting in a socially inappropriate way, he or she invites social disapproval or at least signs of non-approval. It is difficult to persuade people to change their behaviour if to do so conflicts with reference group norms. Hence it is advisable to couch suggested changes in behaviour in language that upholds these norms. Sometimes words can be used in a way that suggests adherence to group norms even when they are being violated; thus choice of words can be instrumental in changing perspectives. Bhagwati shows how the US government devised the phrase 'fair trade' to cover up their violation of free trade agreements to protect domestic industries that were having difficulty competing: 'fair' trade resonates with the public's sense of justice and offers a different perspective on what would otherwise seem an outrageous breach of agreements.[10] Similarly, the Federal Communication Commission defined cable internet access not as telecommunications but as an 'information service': a perspective which, if accepted, exempts cable companies from any necessity to act as common carriers. Marvin Bower, the man mainly responsible for establishing the consultancy firm of McKinsey, insisted that jobs were engagements and that the firm (not the company) had a practice, not a business, while employees until very late on were required to wear hats. His target audience was the business world and he wished to generate a certain image of McKinsey.

Conformity to group norms is reinforced by the desire for both *social conformity* and *informational conformity*. Social conformity proceeds from the desire for acceptance. People want to harmonize their relations with others and social conformity is one way to do this. When beliefs are not something that can be confirmed by a physical check because they relate to social reality (e.g. status symbols) where things are more ambiguous, social conformity offers a safe anchor. Most purchases that are worn on the person or are visible in some way, like a dress or a car, tend to require the seal of social approval as people are never quite sure of their taste. *Informational conformity,* on the other hand, stems from the desire to make sense of the world around one. While social (normative) conformity to group norms emanates from the desire to be accepted, informational conformity is based on the desire for an accurate view of the world by accepting the information generally believed to be true. But the distinction between social and informational conformity is less secure than it might seem since information has to be interpreted and this gives scope for social persuasion. Most conformity in fact involves both informational and normative influence.

Social groups are communication networks and the informal *word-of-mouth* communication that occurs within them can be more persuasive than mass advertising in determining what is bought. We are more impressed by what others say as independent sources than we are by an ad. Identifying strongly with a group tends to reduce individual self-awareness and, as a consequence, less attention is focused on the individual's own feelings, beliefs and wants. This inhibits deliberation while encouraging compliance with group views.

Social class

A social class is usually defined in terms of the socioeconomic status of its members relative to other strata of society. Occupation and income are the typical criteria for distinguishing social classes in marketing but some researchers stress other factors such as education, lifestyle, prestige or values as better descriptive measures. Consumers who are very conscious of social class use it as a reference group. A strategy of persuasion that is successful with one social class may not be successful with another. This is well accepted in advertising and knowledge of the social class of the target audience is essential information for any campaign. Throughout the world social class is a guide to values typically relating to patterns of buying or it can even be a discriminator in the purchase of such products as clothing, food and cars.

It is frequently argued that as consumerism develops, with many of the same images reaching society's consumers, class distinctions and ideological distinctions disappear while other forms of social differentiation, like gender, ethnicity and age, become of greater concern. In the United States, since the American Revolution, class divisions have often been denied. This originated by contrasting America with England where, at the time of the American Revolution, social class was something virtually determined at birth. But social class remains a guide to values and, since these in the final analysis determine the major trade-offs in buying, it is considered crucial in marketing as an indicator of what is likely to appeal. What Melvin Kohn said about social class or hierarchical position in the social structure is still true today:[11]

> hierarchical position is related to almost everything about men's lives – their political party preferences, their sexual behavior, their church membership, even their rates of ill health and death. Moreover, the correlations are not trivial; class is substantially related to all these phenomena.

It has been claimed that the mass media, higher incomes and more global brands have meant more homogeneity of tastes and thus fewer outward signs of social class. In the 1970s, the young seemed to detach themselves from their roots and become a new class where entertainment was concerned. The middle classes, once distinct not only in income but in taste in clothes, social behaviour, housing and choice of reading and, in the UK, in speech, were invaded by masses of people who had middle-class incomes but adhered to lower-class values. But social class persists. This is because higher social classes possess higher social status and this is extremely desirable as a reflection of a person's position in the social pecking order. What has been changing is the ranking within the middle classes in that profession has become less important than income in establishing status. This is probably a reflection of the decline in the social worth of 'respectability' vis-à-vis that of money.

Inequality in income is growing in both the United States and the UK, following a sustained rise throughout the 1980s and 1990s.[12] No Western democracy is less equal than the United States, though the UK is not far behind. This spells a lot of differences in social behaviour as large income differences mandate differences in spending patterns and these, in turn, contribute to class perceptions. The children of the deprived in both the United States and Europe regard the upper classes as being from another planet. Social stratification remains as people seek status and visibility and attempt to rise above the masses.[13] It may be claimed that gender, ethnicity and age are assuming greater importance than class, but the facts can only be found by research or validated theory showing why these things are inevitably of more concern today. We should not be misled by the universal popularity, among all classes of the young, of pop stars and sports celebrities, into believing that class is disappearing and no longer useful for segmentation purposes. Conspicuous consumption which goes with wealth also gives rise to different spending patterns even if 'the habit of acquiring more becomes detached from the value of having more'.[14]

Emotionally grounded experiences

How we see, interpret and react to something is coupled not only to circumstances but also to the general and unique experiences of the individual. The most important experiences in life are emotional since these are etched in the memory to be resurrected when a person is roused, in dealings with others . . . and when reading or viewing advertisements. Someone who has had a bad experience with a company or its products is much less open to persuasion about the merits of what it has to offer. Bad experiences linger in the memory and can leave emotional scars; good experiences linger too, but stir less feeling.

Internal shields: overall perspective

Current beliefs and values

Unless we take account of the target audience's social attachments, we fail to be mindful of the resistances to be overcome. Social attachments mould the consumer's overall perspective which is composed of a set of beliefs and values. Thus in the early twenty-first century perspectives in the United States and Europe are at odds over genetically modified foods. In the United States there is little resistance to such foods while throughout Europe the metaphor 'Frankenstein foods' has been given to gene-altered food. As Europe could be the greatest overseas market for such foods, the US government is intent on taking all sorts of legal remedies to get Europe to change. There is a failure here to appreciate that the problem lies with European perspectives on such foods and not with European governments.

While Zoellick calls Europe's stance on genetically modified foods 'Luddite' and even 'immoral' (on the grounds that the European attitude has caught on in Africa where such foods could do so much good), nothing really has been done to tackle the basic problem of perspective.[15] Europeans are naturally suspicious of such foods, given the scandals that have occurred: 'mad cow disease' in the UK, dioxin-infested chickens in Belgium and so on. In all these cases there were government assurances that all was well. Once bitten, twice shy: scientists no longer have credibility on food matters, so better safe than sorry. Whatever pressure the United States puts on European governments to import gene-altered foods will not work until something is done to change perspectives. Until some effort is made to understand the underlying perspective of Europeans on gene-altered food, what the US government is doing will be of no help to firms like Monsanto.

Different perspectives are often captured by pictorial metaphors. Thus one reader's letter in *The New York Times* on 5 November 2002 described the Germans' view of the United States:

> the friendly but overweight neighbor who owns a big house and a big car, has a pile of junk in his backyard, thinks he owns the block and walks around waving his gun. This neighbor doesn't bring on envy, but he sure does raise some eyebrows.

An individual has many perspectives according to the issue at hand. Every social scientist in fact operates from a distinct perspective. The behaviourist views the consumer as simply responding to the push and pull of past impressed events and immediate stimuli, claiming all behaviour is the result of conditioning. Those subscribing to behaviourism in the form of operant conditioning (see pp. 102–10) believe that humans emit behaviour all the time and those emitted behaviours that are reinforced recur while those that are not reinforced die away. The behaviourist centres on reinforcement as a change agent without feeling the need to take account of mental processes associated with being persuaded. On the other hand, the cognitive psychologist believes that behind behaviour lie influencing mental processes, so the focus should be on the processes of perceiving, knowing, remembering, paying attention, language use, problem solving and so on. Given the cognitive psychologist's beliefs, value will be placed on studying the 'software' of the mind, studying, say, how information is processed.

Persuasion involves arguing *for* a certain point of view or perspective even if that perspective is not tied to any particular theory. But we also argue *from* a certain point of view or perspective emanating from the influence of social attachments. As a consequence, the persuader's perspective needs to be reconciled with the perspectives of the target audience. Reconciliation is needed because persuasive appeals assume that both the persuader and the target audience are on roughly the same wavelength. Different perspectives indicate potentially different views as to the significance of things and what they symbolize. Thus the Republican and Democratic perspectives on the role of government and its role in the marketplace differ, so it is not surprising that at the time of writing Democrats perceive the recent scandals in corporate America as symptomatic of a deep malaise, while the Republicans perceive them as due to a few rotten apples with nothing wrong systemically. This leads to different policy recommendations.

Perspectives affect every level in society and affect international relations. Kammen points out that after the war of 1812, Britain's perceived condescension gave rise to a perspective of Anglophobia that coloured outlooks and prejudiced decisions involving Britain. A series of friendly acts by Britain led to a perceptible shift in the twentieth century and Anglophobia gave way to lukewarm

15

affection, and eventually detente and alliance.[16] Yet even in the 1920s school boards banned the use of any textbook containing the slightest hint of sympathy for Great Britain in the American Revolution. A number of supportive acts by Britain, and the fact of the two countries being allies in the First World War, finally turned Anglophobia into Anglophilia. This also illustrates how, over time, supportive interaction softens hostile perspectives or even transforms them. But getting another country to appreciate a different perspective which lacks consistency or equity is problematic, as the United States has found in many areas of international relations. For example, from the perspective of the US government, there is nothing odd in bringing Milosevic before an international court of justice while at the same time refusing to endorse the setting up of an international court which could extend its reach to include Americans.

To take a very different example, Hacking shows how, in psychotherapy, 'disease and disorder are identified according to an underlying vision of health and of humanity, of what kinds of being we are, and what can go wrong with us'.[17] He illustrates how the emergence of new theoretical perspectives gives rise to the emergence of corresponding psychological disorders: we see what we have been taught to see according to our perspective. Every model in social science is both a way of seeing some aspect of the world and also a way of not seeing, in that the adoption of one perspective eliminates others. We typically 'see' what we have been taught to look for.

Park, a physicist, characterizes as 'voodoo science' theories such as astrology, psychokinesis and precognition, UFOs and irrational projects like the search for perpetual motion machines; yet belief in such theories can be very strong.[18] If our target audience's global perspective sees the world as mysterious and unintelligible, as a place where just about anything can happen, a receptive window is opened for a voodoo science that caters to the desire for wonder, surprise and novelty. Advertisers have been known to build an ad campaign on this perspective. But perspectives may also be shaped by self-deception. Gratzer, a biophysicist, illustrates this with the story of the non-existent N-rays invented by French scientists in 1903 to counter-balance British and German successes in the natural sciences.[19] Although carefully conducted experiments failed to endorse any of the claims, many first-rate French scientists said they were convinced. Park characterizes voodoo science as being in violation of fundamental scientific procedures; no testable theories are put forward; appeals are made to the mass media by-passing scientific review; criticism is not tolerated (as with cold fusion); appeals are made to authority not evidence (as in astrology) and so on. However, such indicators are unlikely to dissuade believers since *ad hoc* rescue hypotheses can always be cited to uphold whatever is believed. The indicators themselves can sometimes be used to support voodoo science, for example by using the argument that major scientific revolutions inevitably violate established laws, and going direct to the media is the only way of getting a hearing, given the prejudices of the scientific community. Distorted perspectives give rise to irrational actions such as Mao's Great Leap Forward of 1959 when in a collective self-deception it was believed that 'miracle crops' could just be 'willed' and iron could be produced in domestic backyards. Such faith contributed to the deaths of twenty million people through famine.

No persuasive communication falls on minds that are passive, blank slates (*tabulae rasae*), ready to receive uncritically the views of others. People order the world and develop a set of beliefs and preferences in order to have some control over their lives. It was Nietzsche (1844–1900) who claimed that all thinking arises from perspectives and, as a consequence, there are no 'facts', only interpretations. Whether we agree or not about there being no facts, only interpretations, it is true that perspectives constitute a framework or conceptual schema within which we think. Consumers, indeed people generally, have a cognitive orientation, a way of seeing a situation from some conceptual, physical or temporal viewpoint with corresponding preferences. A fundamental change in a person's perspective is captured by the metaphor: 'the scales fell from my eyes'. Sometimes a perspective changes simply when people 'get the hang of' something, that is understand what it is all about. Perspectives are always important to the design of a persuasive appeal since they mould the perceptions which result from the interplay between sensory signals and the stored information where perspectives are embodied. If perception can be described as unconscious inference, it is based in part on information tied to one's perspective. Persuaders focus their interest on how things are perceived, and this is connected to perspective. Thus at the time of writing Nissan is seeking to change consumer perceptions of its brand image ('O.K. car, O.K. brand, with quality not as good as Honda or Toyota') by changing the brand theme from 'Driven' to 'Shift' to celebrate the values of achievement, non-conformity and the defiance of expectations. The advertising campaign is premised on the need to make an emotional connection with consumers because value and quality are not enough when every car manufacturer offers them.

A view put forward by Kelly in his *personal construct theory* has relevance to the notion of perspectives. The Kelly perspective on human beings is that of the *person-as-scientist*: people's behaviour is best viewed as essentially experimentation; arising from their 'theories' (perspective), people have expectations which they modify as a result of comparing expectations with unfolding events. People behave like scientists, trying to predict and control the causes of events by setting up hypotheses, testing them and weighing up the evidence.[20] For Kelly, people's 'theories' constitute personal construct systems: these constitute perspectives. They are personal in that they are based on a person's own interpretations of the world while the constructs (a person's own set of concepts) constitute a conceptual lens or set of hypotheses by which he or she makes sense of the world.

17

Unfolding events may or may not validate a personal construct system(s). If not, the person's construct system will change. All this means that perspectives are not set in stone but are constantly being modified with experience.

Although it is easy to show that people do not always behave like scientists, it can also be shown that they commonly do behave in this way in order to establish valid beliefs, necessary for evolutionary survival. People who constantly make bad judgements are less likely to survive to pass on their genes. Nonetheless, people vary in their susceptibility to persuasive endeavours. High susceptibility to persuasion goes with a lack of self-confidence, low self-esteem, submissiveness and a low anxiety threshold. But all of us are to some extent susceptible. In fact, Boyer makes a strong case for claiming that we all have a built-in disposition to believe in gods and a spirit world in spite of protests to the contrary.[21]

We have not discussed consumer 'attitudes' though marketers are more likely to substitute 'attitudes' for 'perspective' and thus envisage persuasion as influencing/changing attitudes. While a person's perspective on an issue constitutes his or her point of view, an attitude is traditionally defined as a disposition to respond positively or negatively to some other person, item or event. Unfortunately, no measures of attitude adequately capture this idea of a 'disposition to respond' and attitudes, as commonly measured, are built up from belief statements about the issue in question. The chief use of attitude measures in marketing is to place attitudes towards a product or brand along a favourable/unfavourable continuum as a basis for predicting behaviour or influencing/changing attitudes on the assumption that attitudes relate to buying. Of course, a product may have many properties on which the consumer has an attitude and this makes it difficult to obtain a valid summary attitude measure. Even if we could obtain a summary measure of attitude, it is unlikely to be highly predictive because attitudes are captured by belief statements; beliefs alone, without knowledge of values/wants/motives, are not sufficient for predictive purposes. We may have a very favourable attitude towards bicycles (environmentally clean, etc.) but still not buy one as we have no need of one. Attitude measures in marketing tend to be better predictors of behaviour (or at least, of buying intentions) than they are in the social sciences generally because the relevant wants can often be assumed. The more specific the attitude measures, the better the prediction. Thus a measure of attitude towards purchasing product X at this very moment is likely to be more predictive of purchase than a simple measure of attitude towards X. But this measure may be no better than asking someone what he or she is about to buy. But to return to the subject of attitudes and perspective, we would endorse the view of Deanna Kuhn that attitudes can only be fully understood as a part of the broader theories (read 'perspective') that people hold about the world, and it is in that framework that they need to be approached.[22]

In seeking to understand a person's perspective we inquire about relevant social attachments and about the target's overall viewpoint on, say, buying a car. We encourage them to talk 'off the top of their heads' to allow us to infer an overall point of view. From this understanding of a perspective, certain attitudes can also be inferred but seeking out the overall perspective itself is likely to be more useful to the development of persuasive strategies. This is because identifying a perspective taps beliefs and values.

Scheibe uses the metaphor of the 'box' in talking about changing perspectives.[23] He prefers 'box' to 'frame' (favoured by Goffman in talking about self-presentation strategies) on the ground that boxes are frames but with a third dimension. He reminds us that we have many perspectives depending on the box we are in at the time. Thus the perspective displayed in the classroom can appear quite different from that displayed at faculty meetings. Thus one way to change perspectives is to put people in a box where the role they have to play is supportive of the perspective we wish to promote. Scheibe reminds us that the intended function of propaganda is to make us concerned about what we otherwise might be indifferent to, so his other view on changing perspectives concerns bringing issues vividly into others' 'circle of meaning by words and pictures, dramatically composed and frequently repeated'.[24] We will be returning to the theme of changing perspectives later, though it is by no means clear how often an advertiser needs to bring about a complete change of perspective: we suspect not often.

Ranking a person's values on the basis of intensity reveals his or her *value system*, and the hierarchy of values that determines the trade-offs made in choices, given that trade-offs implicitly involve an appeal to values. Value systems are emotionally grounded, so what makes people emotional is a guide to their values. Whenever we make major trade-offs in our decisions, they are connected to values. If we are able to convert trade-offs into a money scale, we are able to make the best choice, but only if we want economic values to dominate. When people reject value judgements in making choices (following the assertion of Jeremy Bentham (1748–1832) that 'Pushpin is as good as poetry'), they are demonstrating an indifference to the choices, not some adherence to principle.

Although values and value systems tend to be stable and enduring, being grounded in significant life experiences, they do change. For example, values have been changing in Western societies in respect to marriage, community, piety and so on. But some values remain, with advertising, explicitly or implicitly, appealing to the durable values of being healthy, beautiful or slim while people in their buying and in their actions continue to exhibit values related to enhancing self-image, self-esteem and self-confidence.

- *Self-image* consists of the properties a person believes apply to him or her. Thus typical properties are gender, ethnicity and social class. They can be intrinsic ('I am blond') or comparative ('I am slimmer than any of my friends'). In buying, consumers seek to reinforce an image. An individual's self-image arises both from within herself and from external influences such as feedback from others. But comparisons with others are never objective since we bias them for purposes of self-enhancement.

- *Self-esteem* is the subjective counterpart of the ego and depends on the private valuations we put on the properties constituting our self-image. These valuations are tied to societal values, acquired through socializing with others. Self-esteem is not a constant but varies according to the type of people (introvert versus extrovert) we are with and to the situation (social or in the exam room) we are in, since different people will be perceived as judging our 'assets' differently. In any case, low self-esteem tends to be tied to greater susceptibility to external influence. Purchases are more likely to be made if they are perceived as enhancing self-esteem.
- *Self-confidence* entails as one of its aspects the feeling of being able to have an impact on others. A good deal of advertising, e.g. of personal toiletries and cosmetics, is tied to enhancing self-confidence.

NO CERTAINTIES IN SOCIAL SCIENCE

There are no universal laws in social science and none of its claims can be said to be universally true, except those that are truisms, requiring no social science to justify them. An example is the assertion that no one likes to be cheated. McGuire argues that social scientists who look for universal truths find themselves confined to testing hypotheses that are sterile truisms without the seeds necessary for theory development.[25] His alternative to the 'positivist view' is 'perspectivism' which acknowledges that there are no laws when it comes to social behaviour or intentional action and that no hypothesis is perfectly true (as we inevitably misrepresent reality to some extent) but may be reasonably true on occasion. McGuire recommends exploring the pattern of contexts in which a hypothesis does or does not obtain and identifying the reasons why this is so. Flyvbjerg also stresses context-dependence, denying the possibility of laws in the social sciences which are novel, reliable and accurately predictive. He claims that social science nonetheless matters in the realm of practical knowledge.[26]

McGuire's stress on explanation is important. Prediction is also significant but there is a danger in all social science inquiries of focusing on prediction as if it were all that mattered. As Deutsch says:[27]

> Whereas an incorrect prediction automatically renders the underlying explanation unsatisfactory, a correct prediction says nothing at all about the underlying explanation. Shoddy explanations that yield correct predictions are two a penny, as UFO enthusiasts, conspiracy-theorists and pseudo-scientists

of every variety should (but never do) bear in mind. . . . I have already remarked that even in science most criticism does not consist of experimental testing. That is because most scientific criticism is directed not at a theory's predictions but directly at the underlying explanations. Testing the predictions is just an indirect way (albeit an exceptionally powerful one, when available) of testing explanations.

Context tends to be all-important to the applicability of social science findings, so judgement nuanced by experience is always needed. Why social science is important in practical matters is because the discipline has not only given us findings that can point to explanations but also offers a wide range of sensitizing concepts that offer expectations and insights and alert us to what to look for in various situations. Thus the concepts explicated in this book sensitize us to notice situations where they apply and this helps fine-tune our judgements in evaluating a situation.

Economics is often quoted as the social science that has been able to maintain rigour and applicability. But as Toulmin says, the excessive (mathematical) rigour of economics has weakened its claim to practical relevance: reliance on pure economic theory is a bankrupt approach unless full consideration is given to the social, cultural and historical conditions in which the theory is applied. With its search for an ideal form of theory, economics has copied a model of physics that never was. The result has been a focus on 'doing sums right' instead of 'doing the right sums'.[28]

Chapter 2 describes the role of rational versus emotional appeals in persuasion; it discusses changing perspectives and the differences between quantitative and qualitative approaches to persuasion. Subsequent chapters are concerned with delineating the various persuasive appeals, assessing their basis in social science and evaluating their pragmatic and theoretical worth.

The book is only concerned with categorizing and explaining persuasive approaches rooted in psychology or the social sciences. Thus it does not discuss how to define a target audience, set advertising goals, determine the message focus (whether on some unique selling proposition, brand image, positioning in the mind, or match between want and offering). There is also no direct discussion of whether advertising appeals should be put across in an emotional, rational or dogmatic way. Finally there is no explicit presentation of tactics for executing an advertising strategy – whether to entertain, be simply factual or use celebrities, slice-of-life advertising or comparative advertising. Finally, nothing at all is said about media planning and budgeting, essential considerations in developing an overall advertising strategy, as these are discussed in detail elsewhere.[29] That said, this book has implications for all these elements of advertising strategy, implications that are pointed out in the body of the text and in the Key Assertions at the end of each chapter.

**WHAT COMES FIRST,
THE CHICKEN OR THE EGG?
WE THINK IT'S THE CHICKEN.**

The welfare of our chickens is always a priority at McDonald's. And that means when you're enjoying one of our breakfasts, you can be sure you're only eating free range eggs. Talking of good eggs, we recently received the Good Egg Award from the British Free Range Egg Producers' Association which recognises our commitment to animal welfare. All our eggs also carry the Lion mark, an independent assurance of food quality. Which goes to show that like the chicken, the customer always comes first at McDonald's.

©McDonald's Corporation 2005. The Golden Arches logo is a trademark of McDonald's Corporation and its affiliates.

■ *Plate 1.2* *Managing our perspectives: McDonald's*

Source: Courtesy of McDonald's

The welfare of our chickens is always a priority at McDonald's. And that means when you're enjoying one of our breakfasts, you can be sure you're only eating free range eggs. Talking of good eggs, we recently received the Good Egg Award from the British Free Range Egg Producers' Association which recognises our commitment to animal welfare. All our eggs also carry the Lion mark, an independent assurance of food quality. Which goes to show that like the chicken, the customer comes first at McDonald's.

KEY ASSERTIONS

- Persuasion, defined as the process of trying to alter or modify the values, wants, beliefs and actions of others, is a major focus for marketing.

- If marketing is to persuade, it should frame all its persuasive endeavours as signalling a desire for affiliation and bonding with its target audience and avoid coercive strategies, because they undermine the offer of affiliation that is basic to all types of persuasion.

- If marketing is to persuade, it should distinguish between intentional persuasion and the other ways a target audience is influenced, since the intent to persuade may be frustrated by other factors (e.g. poor service) that emanate from the organization. Persuasive appeals that are contradicted by other aspects of the firm's behaviour amount to saying one thing and doing another.

- If marketing is to persuade, it assumes some degree of trust by the target since signalling the desire for affiliation presupposes the other party believes the intention is sincere; influence *per se* does not presuppose trust.

- Marketing should assess whether persuasion can be a simple matter of presenting its case or whether there is a need to overcome resistance to being persuaded due to protective shields. These shields are both external and internal:

  - *external:* social attachments to culture, reference groups, social class and emotionally grounded experiences.

  - *internal:* an overall perspective or view of the world tied to some constellation of interrelated beliefs and a set of values.

- If marketing management is to persuade its target audience and resistance is predicted, it must form an understanding of the target audience's culture, reference groups, social class and the key experiences likely to have been influential. Some understanding of these influences makes it easier to understand the target's overall perspective.

- If marketing management is to persuade on the basis of understanding things from the target's perspective, identifying relevant beliefs and values is important because beliefs map the target's picture of how the world is, and values (like wants) target things to aim for.[30] Values are important since all major trade-offs in buying reflect value rankings.

- If marketing management seeks to persuade, the universal evolutionary values that need to be considered are the target audience's self-image, self-esteem and self-confidence.

cont.

■ If marketing management seeks to apply the findings of social science, context tends to be all-important in considering applicability, so judgement, nuanced by experience, is always needed. Social science's most important contribution is its stock of sensitizing concepts as these offer expectations and insights and alert us to what to look for in various situations.

Chapter 2

Rationality, symbolism and emotion in persuasion

THE RATIONAL VERSUS THE EMOTIONAL

Every ad aims to make the target audience construe it in the way intended. However, while every communication invites a certain interpretation, this invitation can be refused. It may be refused because the target audience does not have the necessary perspective to be receptive to it. If this perspective is missing, initial persuasion has to be directed at inducing the 'right' perspective. In other words, there is a need for 'consciousness raising', getting across a certain viewpoint, a certain definition of the situation, or showing an alternative window through which to view the problem. It is difficult to persuade people to stop smoking for health reasons unless they first accept the orthodox medical perspective of a link between smoking cigarettes, lung cancer, heart attacks and the more immediate effects on their looks. Once the perspective is adopted, persuasion can focus on activating change.

There is constant debate in public policy (and in marketing) over whether the most effective persuasion is rational or emotional. For example, some would deny single mothers welfare benefits on the ground that young women, acting rationally, would then, as a consequence, take precautions to avoid pregnancy and be more likely to seek a marriage partner. This is in line with the economist's rational choice model. Others claim such familial decisions are shaped by emotional impulses, not by calculations of economic self-interest. Similarly, some claim the problem of teenage pregnancy could be solved by providing more education about sex. This, too, is founded on the basic idea of rational persuasion, ignoring any emotional factors at work. But the debate over the relative efficacy of the rational versus the emotional is misleading: both are needed.

Persuasion motivates people into action through influencing beliefs and desires. It is not enough just to change beliefs. It may wrongly be assumed, for example, that if we put across the findings and recommendations endorsed by the 'hard' sciences, people will follow such recommendations. This assumption commits the Platonic fallacy that 'with knowledge, comes virtue'. Thus people continue

SMOKING CAUSES HEART DISEASE

Chief Medical Officers' Warning
5 mg Tar   0.5 mg Nicotine

Plate 2.1 Symbolizing the brand: Silk Cut

Source: Courtesy of Gallaher plc and M. and C. Saatchi

to smoke though surveys show that smokers are more aware of the health dangers than non-smokers.[1] When any close-knit group or subculture holds certain beliefs in common, the psychological defence mechanism of denial induces members to reject rational, objective arguments if these give rise to unpalatable truths.

In a sense, all persuasion is self-persuasion in that we are unlikely to be persuaded unless we reflect (or fantasize?) on the meaning of the persuasive communication. As the saying goes, 'A man convinced against his will is of the same opinion still'. But self-persuasion can be helped along. Examples abound in marketing promotions. Thus a questionnaire for an animal protection society invites the public to complete and return it as part of a survey. In fact, filling in the questions (e.g. 'Do you think cosmetics companies should be allowed to test on animals?', 'Are you aware of our National Cruelty Phoneline?') is a 'consciousness-raising' technique designed to induce an emotive reaction to the ill-treatment of animals, and consequently a donation to the organization. A competition for a Mercedes car asks potential buyers to choose from a number of pictures (e.g. of the Parthenon in Athens) the six that best represent the new Mercedes. This results in thinking about the Mercedes in association with the images chosen and creates the likelihood of self-persuasion. A common device in American electioneering is to engage in bogus polling as a means to persuasion. This tactic recognizes that every question is in fact a persuasive message which can trigger an answer that can become a choice. Advertising gives new meaning to a product if it can induce self-persuasion by getting the target audience to imagine using or consuming it.

THE PERVASIVENESS OF EMOTION IN PERSUASION

Anything that concerns us has the potential to arouse our emotions and, as Margalit says, emotions engage us with their objects in such a way as to make them lose their neutrality: they become marked by being lovable, disgusting, exciting, fearful and so on.[2] The same applies if the object of the emotion is a market offering: we are no longer indifferent to it. To describe an emotion is to describe the circumstances that generate it. Thus anger is associated with circumstances that are perceived as insulting and threatening to one's interests, while pride is aroused when something happens that increases one's sense of standing in the world and exceeds expectations.

Emotional messages have an impact at every stage in life. Even young babies are influenced by emotional messages communicated through the TV screen. Emotion is a major factor in persuasive advertising that aims to change viewpoints and not simply to demonstrate the logical implications of data. In the grip of an emotion, a person not only feels differently, but tends to think differently. Advertising that resonates emotionally stands more chance of inducing a change in beliefs and values/motives/wants/desires than one based on logic alone.

27

Murray Smith neatly sums up why the emotions, which on occasion can undermine rational behaviour, were necessary to evolution:[3]

> First, emotions provide us with a kind of motivational gravity, allowing us to grasp the world and act decisively in it, rather than drifting among an array of equally weighted options. Second, emotions provide a rapidity and intensity of response to a changing environment which reasoning alone cannot provide. Given that we live in a changing and sometimes hostile environment, our chances of survival are enhanced if we have a kind of in-built 'rapid' reaction force alongside our more precise, but much slower, mechanisms of reasoning. Whether it's a wild animal or a car suddenly bearing down on us, it is mighty handy that we have an instinctive fear reaction to unexpected loud noises and fast movements – that we leap out of the way immediately, rather than calmly trying to assess the nature of the moving object, its size, speed and intentions.

There are many who have written on the role of emotion in persuasion: for example, on advertising,[4] on attention to an advertisement,[5] on emotions and affective responses,[6] on emotions and attitudes,[7] on memory of brands and advertisements,[8] on patterns of emotions,[9] and on the influence of emotional appeals across cultures.[10] Nonetheless, emotion in advertising, while fully acknowledged by those in the business, is still under-researched in consumer behaviour.

The employment of emotion in advertising

Tony Schwartz, a pioneer in political advertising, argued that advertising's role was to impel action by striking a responsive emotional chord in the target audience.[11] This is another way of saying that advertising should connect with what concerns the audience. A political advertisement he designed opposing Barry Goldwater, then running for President, showed a small girl happily playing in a field counting petals: her voice was replaced by a man's making a nuclear countdown following an image of a mushroom cloud. The vulnerable image of the little girl, a symbol of the country's future, contrasted with the soulless male voice in the nuclear countdown. What more needed to be said to bring out the stakes: whether to make a world in which all of God's children can live, or go into the dark? But direct persuasion can also 'strike a responsive chord': a person may be persuaded by direct argument that something is, say, threatening, even though this may not be the case.

Reframing an issue so it arouses feelings is also a way of connecting to the concerns of the target audience. Reframing amounts to putting a 'spin' on something to connect to these concerns; for example, to broaden their constituency, environmentalists stress the medicinal properties of rare plants threatened by extinction. Anything that impacts on core concerns or values has the potential to stir the emotions, perhaps giving rise to a sense of not being in control, inducing on occasion an acceptance of some bizarre explanation of our experiences which, in turn, can give rise to changes in perspective.[12] Curiosity can be an emotional motivator to explore further while the satisfaction of curiosity can act as a positive reinforcement. But no one is curious about everything that is different, so the trick lies in arousing curiosity, a process likely to involve the presence of novelty.

Different words for the same phenomenon (e.g. 'smell' versus 'stench') evoke different images in the mind and so have a different impact. Some changes in terminology are designed to change perspectives. For example, the tendency today in psychiatry is to speak of 'mind-ordering' drugs instead of 'mind-altering' drugs, a phrase that evokes Orwellian fears. Some words like 'new' get attention as they appeal to curiosity and the desire for novel experiences. Tony Blair, the British Prime Minister, in fifty-three speeches used the term 'modernization' eighty-seven times, even though the modernization of welfare meant simply continuing the reforms initiated by the previous government, while the so-called modernization of the constitution simply added up to a confused devolution of power and changes to the House of Lords that made it seem nothing like a reformed second chamber.

Emotion plays a part in the academic acceptance of ideas since these often resonate with core concerns. Thus one reviewer in *The Times Literary Supplement* (*TLS*) pointed out that when Edward Said's *Orientalism* was published in 1978, historian after historian put it down without finishing it as it was technically bad: in its use of sources, in its deductions and in its lack of rigour and balance.[13] It was, according to this reviewer, a caricature of Western knowledge of the Orient, yet it has had immense popularity and influence as it 'touched a deep vein of vulgar prejudice running through American academe'. Book titles that capture the popular mood are important to sales, for example *The Closing of the American Mind*, *The Greening of America* and *The Decline of the West* and so on.

Prejudice means a viewpoint unjustified by the facts; a prejudiced person is unwilling to question the viewpoint by examining the facts. A prejudice can be embedded in a perspective and anyone holding that perspective will see not prejudice but just objective facts. Certainly even academics are not aware of their prejudices:

In the early decades of the 20th century the most professionally accomplished work on the Reconstruction – work hailed by the profession as the most objective, the most balanced, the most fair – was viciously racist; antiracist accounts were for the most part crude and amateurish.[14]

Effective persuasion typically uses emotion in changing perspectives as rational appeals implicitly assume the audience is already *emotionally* in tune with the message. A dramatic metaphor is always an important way of changing perspectives, just as saying the brain is a computer may switch the perspective of a behaviourist. Advertisers use metaphors all the time for this purpose: Lacoste talks of its men's fragrance as 'Style on skin' and Toyota calls its car 'Sheet Metal Magnetism'. The 'war on terrorism' is a metaphor since there is no war in any conventional sense but the imagery of the slogan has done much to win support for President Bush. But how far will such a metaphor sustain a change in perspective? And, if so, is it the novelty or insightfulness of the metaphor that convinces or strikes an emotional chord? Creating strong emotional appeals to change perspectives is never simple as such appeals presuppose knowledge of the existing mindset of the target audience in terms of their values and beliefs. Yet metaphors can be fundamental to persuasion. Gibbs points out that much of our language and cognition (thinking) is metaphorically structured and that there is considerable evidence showing that a metaphor can significantly change attitudes and perspectives.[15] For example, in California attitudes towards compulsory seat belt legislation were changed significantly when people of that state were presented with ads using the metaphor that such a law was like having Governor Deukmejian in your bathtub telling you to wash behind your ears. A metaphor is more compelling than a simile and there is generally more scope for extracting meaning.

EVERY AD CAN BE GIVEN A PERSUASIVE TWIST

All the following types of argument can be the bases for persuasive advertising and all are in fact used in advertising.

Statistical evidence

How statistical evidence is presented can be key to its persuasive impact. It is not surprising that many books have been written on how deceptive statistical presentations can be. The presentation of statistical data influences the meanings drawn from it, with some meanings resonating more emotionally than others. Thus Eysenck, an advocate of IQ tests, claims that IQ scores predict scholastic performance with 'considerable precision'.[16] With the correlation between IQ scores and scholastic performance being around 0.5, this simply means that 25 per cent (0.5 × 0.5) of the variance or differences between people is accounted for by IQ. An opponent of Eysenck could, with more justification, claim that IQ does not predict with precision since 75 per cent of the differences between students in scholastic performance would still be present (to be accounted for) even if all the students had the same IQ. Advertisers quote statistics as they sound like hard evidence even though most of the audience may be mathematically illiterate. Just think of the difference in the impact of an ad claiming 90 per cent customer satisfaction compared with one saying a company had 10 per cent dissatisfied customers.

Narratives and anecdotes

A narrative does not simply chronicle events or facts but tries to make sense of them. While an anecdote is a short illustrative story, a narrative is a story that accounts for the sequence of events. Both narratives and anecdotes can be very persuasive. President Ronald Reagan was a past master at using anecdotes to persuade. Stories of welfare abuse are the stock-in-trade of conservative politicians and right-wing newspapers as they are guaranteed to cause public fury. Stories attached to products, for example how a product is made or how it was discovered or invented or the successes consumers have had with it, add to perceptions of authenticity and credibility. Lee Iococca, as CEO of Chrysler, featured in commercials in which he took viewers around his car plants; the work force were shown while the story of the company's achievements in car manufacture was narrated. Such stories create a warm feeling of reassurance which tends to mute criticism.

Narratives can be a powerful tactic when used to persuade, as they can highlight key persuasive elements and conjure up emotional visions. Simmons shows how stories help managers inspire, persuade and give direction in a way that is far more effective than purely logical argument.[17] It is the stories in the Bible that people quote and ministers use to illustrate their sermons. Stories, like good jokes, stick in the memory and set themes for our thinking. Well-chosen examples can be stories in miniature and effective persuaders. Stories tend to work by transforming into a different context what are typically familiar ideas. The presence of the familiar reassures and lowers defences. Stories like the Enron scandal can be ideal for teaching values and ethics.

Sartre (1905–80) was very successful in using lucid vignettes rather than logical argument to establish his claims, e.g. that all values are relative. Many 'theories' succeed in this way. Freud commonly used vivid stories to illustrate his theories. 'Repression' was, for example, shown as analogous to someone interrupting a lecture and, after being escorted out, continuing to bang on the door. An extended metaphor like this is not uncommon in advertising and is a powerful persuasive device. All target audiences seek maximal relevance for information to be absorbed – that is, maximal cognitive effect for minimal processing effort.[18] Stories require little cognitive processing effort.

A persuasive story brings together the relevant known facts into a supportive framework. Pennington and Hastie studied how jurors made sense of the evidence presented during a trial when just to remember all the facts was impossible.[19] What they did was to bring the evidence together into a story that made sense for them. They then used this story to evaluate the stories told by the prosecutor and the defence. It was on the basis of this evaluation that jurors accepted or rejected what they were being told. However, just because listeners or viewers make sense of a story, it does not follow that the actions taken make sense in the circumstances. A juror may make sense of the sequence of actions carried out by the killer but still reject the killing as in any way justified. Similarly, in slice-of-life advertising, the sequence of events can make sense without the viewer thinking that buying the brand would make sense for him. There is a need to dramatically connect the two.

A genealogy is a form of narrative. It explains by describing how something came about. In advertising, it is not uncommon to show the whole of the manufacturing process, from input of raw materials to outputs to customers. This is an effective way of showing the product to be authentic and gives it a richer background and identity.

Description

Any description has the potential to arouse emotion by connecting with concerns and in this way to generate changes in perspective. Contrary to rational choice theory, the words used to describe are very important. We buy a product not *per se* but as the bearer of a description of benefits, and such descriptions can vary widely in persuasive appeal. In persuasion, everything depends on how things are put, that is on rhetoric. For example, to say something is 'authentic' conjures up associations that an identical replica (e.g. a copy of the Elgin Marbles) does not. A market trader selling counterfeit Rolex watches in Mexico described them as 'authentic replicas' to exploit the adjective. The names given to features of a product (like *anti-ageing* cream) do not just declare a benefit but create perceptions. This can be effective since consumers are disposed to react on the basis of the names used to describe, as these are categories used to organize our thoughts. It is simply not true that a rose by any other name would smell as sweet. Words can bias behaviour in the wrong direction: for example, the term 'recreational drugs', makes the whole drug scene sound harmless. When we lump together, as simply 'recreational drugs', marijuana and heroin, the harsher associations of hard drugs evaporate. Morphine, opium and heroin may all be refinements of the same drug, but the meanings, imagery and ethics that attach to them are radically different. Perception goes beyond what is received via sensory stimulation as it involves interpretation influenced by a person's perspective. There can be emotional reactions to a perception without conscious awareness. On these grounds, the term 'apperception' is the word used in psychology for conscious perception with full cognitive awareness.[20]

Appeals to emotion by the right choice of words have always been endemic to war propaganda, the tendency being to dehumanize the enemy by the words used to describe him (e.g. gook) and to avoid facing up to the human suffering (e.g. the use of words like 'collateral damage'). The recent Balkan wars witnessed the Serb rhetoric of denigration, Bosnian Muslims becoming 'Turks' and the Croats 'Ustasha' (fascist allies of Germany in the Second World War). Emotive exhortation in politics has a long lineage. For example:

The Budget should be balanced, the Treasury refilled, Public debt reduced, the arrogance of officialdom tempered and controlled and assistance to foreign lands reduced, lest the state becomes bankrupt. The people should be forced to work and not depend on government for assistance.

This was actually said by Cicero (106–20 BC).

How we react to some event, person or attribute is very much tied to how it is described. Thus to call a car a 'hairdresser's car' undermines its symbolism in the eyes of the consumer, even though there are many rich and successful hairdressers.

Visual evidence

Pictures can indeed be more persuasive than a thousand words. The horrific photographic evidence of poverty used by Roosevelt to promote the New Deal struck the right emotional chord to change perspectives and obtain agreement for the project. Photographic images from the Vietnam war had considerable influence on international opinion: the image of a little girl running covered in napalm, the Vietcong suspect being shot in the head by a South Vietnamese general, the Buddhist monk aflame, the last helicopter leaving the US embassy surrounded by panic-stricken crowds left behind, etc. These images made Americans begin to question the assumptions behind the war in a way that little else could have. Similarly, in the US student protests against the Vietnam war, we saw a girl cradling a dead body in the Kent State massacre of 1970. Visual evidence is common in commercial advertising to show the effects of some cosmetic or other, but in not-for-profit advertising pictures can be the key to encouraging public donations or outrage, as when they show baby seals being battered to death in Canada, or dogs in a hunt tearing apart a fox, or the skeletal form of a malnourished child in Africa.

Comparison and contrast

Contrasts/comparisons are often used to arouse sympathy and action. For example, dramatic comparisons between wealth and poverty arouse indignation, while the before and after illustrations in cosmetics or diet food ads prompt interest and buying.

Analogy

Analogies in persuasive appeals can be false but nonetheless effective, as many in the target audience continue to be transfixed by the image generated by the analogy. An example is the claim that taxation of the rich to pay for welfare programmes is analogous to communist confiscation. This analogy provides the 'framing' that arouses the emotion of outrage. Similarly, the American Medical Association refers to 'socialized medicine', the Republicans talk about 'confiscatory taxation', or Democrats talk about tax reduction as a 'gravy train for the rich'. Analogies have the same sharpening and blurring effects as words do in general but more so. In commercial advertising analogies are common: as Mercedes-Benz says, 'once you drive one, there is no turning back' and takes as an analogy the marriage vow.

Classification

Classification can persuade by associating the subject with the image conjured up by the category in general. Thus categorizing a product as a health food associates it with the connotations of 'health'. Attached to all categories are certain connotations ('junk food') which get transferred to anything we put into the category (e.g. all fast food). Getting a target to accept a certain categorization (e.g. genetically modified food as 'Frankenstein food') contributes to inducing the desired perspective. Thus one ad talks about dealing with 'acid reflux *disease*': the classification as a 'disease' commands more interest and desire to act while the medical jargon of 'acid reflux' provides credibility.

Interestingly, the way people are classified (e.g. as house-proud) tends to induce them to behave according to the category in which they are placed. In other words, people are apt to grow into the labels given to them, particularly the labels attached to them by authority figures like teachers. The British in India, like the Mughals before them, believed firmly in the so-called 'martial races', the tribes from which they drew their troops. The need to recruit 2.5 million men in the Second World War meant recruiting from non-martial peoples in India, who nevertheless performed just as well when accorded the title of soldier. Advertisers exploit this tactic when, for example, they label today's woman the 'liberated woman' (e.g. in the Charlie perfume ads) and then identify 'liberated' with the use of a certain perfume or other. There is also the exploitation of the 'granfalloon' effect whereby a group of consumers is addressed as if they had some distinguishing characteristic in common that needs to be addressed in the attributes of the product they buy. The classic example in advertising is the suggestion that heavy users of detergents need a particular kind of detergent. Labelling a group of people as having something in common will induce them to act as if this were so. As the resulting sense of sharing is highly valued, consumers may unquestioningly accept that they do have that something in common.[21]

DEFINITION

Analytic definitions purport to give the essential features of whatever is being defined; thus man might be defined as a rational animal. Acceptance of the definition means acceptance of its implications or consequences: in this lies the persuasiveness of the analytic definition. Thus there is the age-old dispute over whether the 'law' is to be defined in terms of being a 'command' or a principle certified by reason, or just something that emanates from consensus opinion. The controversy is not simply about words. It is concerned with making one rather than another aspect of law central, so the appropriate consequences can be drawn.

Analytic definitions should specify the necessary and sufficient conditions for something to come within their scope. It has often been suggested that analytic definitions should be formulated for concepts but this has proven difficult. In fact most concepts cannot be defined in this way, so it is generally held that under-standing a concept amounts to knowing when it can be used.[22]

It is hoped that how a situation, object or thing is defined will influence how the target audience thinks about it. Getting acceptance of a certain definition (abortion is murder of the unborn child) induces a certain perspective which makes persuasion more a matter of logic, simply an inference from that perspective. A historian's attitude is often indicated by the defining words used, just as whether Christopher Columbus's arrival in the Americas is described as a 'discovery', an 'invasion' or a 'conquest' can be revealing. The term 'persuasive definition' refers to the attempt to attach the value of one thing to the reality of something else, by defining the latter as a true example of the former. Thus defining National Socialism as true democracy, as Hitler did, was an attempt to persuade by making the two concepts equivalent. Ads often claim their product defines, for example, good taste or the complete experience, in the hope that forceful assertion will convince the target audience that this is so.

In the marketing of causes, one of the most persuasive arousing strategies has been to define something as a 'right', the 'right' to buy and consume hard drugs being the latest example. Certain rights may be conferred by law, like the right to privacy, but the rights under discussion here are those taken to be in some way 'natural' rights. The concept of natural rights is a difficult one since it implies the rights are present in everyone and arise without learning. The Universal Declaration of Human Rights has been described by the UN Secretary General, Kofi Annan, as the 'yardstick by which we measure human progress'. The Declaration enunciates rights but does not explain why people have such rights, who conferred them and so on. It is hoped that by simply asserting certain rights to be moral universals, there will be a raising of consciousness (and consciences!) such that perspectives change. The language of rights in this context has done a lot of good though the claim to them has no teeth as there is no mechanism for enforcement.

Strangely for someone from the country which popularized the 'rights language' of the Founding Fathers, Senator John Bricker argued that the UN human rights documents were completely foreign to American law and tradition. This was because, until the Helsinki Final Act in 1975, there existed a

35

socialist and a capitalist conception of 'rights', with socialism stressing social and economic 'rights' and capitalism stressing civil and political 'rights'. Neither side would accept the other's definition, but Helsinki saw the capitalist version triumph. In politics the language of rights is a powerful emotional political stick that continues to be employed, a recent example being the demand that the West concede a 'nation's right to development' which in practice decrees the transfer of resources from the rich West to poorer nations. Such may be a real need but it is not a 'right' in any meaningful sense.

For Mary Warnock, talk of natural rights should be replaced by talk of moral principles.[23] But this more accurate use of language would lose the emotional resonance built into the word 'rights'. While the word 'rights' is overworked, it still carries a lot of emotional punch, and this is often exploited by advertising. Many ads portray their product as cementing or advancing women's rights by showing women taking what has traditionally been the man's role, for example, or by suggesting their product symbolizes women's new freedom ('You've come a long way, Baby').

Warnock, while acknowledging there is a certain usefulness in the claim that there are basic rights belonging to all human beings, argues that the use of the term 'rights' to describe 'ideals' devalues the language in the interest of rhetoric. Peter Singer, a philosopher, popularized the idea of 'animal rights' and coined the word 'speciesism' to mean an irrational prejudice in favour of the human species.[24] This technical-sounding name echoed the word 'racism' and suggested that not treating animals on an equal footing to humans was unethical. It has been persuasive with many people.

THE NEED FOR BOTH THE RATIONAL AND THE EMOTIONAL

Although an appeal that resonates emotionally will get attention and even trigger action, there is usually a need to show that the proposed action (buying or otherwise) is socially appropriate and can be 'rationally' justified. This is because the consumer is not an isolated individual but a social animal. It is as if there were a hidden audience observing our buying and requiring that whatever is bought adheres to social norms and can be 'rationally' defended or at least rationalized.

Since the strength of any motive to act is intimately tied to the level of emotion evoked, the more emotional an issue is made, the more interest (sustained attention) it receives. Hence, advertisers should typically seek messages that resonate with the *values* of their target audience which go beyond mere hedonism. The art of successful political agitation lies in selecting the issues that best resonate with the public. Although Milton Rokeach, referring back to the Greeks, like many before him, speaks of terminal values and instrumental values, values are more usefully viewed as those ultimate concerns which are the final arbitrators in resolving otherwise intractable trade-offs.[25] Values, and the emotions to which they relate, are involved in all trade-offs. As Alasdair MacIntyre says, questions of ultimate goals are questions of values, and on values reason is silent; conflict between competing values cannot be settled by reason – one must simply choose.[26] Reason itself cannot *prescribe* what to do but can *proscribe* what is ineffective or inefficient. This is not to downplay reason, which can be a powerful persuader, but simply to state a fact.

COMMUNICATION, SYMBOLISM AND MEANING

In marketing, persuasive advertising acts to establish wants/motivations and beliefs/attitudes by helping to formulate a *conception* of the brand as being one which people like those in the target audience would or should prefer. Perception involves some conceptualization of the brand, that is a grasp of what features typify it and distinguish it from rivals. Product reality for the consumer is concept-relative: we see what our concepts have taught us to see: things are seen though a conceptual lens. Concepts, perceptions and the resulting perceptual judgements are thus inseparable.

All fields of persuasive communication (including advertising) seek messages that resonate with values. Yet values, like objectives, are typically multiple and conflicting, their ranking constantly altering with changes in circumstance. There is arguably a fault line in America's value system between equality and meritocracy. In our personal lives there is a tension between standing out and standing in, between the need to express individualism and the desire to join and conform to positive reference groups. The most persuasive journalism engages and stimulates the raw feelings of the reader. It conforms to the notion of co-production in postmodernism, being a kind of 'co-production' between journalist and reader.

The values that are likely to resonate are those of the relevant subcultures to which the target audience belong (we tend to belong to more than one subculture) as these are likely to be more galvanizing and influential than those of the culture as a whole. The taking of drugs can be a badge of attachment to some reference group as well as a symbol of rebellion against authority figures: this must be recognized in any anti-drug campaign. If the dominant American cultural values are the puritan ethic, equal treatment for all, individualism, achievement, moral integrity, practicality and efficiency, material comfort and racial and gender equality, they are normative values, not the dominant actual values. A target audience's specific subcultural values are the foundation on which to build appeals as these reflect their members' key concerns.

A *sign* has *reference* in that it refers to something other than itself. A brand name is a sign as it refers to something other than itself, namely the product. But precisely what is conjured up by the sign is not simply its reference but its *sense-meaning*, that is the meanings or connotations attached to the brand. Suzanne

37

Langer, like many philosophers, speaks of the *denotation* of a sign being the common reference we have for it, while the *connotation* of the sign is the 'meaning' it has for us.[27] 'Meaning' as used by Langer is equated with sense-meaning. In any specific instance the sense-meaning of something may or may not have significance for us. If something does have high significance for us, it has 'significant meaning' for us; that is, we believe it has high significance for our values, wants and goals. And anything that has significant meaning for us can influence our actions. As Greenspan points out, to have significant meaning implies salience of the sort that registers with the emotions and demands attention.[28] For Greenspan, reasons for action become more intentional 'when loaded with affect' while emotion itself 'is the initial vehicle of motivational force'. But in directing attention to things that concern us, emotions also distract us from perceiving other things, like perhaps the brand name in an advertisement.

A *symbol* is a sign that conjures up something additional to its reference, namely what it signifies or stands for. Rolls-Royce refers to a particular make of automobile but it is also a status symbol. But what a particular product or brand symbolizes may vary from one person to another and, even more, from one society to another. Thus in the United States and Japan, the Mercedes car symbolizes status whereas in Lisbon (Portugal) it often conjures up a taxi. Symbols embody a complexity of information for those to whom they are significant. Symbols can substitute for vast quantities of direct information and in this lies their power to influence. But even when a symbol is loaded with ambiguity, the power of symbolism can lie in its very vagueness since the audience has more freedom to interpret and map onto it their deepest concerns.

Brands can be *codified symbols* of status, prestige, reliability or quality, or, for some consumers, just the opposite. Many designer labels are bought because they symbolize social reassurance, beauty, the possession of in-group information, social approval and an expressive gesture of the consumer's feelings at the time or merely because they reflect the power of aesthetic attraction. In any case, purchases are made and valued not just for their functional utility but also for their symbolic utility. Approaches to buying that fail to come to grips with symbolic utility will always be unsatisfactory.

It is certainly true that many a once-famous brand name has lost its pulling power. In the early twenty-first century it is even being claimed that McDonald's has lost a lot of its shine. Such decline usually occurs because the brand has not been updated and has ceased to project an attractive, arousing image. This is the case with the Helena Rubinstein brand of cosmetics which has not moved with the times but has remained tied to an older generation. It has failed to reinvent itself for a younger generation that identifies it with products their grandmothers used. This is always a problem for 'older' brand names in that the younger generation typically view the older as a negative reference group where tastes are concerned (think of music), while many of that older generation want to show they are 'with it' by imitating the young. Brand images are diluted by becoming associated with price discounts. Constant price discounts are actually teaching the target audience that price is the criterion to apply when buying, in the process turning the brand into a commodity product.

When brands are perceived as undifferentiated in functional performance, symbolic meanings become crucial. A successful brand is one that symbolizes an image tied to what the consumer cares about. Advertising seeks to fuse the brand with several symbolic meanings:[29]

1 meaning as symbolized by the 'personality' given to the brand, e.g. sophisticated woman. Sometimes this personality is partly the construction of history. Thus the very name Jaguar and its associations with the familiar leaping cat were the invention of advertising people, since the company's previous incarnation as SS cars was deemed inappropriate in 1945;

2 meaning as symbolized by the emotions emanating from using the brand, e.g. self-confidence;

3 meaning as symbolizing the power to complete a social relationship, e.g. with some member of the opposite sex;

4 meaning as symbolizing that certain moves are possible, e.g. social advancement;

5 meaning as symbolizing that the brand makes things intensified, e.g. more exciting.

It is brand image that persuades 'otherwise discerning people that a brown fizzy liquid called Coca-Cola is the symbol of youth and vitality', or leads, 'the young to demonstrate their individuality and rebelliousness by wearing mass-produced clothing emblazoned with the brand names of multinational companies'.[30] Brand image is as important as ever, and can be given sharper meaning by the addition of a logo and a slogan. Some slogans are inappropriate for the product: Windex's opaque slogan 'Inspiration in a Bottle' compares unfavourably with the slogan used by Lexus which says what the product stands for: 'Passionate Pursuit of Perfection'. Some images become lifeless and start fading away. They need sparkle to be revived.

If the consumer has come to accept that all cars are reliable, have warranties undreamt-of a few years ago and so on, there is a danger that all the cars within a segment will be viewed as tokens of each other. In such a situation, brand images distinguish the various makes of automobile in the eyes of the consumer. Products, as possessions, help us project a certain social identity. If the dramaturgical model of Erving Goffman has any validity, products can be likened to stage props in that they help refine and elaborate our act.[31] Although the credibility of a projected brand image requires some substance to back it up (everything cannot be done with mirrors), it is also true that substance can fail without the elixir of a positive brand image. Where there is uncertainty in choosing, as occurs when the market segment is full of brands that look alike, the importance of symbolism is paramount.

What resonates is what a product symbolizes. As Albert says, a glass of warm milk at night is not just a calcium and L-tryptophan cocktail but can symbolize mother and childhood security, while a cup of coffee after dinner may represent a beloved ritual and symbolize a special private time.[32] It is this kind of symbolism that made it take so long for tea bags to penetrate the British market, since 'making a nice cup of tea' was a significant ritual. With increased familiarity, a brand acquires sentimental attachments that arouse nostalgia. Consumers need the familiar, especially in times of change. This is an aspect of brand loyalty and a significant one. One newspaper article records the loyalty of customers of United Airlines: 'Right up until the very end I will stay loyal to them, until there's no United to fly'; or 'Yes, I'm concerned about the bankruptcy. But at the moment, I won't take any other airline.'[33] At the time of writing, media commentators are expressing surprise that corporate sponsors are refusing to sign up for plans to save rare species. This suggests the cause does not resonate with corporate donors or even with the public; otherwise large companies would find it advantageous to identify with it. In fact, the public willingness to save rare species is correlated to the appeal of their names; few, for example, would be willing to strain their finances to save something called the vampire bat.

When we think of emotion in persuasion, we think of symbols arousing toxic feelings like anger and guilt. But any symbolic system can have a tone or texture that touches the emotions by possessing relevant meaning for the audience. This is because all symbolic systems, whether words (spoken or written), pictures, gestures, music, images, art, religion, money, institutions or human behaviour, can evoke relevant meanings by resonating with the concerns of the target audience and so can be instrumental in persuasion. Pope Gregory the Great (c. 540–604) called statues 'books for the illiterate' since so much was 'read' into them. A precondition for all persuasive advertising is the ability to use symbols that resonate with the concerns of the target audience.

Although the most symbolic aspect of any culture is language, some of the most effective emotional appeals are made through pictures and music. Music is 'consumed' purely for pleasure though it taps deep into the emotions through altering mood. While it expresses emotion it is not *an* emotion. Music is powerful for making an emotional evocation of the past and so is common in advertising that exploits nostalgia. The use of classical music in British advertising led to its increased popularity after years of decline in the face of pop music. Vivaldi is a good example of a classical composer made popular by exposure in advertising. Music evokes an emotional sense of sharing – which explains its frequent use at ceremonies – and so is instrumental in changing moods. Music often has the merit of being able to arouse strong feelings devoid of any particular ideological, and therefore maybe alienating, context. Thus the 'Marseillaise' can signify leftist revolution – the bands played it in 1917 as Lenin arrived at the Finland Station – and still be the theme tune of Vichy France. Similarly, 'Lillie Marlene', a song created by Norbert Schultzer who was a favoured acolyte of Goebbels, became a hit with the Allies and indeed almost the theme tune of the Second World War. But there are exceptions. For many Jews, Wagner's music is not pleasing at any time, being so much associated with the Nazi regime.

Pictures (especially films) are typically more effective at persuasion than any book or article. During the Bolshevik revolution, Lenin concentrated on sending trains equipped as cinemas to the illiterate rural population of Russia. And for Goebbels, Nazi control of the cinema was the very foundation of the regime. In the closing months of the war, Goebbels withdrew 100,000 men from the front to make a historical epic, *Kolberg*, about Prussia surrounded during the Napoleonic Wars.

Kenneth Burke argues that if we are to create a sense of identification with a target audience, we must speak to them in their own language.[34] This is not surprising if we view persuasion as an offer of affiliation. As an example of this, the two most successful British Second World War broadcasters were the author J.B. Priestley and Lord Woolton, then Minister of Food. Both were successful because they used the language of ordinary people (e.g. 'belly' for stomach) rather than making the patronizing and obfuscating official broadcasts that were then common. Ronald Reagan, as President, was the most successful of communicators partly because he understood the power of the vernacular in creating common ground between leaders and led. (Some academics thought it was because he knew nothing else.) Thus his well-chosen populist slang, like his description of Colonel Gaddaffi as 'the flake', helped to create Reaganism. This lesson has been well learned by advertisers (except when they want to stress the scientific credibility of a product by using pseudo-scientific jargon), who are quick to use the slang of their target audience. If culture is a man-made, socially constructed reality, it is also a symbolic system, different parts of which have differing emotional significance depending on life experiences.

Making any decision involves doubts, risks and uncertainties. If there were no doubts, no uncertainties and no need for trade-offs, there would be no need for persuasion. In systems of symbolic logic, where there is only one valid solution, we speak of *demonstrating* the right answer or of *exposing* the errors made by those who got it wrong. It would seem odd to speak of persuasion in such a context since, after certain axioms have been accepted, solutions in symbolic logic are simply matters of deduction. But with decision making there are alternative views and different preferences, so persuasion is always involved. We cannot, through logic alone, compel agreement. In the epic nineteenth-century debates between the two outstanding British leaders, it was usually the novelist Disraeli

41

who won through appealing to the ancestral calls of blood and nation, eschewing the logical formulas used by the mathematics graduate, Gladstone. Strong logic is not necessarily compelling. A rational demonstration of the correct conclusion to a syllogistic argument presupposes the target audience have knowledge of deductive logic. But the rules of deductive logic are not innate but have to be learnt.

We may compel assent by logic but not convince if the logical way of persuasion is an alien perspective. This is illustrated by the story of Socrates (470–400 BCE). Socrates was accused of making the weaker argument defeat the stronger. His reasoning compelled his inquisitors to assent but they nonetheless found his arguments unpersuasive because his abstract form of reasoning lacked the *psychological* force of the traditional wisdom. Aristotle (384–322 BCE) feared the power of rhetoric because it could make 'the worse appear the better reason'.

We typically find it difficult to voice views that are not consonant with our own perspective or system of beliefs and values. Hence, we only express a small subset of statements about social life. Contradictory systems of beliefs compete, none defeating the others, because each system of beliefs acquires a coherence or organic wholeness that makes it plausible to adherents. This is the position in religion. People commonly adopt a 'coherence theory of truth'; that is, people judge a statement on the basis of whether it coheres with their current beliefs. While such coherence does not establish truth, for the consumer it does offer a warrant to believe. Supporters commonly invent *ad hoc* hypotheses to explain away any 'falsifying' evidence or arguments. In her studies on skill in argument, Deanna Kuhn found that subjects in her study tended to assimilate any new information to existing theories, with the result that the ability to evaluate the relevance of evidence to challenge their theory was lost.[35] That a coherence theory of truth was being followed was apparent from the tendency to establish the plausibility of some causal chain by spelling out or describing how the relevant causal sequence occurred rather than by providing evidence for the theory's correctness.

Ramachandran, a neuroscientist, argues that it is the function of the left hemisphere of the brain to create a belief system and make any new information fit into it so that it coheres.[36] He argues that if some new information cannot be easily fitted into existing perspectives or belief systems, the left hemisphere relies on Freudian defence mechanisms like denial, rationalization and projection to preserve the status quo. On the other hand, it is the right hemisphere's task to play the devil's advocate by questioning that status quo and to look for inconsistencies. If the left hemisphere is conformist, trying to shut out information that is potentially threatening to the status quo, when anomalies become too great to ignore the right hemisphere can force a complete shift in viewpoint. What advertisers need to try to do is show that their claims and assertions cohere with what is currently held to be true and give no grounds for bringing in the devil's advocate.

A RETURN TO PERSPECTIVES AND PERSUASION

Every argument, every persuasive appeal takes some set of beliefs and values for granted. As stated in Chapter 1, being on the right wavelength is the same as having the 'right' point of view or *perspective*. Different perspectives lead us to classify things differently. Thus if a person's values incorporate animal rights there is no way that he or she is going to endorse fox hunting or the killing of baby seals for their skins.

The perspective from which people view the evidence influences their choice of 'facts' as perspective influences what people see as relevant. The opinions in politics that catch on are those that best define what people are already thinking, that is, exploit a common perspective, or, in the words of the eighteenth-century poet Alexander Pope, 'what oft was thought but ne'er so well expressed'. A political party leader, Andrew Bonar Law (1858–1923), once exclaimed: 'I must follow them, I am their leader'. What we mean by being a good 'politician' or a 'good journalist' often amounts to the gift of eloquent expression of popular prejudice, elevating it from its origin on the bar-room floor. When we have the same perspective as the speaker or writer, we enjoy listening/reading and being further persuaded. This is why a rallying sermon is so much more satisfying than a church ceremony. The sermon has always been an instrument of persuasion. And its effectiveness cannot be assessed from reading it in print. The very act of being with others in an audience, collectively listening and sharing words that resonate, can be very emotional, and being 'persuaded' very enjoyable[37] because, at its best, it provides a sense of sharing and an offer of affiliation. The sense of sharing is important. The Japanese word *amae* meaning comfort in complete acceptance by another, captures this sense of sharing. Its importance indicates that ads must resonate to be effective and subtly make an offer of affiliation.

Researchers in the social sciences are influenced by the perspectives they bring to their task. One example is the well-known controversy between the American anthropologists, Robert Redfield and Oscar Lewis.[38] They both worked in Tepoztlan, a village in Mexico. In the 1920s Redfield found the village an idyllic place in terms of the health and happiness of its inhabitants. Twenty years later Lewis found no such harmony, just suspicion and tension. Commentators dismiss the idea that the village inhabitants had changed. The fact was that Redfield saw urban life as the source of moral and social disintegration and presented Tepoztlan as a contrast to the horrors of the city. Lewis saw peasant life as one of backwardness and extreme poverty. The perspectives of both Redfield and Lewis influenced their research and how they interpreted what they saw.

Perspectives within a culture do change as a result of cultural drift. New cultural perspectives arise and people gradually witness their triumph. Perspectives on sexual matters have changed completely in the last fifty years in Western societies. The writers who first identify what is happening are regarded

43

as astute social commentators. In one sense a brand image can be fruitfully viewed as a particular perspective since it is a distinctive way of seeing and a partial way of understanding. Hence, much of any discussion of the problem of changing perspectives has relevance to changing a brand image as this is an analogous process.

When the perspectives of opponents stem from core values, bringing about a change in them through rational debate is a non-starter that will amount simply to an exchange of dogmatic assertions. As the assumptions of each perspective come into conflict, there are no common mutually acceptable criteria by which one party can compel the assent of the other. Thus we divide persuasive appeals into:

1 persuasive appeals addressed to an audience that can be counted on to have the right perspective. Here we argue within the agreed perspective to show our solution most coheres with it. Sometimes the term 'persuasion' is itself defined in this way. Thus Meyer defines persuasion as the process by which all the questions raised by an audience are answered as well as those they had in mind.[39] But a persuader can satisfactorily answer all of both sets of questions, yet the audience remain unconvinced;

2 persuasive appeals designed to induce the required perspective as a prerequisite to persuading the target audience. This means knowing something about the social attachments that have influenced the target's beliefs and values. Established perspectives in science are its paradigms or what Gilbert (following Kuhn) calls one's position or matrix of beliefs, attitudes, emotions, insights and values connected with some claim.[40] The acceptance of some basic paradigm makes persuasion in line with that paradigm much easier. Thus any psychologist who accepts behaviourism will look for a solution in operant conditioning and will not question such a solution. Sometimes the persuader needs to take account of an entire perspective and not just one single claim. The first requirement in all cases, where perspectives differ, is to induce the 'right' perspective, so an advertisement's appeals or arguments are perceived as good. This means discovering what the perspective of the target audience is and understanding it. Aristotle recognized this need for common ground and in particular argued for the need to understand the *feelings* of the audience on any issue so these could be taken into account. The word 'peasant' to describe agricultural workers would be regarded as snobbish by an audience of British or Americans, yet it is a legitimate term in many countries and would be deemed an objective description with no suggestion of social condescension. Aristotle recognized that there were events outside the persuader's control (*atechoi*) which can be crucial in a final decision. As Quine points out, there is no 'unvarnished news' of the

world and our perceptions inevitably involve judgements as to what concepts to apply.[41] Without the right perspective, neither the questions asked nor the answers given can be very meaningful. After all, any question asked is ambiguous until you know what the questioner is getting at and this assumes knowing where he is coming from. Perspectives on occasion can be cast in stone when strong vested interests are at stake. Thus, as we look back at the six demands of the Chartist movement in the nineteenth century – manhood suffrage, equal electoral districts, annual parliaments, payment of MPs, the abolition of the property qualification to vote and voting by ballot – it is difficult to understand the perspective that responded with intense opposition. One of the advantages of one-to-one marketing (relationship marketing) is the learning opportunity it provides to get to know the individual customer's perspective.[42]

QUANTITATIVE AND QUALITATIVE APPROACHES TO PERSUASION

Quantitative approaches to persuasion are associated with 'principles' of persuasion derived from social science. *Qualitative* approaches are typified by *rhetoric* which deals with questions and issues where there is a conflict of opinion and where judgement or social norms predominate. It is not just confined to poetics, the analysis of style or literary effect, as is commonly supposed. Rhetoric is not empty but provides additional pros and cons on an issue and covers methods for overcoming objections. Since changing perspectives involves indirect means of persuasion rather than logical appeals, rhetoric tends to be more useful. In general, all rhetorical and emotional means of persuasion are contrasted with the use of reason since they exploit feelings rather than logic. Persuasion here uses a sense of shared interests, a sense of solidarity, or, alternatively, creates a connection in the mind of the audience between feelings evoked and action to take. Rationality alone is insufficient since all decisions involve goals or purposes and the selection of goals and purposes involves values. The best recipe for decision making is a mixture of reason and emotion.[43]

For Aristotle, persuasion was identified with rhetoric. In rhetoric, emotional appeals are as relevant as rational appeals, and Aristotle saw rhetoric as integrating emotion and reason.[44] He stressed, as many have done since, that rhetoric is about opinion (*doxa*) rather than knowledge that is certain (*episteme*). He viewed persuasion as composed of:

- *ethos*, which depends on the characteristics of the source of the persuasive communication and the source's corresponding credibility (reputation, technical expertise, trustworthiness), including indicators such as

45

cleverness of argument, choice of words, gestures, dynamism, eye contact and so on.

- *logos*, which depends on the evidential base of the argument and refers to the message's rationality or to appeals based on rational argument;
- *pathos*, which depends on inducing a certain frame of mind in the audience through appeals to the emotions.

The above classification finds an echo in today's approach to persuasion, though postmodernists like Foucault claim that any distinction between rhetoric and logic is false because all forms of communication are rhetorical.[45]

▓ *Plate 2.2* *Rational argument: Pilkington Glass*

Source: Courtesy of Pilkington Glass

Introducing the first glass to clean itself continuously.

The unique dual-action process of Pilkington Activ™ makes it the most effective self-cleaning glass. An invisible layer, on the outer surface of the glass, reacts with natural UV energy to break down organic dirt continuously. At the same time it causes rain to run in sheets down your windows, washing away dirt without leaving streaks. Pilkington Activ™ is the latest inno-vation from a company that has been at the forefront of glass technology for over 170 years. For further details visit www.activeglass.com

Pilkington Activ™. The world's first self-cleaning glass.

This window hasn't been cleaned for 6 months.

Neither has this.

Introducing the first glass to clean itself continuously.

The unique dual-action process of Pilkington **Activ**™ makes it the most effective self-cleaning glass. An invisible layer, on the outer surface of the glass, reacts with natural UV energy to break down organic dirt continuously. At the same time it causes rain to run in sheets down your windows, washing away dirt without leaving streaks. Pilkington **Activ**™ is the latest innovation from a company that has been at the forefront of glass technology for over 170 years.

For further details visit **www.activglass.com**

 PILKINGTON Pilkington **Activ**™ The world's first self-cleaning glass.

Pilkington **Activ**™
self-cleaning glass

Case study:
STELLA ARTOIS

Advertising can create a mythology to surround a product. This has been pre-eminently true of the Belgian lager Stella Artois, for which a long series of advertisements set in historical contexts and celebrating the drink have been created. The effect is really to provide a bogus pedigree or manufactured ancestry; the product is encased in a nimbus of ancient-seeming tales that attest to its astonishing status, tradition and exclusivity, embodied in the daring slogan 'Reassuringly Expensive'.

Epic/cinematic production values

The visual qualities of these advertisements are high, indeed they mimic scenes from epic Hollywood high-budget movies. But they are minutely observed, a kaleidoscope of traditional costumes, ostentatious colour schemes and massively characterful faces: for each one, a vivid narrative is fabricated which attracts, beguiles and sustains attention.

The *Guardian* (www.media.guardian.co.uk) described the production values thus:

> Stella Artois is a *Jean de Florette*-inspired campaign, now in its twelfth year. When the Stella script comes in, you know it's not going to be just another commercial, but a mini film, with a story, characters and a punchline. Perhaps most importantly, it's not just the beer that is reassuringly expensive; these ads come with a healthy production budget that gives directors the free rein they so desperately want and a serious bit of showreel for when Spielberg finally makes the call. Stella's advertising agency, Lowe, has been producing these mini epics ever since 1991, when it first came up with the idea of parodying the hit French film. The first of them, 'Jacques de Florette', was directed by Michael Seresin, an established film-maker who . . . had previously worked on *Midnight Express* and *Bugsy Malone* . . . Matt Edwards, account director at Lowe, says the ads appeal to top directors because they are short films as much as commercials. 'The Stella Artois ads are very good preparation for directors because they give you the chance to do things on a scale you've never done before; they are like mini movies. The new advertisement, "Devil's Island", probably cost more than £¾ million to make and was shot in Argentina with more than 850 extras and an 80 year old ship which had to be made seaworthy; four blocks of downtown Buenos Aires had to be closed.'

Two texts examined

First, we will examine two advertisements in the series in detail, in order to give a sense of why they were both attention getting and memorable. Both these texts resonate:

they celebrate the exclusivity of the product, but they also successfully integrate the identity of the product into the narrative by making it the star of the drama, rather than telling a story that is incidental to the meaning of the product.

A

One of these advertisements begins with a sequence from the First World War. Two soldiers are seen in a battle in a shattered and blasted landscape: one saves the other's life. It is a classic and timeless image of the Great War. The scene then moves to a crowded bar, owned by the father of the saved man. Exhausted by war and the battlefield, the saved man enters the bar. His father pumps him a Stella Artois and he proudly introduces the friend who saved him, his face a picture of thirsty yearning. But we are taken behind the bar to show how the father shifts the tap, pretending it has run dry, so that only his son gets to drink the Stella Artois. The rescuer is only given wine. The message is that Stella is too precious to give free even to those who save your boy's life. Others see a different meaning: 'The moral of this must be never do a Frenchman a favour, which is good advice at the best of times!' (www.dooyoo.co.uk)

What is remarkable about the ad is the contextual detail: the *patron*, a mix of benevolence and shiftiness, the huge thirsts generated by the battlefield, the dourness – all greys and browns, roughness and muted colours – and the creation of a picture right out of a movie set; the explosions, mud, charging soldiers, followed by a scene of battle-fuelled weariness and the mighty thirst this generates. There is no discordant note. The war scenes are epic, the pubs scenes domestic, but all this locates the product in time, tradition and history. The way you dealt with the trauma of the First World War was with the help of this product, the drink, Stella Artois, through whose sublime agency order is restored and renewed. It all evokes a naive Gallic world of simple pleasures, the terrors of the crowded battlefield giving way to the joys of the crowded tavern.

B

The second advertisement ('Good Doctor') is equally one where shock is balanced against the deep satisfying lenitive of consuming the drink, Stella Artois. Here, plague strikes a village. Bravely the doctor has worked through the night. Exhausted by his lonely vigil, he enters the village tavern and is told to leave by an elder, fearful that he is *contamine*. But the priest goes to his aid, declaring that he is free of the plague. The frightened villagers meanwhile have retreated in growling suspicion and produced a blunderbuss. The situation is tense, terrifying and again relieved by the priest's call for Stella Artois: the doctor takes a drink, the priest drinks from the same cup and manfully hugs the doctor. Soon everyone begins to imbibe quantities of Stella and there is pleasure all round. Then the doctor coughs. Suddenly the look of abject fear fills all faces.

Again there is a similarity to a film set and minute observation: everything is portrayed in earth colours, craggy brown skin, brown land, brown buildings dimly lit in the lengthening shadows. It is all about creating a pseudo-history for the brand and weaving a narrative round it. The scene appears to be from a quite remarkably good movie and the characters are hyper-real, every one of them exaggerated. They are not just stereotypes, but antiquated clichés, peasant figures with bushy white eyebrows and glowering countenances, thick-set and clad in pastiche traditional rural clothing, high hats, long socks, etc. The scene is set in some mythical time in the late eighteenth century. The peasants are bigoted and suspicious, ready to break out in anarchic violence or to run away in terror. They have a particular ancient horror of plague and its victims are treated ruthlessly. They are caricatures of traditional Euro-peasant types, their personalities and minds a mass of scorching superstitions. The village doctor by contrast is younger, fearless and fearful. But the commanding symbol is the priest: biretta-clad and stentorian of voice, he is the repository of authority and courageous, a father to his people. Only he can bring order. His hugging the doctor and also his drinking from the same glass promise resolution of the crisis. The doctor then coughs and splutters, leaving us with the possibility that pandemonium may break out again and fulfil its destructive potential, or that order will resume; we are left guessing the end of the story.

These advertisements, with their cult-like aura, excited public interest and comment. Their accumulated imagery was connected by the common themes and symbols of an old, simple France, peasant-poor, cruel, earthy and sensual, yearning for the oblivion induced by that ultimate drink. The authenticity of backgrounds suggested the genuineness of the product itself – and a product displaying authenticity is analogous to a person displaying sincerity. Several more advertisements amplify these points.

Other examples from the series

Various commentators discuss their favourite Stella commercials in cyberspace (www.dooyoo.co.uk):

1

My favourite ad in the series must of course be the one with the vicar. This involves an old man seemingly on his deathbed. An obliging relative fulfils the various last wishes such as getting a flower for the dying man. When he expresses a wish for Stella Artois the assembled relatives grumble as they have a whip-round for the old man's last beer. Our hero is dispatched to fetch the beer but succumbs to temptation on the way home and quaffs the lot. On his return he is met by the local priest who presumably has arrived to deliver the last rites. Our hero takes the priest's coat and hands him the empty glass to hold. As they enter the dying man's room he sits up to see the priest with his empty glass with our hero doing the drinky drinky motion over his shoulder, suggesting that the cleric has guzzled his last beer.

2

The flower seller parks his cart of flowers and stops outside a pub and addresses the landlord, he allows him into the pub and he sits. The landlord goes behind the bar and the flower seller is rooting for change in his pockets. The soundtrack is put to good use as it conveys the mood very well. We then see the next shot with the flower seller on his own supping some Stella. And the landlord is laughing. Gradually, it is revealed that the pub is decorated solely by the flower seller's flowers.

3

Two of the best known Stella ads in the mid-nineties: 'Red Shoes', in which a thirsty Provencal peasant trades a pair of red silk shoes for a glass of beer, and 'Good Samaritan', in which a local tramp does a series of good deeds for his neighbours who offer to buy him a drink, but leave him to settle his own tab when he orders a Stella.

And the *Guardian* (www.media.guardian.co) has revealed a promising new episode in the series:

4

'Devil's Island', which will hit screens next month, tells the story of Didier, a prisoner bound for the notorious French penal colony. On the ship he witnesses one of his fellow inmates attacking a guard with a metal soup ladle and knocking him unconscious. As the prisoner is thrown into the ship's cooler for a spell of solitary confinement, one of the soldiers becomes distracted and drops a bottle of Stella. The bottle rolls to the other end of the deck, where Didier, unable to believe his luck, stashes it away in a rolled-up blanket and waits for a quiet moment to enjoy his discovery. Unfortunately, the prisoners never have a moment alone, and every time he tries to sneak the bottle out he is eyed suspiciously by the others. Then, in a moment of inspiration, he grabs the cook's metal ladle and whacks the guard with an apologetic shrug. He is then dragged over to the hold, clinging tightly to his blanket with a private smile of anticipation on his face, as the words 'reassuringly expensive' appear on the screens.

The appeal of the Stella Artois advertising may be examined from a number of theoretical approaches. One perspective would be that the entire series is, in essence, a luminous theatre of symbolism. The message is elaborated through compact narratives that express a culture's evaluation of its heroic liquid. Serial, semi-ritualized symbolic enactments proclaim (a) the exclusivity and rarity, and (b) the desirability of this drink. The series creates as a result standardized expectations of its narrative product. These dramas are symbolic parables about the uniqueness of Stella Artois, their events carry above all else the central meaning, bequeathed to memory, of the almost sacerdotal status of this drink.

References

'We're only here for the beer', www.media.guardian.co.uk, 3 February 2003.
Stella Artois-Flowers.
'It's ruined Jean de Florette for me' (Kingmaker, 27 August 2000), 'I prefer ir-rever-and' (Buttonman, 14 September 2000, March 2001), www.dooyoo.co.uk/tv/misc_tv/stella_artois_flowers/_review/86626/.
www.adforum.com D & AD 2002.

KEY ASSERTIONS

- In its communications, a company tries to get a target audience to assent to its intended meaning and have its message strike a responsive chord.

- If marketing seeks to persuade, straight logical argument may not be successful as the issues need to be reframed or put into a form that coheres with the audience's beliefs and wants. All types of argument can have a spin put on them to make the message more palatable. This is true whether the argument is: (a) statistical evidence, since presentation can be all-important; (b) anecdotes, since all types of stories direct attention to certain facts and not others; (c) description, since the words used can change perspectives; (d) visual evidence, since one picture can indeed be better than a thousand words; (e) comparisons to highlight differences and contrasts; (f) analogy, since analogies switch normal ways of thinking; (g) classification, since reclassifying a phenomenon changes the focus, with different categories suggesting different connotations; (h) definition, since definitions always endorse a particular perspective or way of looking at a subject.

- If marketing is to get its message accepted over the long term, emotional appeals should be backed by implicitly or explicitly showing that the action being sought is socially appropriate and rationally defensible and coheres with the target's perspective.

- If a new product is being promoted through advertising, the aim is to get the target audience to conceptualize the brand as being one which its members would or should prefer.

- If emotional appeals are to be emphasized, they should be founded on the values of the target group, and use the language of its subculture.

- If a brand is to be promoted, it is important to view it as a symbol and ask what it signifies or stands for, since all established brands are codified symbols of benefits whether functional, expressive, aesthetic or symbolic. The gratification arising from buying, using or consuming a brand cannot be divorced from the images with which the brand is associated.

- If the brand is physically undifferentiated from its rivals, the other aspects of the offering should be examined to establish a competitive advantage, since it is in such markets that brand image counts most.

- If the market is in a state of flux and characterized by consumer uncertainty, brand image is also key, since it gives the consumer something to go on. Brand image offers a perspective and a partial way of understanding the product category.

- If marketing is to develop a persuasive appeal, it must establish whether the target audience can be counted on to have the right perspective or whether there is a prior need to induce the right perspective.

Chapter 3

Persuasive advertising appeals, 1

- Association with social norms, values and valued images
- Solidarity with others
- Status and prestige

This chapter and subsequent chapters discuss approaches to developing effective advertising appeals. The focus is on broad strategies rather than tactics. This means that previous chapters cannot be ignored since there is a need to know about the social attachments (culture, reference groups, social class, experiences) and perspectives (current beliefs and values) of the target audience (Chapter 1), while taking account of devices in persuasive advertising content (Chapter 2). This chapter and Chapter 4 explain the effective use of 'association' in persuasive appeals. The role played by associations in influencing thinking has a long history, with Aristotle (384–322 BCE) proposing that three relations led to associations: (a) when things are similar; (b) when things are contiguous; (c) when things are sharply contrasting. This is still part of thinking today, with the strongest emphasis on contiguity.

When psychologists think of association they think of 'association theory', which describes how one thought leads to other thoughts, just as the thought of a sports car might bring to mind some particular make of car such as the Mazda Miata. Such 'thought networks' dominate thinking, with particular connections depending on relevant experiences. Historians of psychology credit 'associationism' with initiating experimental psychology, and association theory influenced behaviourism and Freudian psychology. In the heyday of behaviourism (see Chapter 4) most theories of learning were described in terms of association between stimuli (S) and responses (R) while Freud believed that the unconscious harboured a vast pool of repressed associations that censored our thinking. While association theory has endured as a principle, it has lost its sparkle, given that cognitive processes are much too complex to be explained purely in terms of associative connections. That said, the parallel distributed processing model of cognitive functioning, concerned with developing principles of mental functioning, has strong echoes of associationism or association theory. This chapter

Plate 3.1 *The call to solidarity: Bombardier*

Source: Courtesy of Charles Wells and Team Saatchi

and the next do not focus on traditional association theory but on how fusing certain associations with a brand in advertising can affect brand image and brand choice.

ASSOCIATIONS, SYMBOLS, BRAND IMAGE, BRAND CHOICE

As Margalit says, animals other than humans relate to each other through face-to-face attachments, tied to licking and smelling. In contrast, humans can form purely symbolic bonds with others, just as they bond together under the symbolism of the national flag: human beings have collective existences built on symbols that encapsulate shared memories.[1]

Anthropologists are apt to view culture, above all, as a system of symbols; not symbols in the abstract but *the* symbols (e.g. language) used to convey meaning in social situations. Consumer advertising most commonly associates products with symbols that exemplify values, group feeling, prestige, status, power, achievement or just plain hedonistic pleasure. Whatever a product is associated with affects perceptions of the product. Association can be powerful. One mouse or a cockroach running across the floor of a restaurant can, through association, ruin a meal, while the presence of a celebrity can enhance it.

Brand names themselves carry associations. There is no such thing as choosing a name that has no associations. A name may have no *concrete* reference but this does not mean it has no *sense*-meaning. A name can have lexical meaning without having any concrete reference like the word 'blue', though it still has sense-meaning. 'Terytak' and 'Lamolay' have no concrete references but which would be more appropriate as the name of a toilet roll? The sharp sound of 'terytak' makes the name unsuitable in contrast to 'lamolay' which conjures up softness.

Pfizer turned to a consultancy firm to invent a name attractive enough to get over the 'stigma' associated with impotence, yet solemn enough for doctors to take seriously. This was how the name 'Viagra' was born. It seemed to suggest vigour and strength, also rhyming with Niagara which evokes images of free and forceful flow.[2] On the other hand, Eli Lilly chose the soft-sounding name 'Cialis', meant to reflect the potential for spontaneity and intimacy in its use. Bayer and GlaxoSmithKline (GSK) chose the name 'Levitra' for their rival joint product which plays upon 'le' (the French for 'the') and 'vita' (Latin for 'life') while also suggesting 'levitate' as a reminder of the drug's primary function.

Traditionally, drug companies have named their drugs to indicate their chemical composition or their mode of action, even if these names are difficult for the consumer to remember and pronounce. Equally if not more important, difficult names stymie word-of-mouth communication about the brand. And word-of-mouth can on occasion be the key to success. The film *My Big Fat Greek*

57

Wedding was shot on a tiny $5 million budget and had to forgo any big studio advertising campaign but grew into a $240 million blockbuster through audience word-of-mouth. Any product with novelty appeal that has an advantage for the function for which it is being bought is a candidate for word-of-mouth. Easily pronounceable names aid this word-of-mouth. The brand 'Unguentum M', a worthy non-prescription cream for eczema and dermatitis, has a name that is difficult to pronounce (without help) and even more difficult to remember: a recipe for deflating sales. But to return to the names quoted earlier, why do name-consultants link names to clever but obscure origins as if these were immediately apparent to members of the target audience? How many runners even knew the origin of the name 'Nike'? The origin of a name can be a talking point in ads, suggesting something authentic about the product. But this can be a very small gain when set against (a) the name not being easy to remember; (b) the name not being easy to pronounce so too embarrassing to ask for; (c) the name not suggesting appropriate connotations. The name needs to resonate with the sense-meanings that the firm wants to project so that the unity and uniqueness of the sense-meaning suggest the unity and uniqueness of the brand itself. Too many names are conjured up in an observational vacuum without recognition that the appropriateness of a name is an empirical question that needs to be tested, and any idea that 'experts' know already must be rejected. Does the name 'Viagra' really conjure up in the mind of its potential users or even doctors the attributes of vigour and strength and images of free and forceful flow? Names are suggested on the grounds of favourable linkages as if these linkages will be the ones most likely to be inferred by the target audience. The perfume industry often just selects a name that captures the spirit and feelings of the time and builds a perfume to match.

One way brand names acquire positive or negative associations is through coming together in time or space with things that have positive or negative connotations. This is because spatial and temporal contiguity influences perceptions. Whenever a brand acquires a new set of associations, it is in effect placed in a new context and a new context demands a reconsideration of old meanings. Consumers, in buying a piece of clothing or any other product, are associating themselves with that brand's connotations. This can affect how others perceive them and how others come to think about the brand. Consumers do not want to be associated with any brand that detracts from their public image. As Leary (1995) says, people want to be associated with the successful, the powerful, the popular and the attractive, and they may connect themselves, not directly but symbolically, to things that have these attributes.[3] Such associations allow them to bask in reflected glory. All this, of course, assumes advertising has been effective in passing on to the brand the appropriate connotations.

Any brand that continues to be associated in advertising with something desirable like a luxurious, exciting lifestyle will be infiltrated by some of the prized qualities: the desirable associations become attached to or fused with the brand in forming its image. The association of a brand with 'sex' in ads is common because sex is powerful in arousing emotions. Typically, consumer advertising is designed to transfer positive meanings to a brand by transferring meanings from cultural icons, for example from the pop world to Calvin Klein jeans. The danger is that these associations will identify the brand indelibly with a particular generation, so the brand ages and loses its appeal to the young. A good example is the hair cream Brylcreem which was so strongly associated with the older generation that younger generations were uninterested. Hence the attempt in 2003 to update its image with David Beckham.

Appeals to nostalgia are another matter. They have enormous potential in emotional resonance as their essential element is sentiment. Nostalgic appeals are common in times of uncertainty and change as nostalgia uses the past to project a contrast between certainty and uncertainty, solidity and flux.[4] When all the old informational anchors are disappearing, people feel vulnerable and insecure, with less control over their lives. In such conditions they reach back to symbols of past times, the period which they understood and which included the brands they had learned to trust. Advertising which exploits nostalgia typically does so by idealizing the past as a time of pure innocence. It evokes memories of past emotions associated with events or songs or other things symbolizing a particular period. Nostalgia is involved in welcoming back brands which were familiar in past times. In 2003 Sears in the United States have an ad campaign that recreates scenes of day-to-day life in the twentieth century, showing Sears then and now. Nostalgia here is allied to showing the authenticity of Sears' heritage. Other blue-chip brands like Ford are following suit.[5] Old neglected brand names like Breck shampoo, Sea & Ski sun-care, and St. Joseph aspirin are being resurrected for their nostalgic appeal. Rheingold Brewing Company is reintroducing Rheingold beer to 'rekindle the romance between the beer and New York City'.[6] It goes without saying that appeals to nostalgia alone are unlikely to be sufficient: there is usually a need for updating, adding a little novelty to ensure relevance to the consumer today. In the case of Rheingold, the beer has a new slogan '100% New York by volume', with a new clear glass bottle with a label that links to the packaging of the 1920s, including a bottle cap on which appears the 1930s slogan: 'Good Beer'.

While 'sensation' is the apprehension of isolated sense-*qualities* like smell and taste, 'perception' is the apprehension of ordinary sense-*objects* such as houses, horses, chairs and so on. It is perception that is basic to any reactions to a brand and it is shaped by association. Consider a study by Rozin et al.[7] in which their experimental subjects were quite happy to eat fudge when it was moulded into the shape of a disc but extremely reluctant to eat it when moulded into the shape of animal faeces. Similarly, subjects were reluctant to eat sugar labelled 'sodium cyanide' in spite of the fact that they had seen it being poured from a sugar box and arbitrarily labelled with that name. The thoughts arising from the negative associations generated an emotional reaction which the known facts (true beliefs) did not overcome. When a product has been used exclusively in one way, it may be difficult to get the consumer to use it for another function. The usual reason given for this reluctance is that the consumer has difficulty in reclassifying the product as also suited for the second function. This is one reason but the reluctance can also arise from the initial use being associated with some unpleasant but necessary task and the new use having that association to overcome. Thus initially paper tissues were used for cleaning car windows and so on and this association did not facilitate the transition to their use on the face.

If a tarnished corporate image is part of the brand image, however 'functionally good' the actual brand, there are negative marketing consequences. For example, there were negative consequences for ITT when its association with the overthrow of Salvador Allende in Chile became known; negative consequences for United Fruit (now Chiquita Brands) when its association with the overthrow of the democratically elected government of Guatemala in the 1950s became known; British Petroleum (BP) similarly suffered from its association with the overthrow of the government of Iran at the same period. Fortunately, the public has a short memory and tarnished images can be polished. Who remembers that those Nazi storm troopers were fitted out by the original Hugo Boss? Nonetheless, past associations that tarnished an image sleep lightly and are easily awakened by further scandals.

Whatever is associated with a brand has the potential to affect its image. Anything pleasant such as music has a positive effect. What would appear dysfunctional is the current linking of anti-establishment lyrics with affluent living. Ads for Wrangler jeans involve images of denim-clad Americans with lyrics from 'Fortunate Son', a scorching Vietnam-era protest song. Ads for family cruises with Royal Caribbean use Iggy Pop's 'Lust for Life', a stirring lyric to the drug life. Some potential customers see the incongruity and protest, just as they protested the use of the Beatles' 'Revolution' by Nike in 1987. But music tends to be absorbed as simply pleasant or unpleasant, the words often not registering at all. A new context is apt to change the perceptions, giving the songs new meanings for the audience.[8]

A positive brand image can be reason enough for choosing a brand. Brand image is used on occasion as a heuristic or judgemental short-cut when a choice is made. Buying on the basis of image saves cognitive energy and 'relieves the tensions of doubt and hesitancy'. Consumers are cognitive misers and often act on what comes most vividly to the mind, 'at the moment when the impulse to decisive action becomes extreme'. In buying purely on the grounds of liking (a common occurrence), consumers are employing the *likeability heuristic* − in just going along with their gut liking. Where a brand or firm is associated with one highly visible individual, whose image then becomes tarnished, both the firm and the brand suffer. Martha Stewart is a case in point as she symbolizes Living Omnimedia. At the time of writing, she is under investigation for insider trading and obstructing justice by lying to prosecutors. Omnimedia, once worth $2 billion, has had its share price reduced by 60 per cent because of the scandal. It is never a good strategy to tie a company's fortunes to the 'charisma' of one individual.

Consumers are put off a brand if members of the target audience loathe the celebrity chosen to promote it or find themselves antagonistic to the ideology of its advertisement. This may have happened with the ad for jeans that featured a youth failing to pay his taxi fare and running away. Displays of social types and lifestyles are not universally admired by all the target audience: advertisements repel as well as attract different audiences. A good example here is the slacker character, Steven, a 22-year-student promoting Dell computers with the antics of a teenager, imploring everyone he knows to buy a Dell computer with the slogan: 'Dude, you're getting a Dell'. He certainly commanded attention and some regard this campaign as one of the most successful ever run by a computer firm. On the other hand, for many he lacked credibility as an expert on computers while his 'fooling around' irritated older viewers, making him singularly un-attractive. Yet it was deemed a successful campaign and Steven got lots of visibility for Dell computers. The campaign, though, was long drawn out and expensive, so the question remains as to whether the resulting sales simply came from the repeated exposure effect. More important, would sales have been much higher if another character had been used who oozed credibility? Or was it simply that most buyers were from the same age group as Steven and could identify with him (he used their lingo), and, given Dell's brand image, went ahead and chose the brand on the grounds of its familiarity and visibility through repeated exposure? Consumers react favourably to a celebrity or TV personality who is similar to some significant other.[9] If people feel very positive towards their mother, sister, brother or a friend, they will have a positive reaction to a new acquaintance or celebrity who appears to be like those of whom they are fond.

Brand associations are not only those put there by advertising. Any associa-tion can affect brand image. Brands that are associated with successful countries have an advantage, more so if the country has a history of being associated with the product in question, as the United States is with films. The word 'German' functions like a brand for many engineering and chemical products, 'Italian' and 'French' for many fashion items and 'Japanese' for many electronic products and cars. These countries have high *reputational capital* in respect to these product categories.

Why can simple contiguity lead to a fusing of associations? Gestalt psychology shows how we experience visual stimuli not in terms of individual elements but as a unified whole. The whole is something distinct from the sum of its separate parts. We have an inclination to organize collections into coherent wholes and so group brands with whatever gets fused to them. In addition, there is the *halo effect* or the tendency to allow one outstanding feature (e.g. the beautiful girl in the ad) to influence response to the total ad (i.e. the ad plus the brand it is endorsing). The halo effect has wide application. While it helps explain why a brand gets a better rating by being associated with highly valued or beautiful images, it also means that the highly favourable image rubs off onto the person buying and using the brand. This association has made consumers willing to display brand logos prominently which, in turn, advertises the brand. Consumers implicitly accept that the association enhances their own visibility and standing.

Damasio's work, among others, has shown there are 'mechanisms' in the brain that classify things as 'good' or 'bad'.[10] As the repertoire of items categorized as 'good' or 'bad' grows exponentially, just about anything contiguously associated with the 'good' or 'bad' tends also to be classified as good or bad. Given that this is so, it is not surprising that older age groups tend to be more 'fixed in their ways' and come to have stronger evaluations over whole sectors of life.

Favourable associations build up over time, leading to a warm feeling about a brand which can be the basis for an *implicit favourite model* and habitual buy. Even before shopping for a new product, the consumer may have an implicit favourite among the brands. Students typically have an implicit favourite when applying to college or graduate school. When advertising appeals fuse the brand with value-laden associations, this brand is commonly recalled first, becoming the implicit favourite model. The implicit favourite model is strong in the stock market. It was Benjamin Graham, in his classical text *The Intelligent Investor,* who argued that choosing stock was something like choosing a wife in that a number of concrete factors were taken into account to which then was 'added a strong and perhaps controlling component of unreasoning favoritism'.[11] With an implicit favourite in mind, the consumer only needs a trivial reason to do what she feels like doing anyway. On the other hand, consumers may converge on a compromise product in conditions of uncertainty and in the absence of an implicit favourite. For instance, Simonson shows how sales of a moderately priced camera increased after the introduction of one at a higher price, consumers rejecting both the very low priced and the premium priced.[12] This is an example of the effect of changing the *anchor* price, that is the price that forms the basis of comparison.

Supportive of the implicit favourite model is the theory of *dominance structuring.*[13] Montgomery argues that information search prior to a decision passes through four stages:

1 screening, where options that do not have certain necessary attributes are eliminated (conjunctive rule);
2 choosing a promising alternative, defined as that which commands most attention;

3 *dominance building*, in which the promising alternative becomes the *dominant* alternative through confirmation bias when assessing the evidence in favour of the choice;

4 restructuring the problem to choose a new promising alternative if the dominance structuring that has already occurred fails for some reason.

Lewicka's work suggests that at least one reason why an alternative becomes the most promising is simply that it is the better known (more familiar). This helps the brand that is the best-known or the brand leader. It also relates to the 'repeated exposure effect' which induces more familiarity and, as a consequence, greater liking.[14] Where two ideas are contiguously associated repeatedly, the association will stick. Thus President Bush time and again associated 'Saddam Hussein–Al Qaeda–9/11' until many in the United States believed Saddam Hussein was connected to the other two. Making a brand familiar by repeated exposure through advertising encourages its adoption. It may even encourage patients to ask their doctors for the particular prescription medicine they have seen on TV. It is worrying to many doctors in the United States that patients insist on Vioxx and Celebrex as their preferred analgesics just because these are the ones being currently pushed by advertising, even though less expensive and equally effective alternatives are available.

Where the screening of options is conscious, consumers focus initially on the elimination of negative alternatives more than on the choice of positive ones. Negative information about a brand influences the final outcome more than does positive information.[15] An evolutionary psychologist might argue that this is only to be expected: the recognition of danger is more important for survival than the recognition that something is pleasing or neutral. This points to the crucial importance of having a positive brand image.

While Gestalt psychology, the halo effect and neurophysiology explain how associations are formed, the effectiveness of an association depends on how well the following are (or can be) exploited:

1 associations tied to the social norms, values or valued images of the target audience;

2 associations tied to a feeling of solidarity with others;

3 associations tied to position and prestige.

The above three sets of associations are the subject matter of the rest of this chapter while the following will be dealt with in Chapter 4:

4 associations tied to the mental modes of excitement and relaxation (reversal theory);

5 associations tied to positive or negative reinforcements (behaviourism/conditioning).

63

ASSOCIATIONS TIED TO THE SOCIAL NORMS, VALUES OR VALUED IMAGES OF THE TARGET AUDIENCE

Values, symbols and images

We commonly contrast fact and value, suggesting values are subjective. Yet values are the ultimate criteria against which trade-offs are made. If in weighing up options, we are able to put all trade-offs on a money scale to choose the most profitable outcome, we would simply be indicating that economic values are our dominant criterion, as opposed, say, to moral, aesthetic, scientific, religious or political values. Whatever decisions are made, they reflect values.

One way to understand what is meant by a system of values is to recognize that we are all sensitive to contrasts in the human condition: rich versus poor; liked versus disliked; happy versus unhappy; healthy versus ill; confident versus insecure; beautiful versus ugly; knowledgeable versus ignorant; being entertained versus being bored; controlling versus controlled; relaxed versus anxious. Listing the more pleasant of these contrasts represents our system of values. There is likely to be a great commonality of values among us. Major differences are over the weighting of the various values. The weighting of values varies widely among different cultures, even between Europe and the United States, as is shown by the differences in their social legislation. Even within the European Community values among nations vary. This is what makes uniformity in legislation a source of controversy. In the United States there is a constant call for state rights, on the ground that people in different states weight values differently. Values are always present in decision making. When people claim that science is value-free, they are saying that it strives to be objective, objectivity being one of the values that scientists uphold but just take for granted.

A good deal of persuasive advertising tries to fuse a company's brand with the target group's values and valued images. Persuasion here eschews facts and arguments and resorts instead to the presentation of symbols that stand on their own as effective persuaders, just as the country's flag might do in battle. This is not to suggest that the same sign symbolizes the same values for everyone within the same culture. The Confederate flag in the United States may symbolize for some a slave autocracy but for others it is a symbol of Southern gallantry. For Freudians, products always symbolize something over and above their physical properties and what they symbolize may arouse the emotions associated with those symbols. But what signs symbolize can change with time. Thus traditionally tattoos were associated with lower-deck (lower-class) merchant seamen while today they symbolize fashion or simply signal non-conformity.

Whenever something strongly resonates with values, it produces an emotional reaction. The importance of this link between values and emotion is often forgotten, however. Kim and Mauborgne claim that The Body Shop created a new market segment by moving away from the traditional emotional appeal of the cosmetics industry to a functional one.[16] In other words, The Body Shop did not exploit emotion but focused purely on function. This is extremely naive. The Body Shop's appeal was steeped in emotion. In justifying their claim, the authors argue that, while the cosmetics industry generally spent heavily on advertising and promises of eternal youth, The Body Shop drew attention to natural formulas using natural ingredients. This, they claimed, appealed to consumers' common sense (suggesting rationality in place of emotion). The fact is that the inspired combination of green (environmentally friendly) cosmetics, a return to native products and help to impoverished indigenous peoples, combined with much political correctness such as condemning the use of animals in cosmetics testing ('animals, too, have rights'), resonated emotionally with consumers. Because of this, The Body Shop received a great deal of favourable publicity which was more effective than any amount of commercial advertising. Strongly held values were involved and The Body Shop saw the latent want that was tied to these values. Though the individual products may have appeared very functional, the total offering was emotionally loaded. As one commentator at the time pointed out, The Body Shop didn't just sell you banana oil but also salvaged your conscience. The real problem for The Body Shop now is whether such a competitive advantage is sustainable when its 'claim to conscience is no longer a unique selling point'. With Estée Lauder now in the segment, with a beauty product range which comes with recyclable containers, high natural content and 'not-tested-on-animals', it is not surprising that The Body Shop is feeling the pinch.

The Body Shop is an example of a business that arose out of the counter-culture of the 1960s and now helps constitute the 'new' establishment; such business forms were able to exploit the prevailing social ideologies in lucrative ways. They could not have existed before our time but nor, unless they reinvent themselves, can they necessarily survive it. There is always a need for some substantive competitive advantage whether in product, price, service, promotion or distribution; or, preferably, a critical advantage, one that is central to the functions for which the product is bought and yet unique to the company. This has been a problem for retailers in recent years. While stores made an effort to differentiate themselves in ways other than location and size after the Second World War, consumers now complain that they are all alike, with no novelty appeal.[17]

Buying certain products may or may not be supportive of social norms, defined as social rules prescribing the 'right' thing to do. But social integration is facilitated by adherence to social norms and the social norms within a person's social milieu influence the buying of all socially visible products from automobiles to clothing, furniture and houses. As a consequence, advertising appeals can be persuasive by claiming that a brand exemplifies the social norms of a particular group.

65

Advertising that stresses the novelty of its product can be persuasive, novelty being a highly prized value. We are motivated to seek novelty to put off boredom and satisfy curiosity, the latter being a reward in itself. Even when we seek rare and exotic experiences, we seek to experience novelty. The expectation, contemplation and anticipation of novelty are exciting as consumers fantasize about what might be. As Scheibe says,

> the human capacity for self-reflection introduces a compelling fascination with the not-yet-known because of its potential consequences for our being. . . . For where certainty exists there is no room for play, for sport, for dramatic transformation. . . . [Sports] are attractive because outcomes are uncertain.[18]

The use of symbols to persuade is what Mayhew calls the *rhetoric of presentation* since the display of symbols outweighs discursive argument.[19] Somewhat illustrative is Eisenstein's film *Battleship Potemkin* which is entirely constructed round symbolic elements, from the Tsarist guards, faceless in the Odessa Steps sequence, to the juxtaposition of the Potemkin's firing cannon with the stone lions guarding the palace, symbols of the *ancien régime*. One famous political ad for Ronald Reagan, 'Morning in America', used no arguments at all for voting Republican, merely a sequence of images symbolic of the 'classic' American way. The target audience is implicitly being asked to respond to value symbols rather than tangible benefits.

Goldman and Papson, point to problems when the focus is purely on attaching symbols or valued images to brands:[20]

1   The first problem arises when advertising associates the same brand with very different images on different occasions. The brand is then in danger of having no core image, symbolizing nothing in particular. Even if the associations provide an aura of pleasantness, there is still no clarity of image. The consumer may like the ad but has no idea what the brand stands for, so it is no longer distinct from rivals in terms of values being promoted. *A brand that stands for something is more memorable, more visible, and more meaningful than a brand associated with a constellation of images.* Sometimes the mixing of radically different images results from changes in marketing managers or advertising agencies, each rejecting the past so as to signal a changed direction and regime. This indicates a failure to recognize the importance of consistency and recognition. Under Sergio Zyman, Coca-Cola promoted multiple messages and multiple images in its advertising. Although Zyman shrewdly revived historical icons of Coca-Cola like the contoured bottle and the disk logo, the brand identities of Coca-Cola Classic and Diet Coke became diffuse and hazy. There should be some commonality of meaning to the images attached to the brand, making it unequivocally stand for something.

2 The second problem with a lack of focused imagery has to do with the cultural images themselves which, through misuse, become debased, just as a country's flag loses its impact when used indiscriminately by all political parties. This is like every brand having the same logo.

Although ensuring a brand stands for something in the mind of the consumer is important, it is also true that familiarity alone can induce liking. If an association is consistent, people favour it as they value the things associated with their way of life. Where there is consistency, familiarity does not breed contempt but, on the contrary, leads to liking. Zajonc talks of the *repeated exposure effect*, defined as the increasingly positive affect (liking) that is felt for any object as a result of mere repeated exposure.[21]. This more positive affect is independent of any conscious cognitive appraisal.[22] This would seem to be in line with the claim made by the sociologist Homans that constant interaction with another person leads to increased liking.[23] Homans was assuming *supportive*, constant interaction or otherwise we would expect fewer divorces. Zajonc also makes no such qualification though it is reasonable to suppose that the object with which we become ever more familiar cannot be something that is inherently threatening or unpleasant. Consumers are more comfortable with products and brands, names and trademarks, as they become more familiar. Advertisers can accelerate this process by associating the brand with attractive logos and pleasing ads. What happens is that with increasingly familiarity, every brand acquires an attractive symbolism as, with repeated exposure, it comes to symbolize a valued way of life.

Leymore stresses that advertising needs to be linked to the most meaningful cultural values. She accepts (following the structuralism of Lévi-Strauss) that people throughout the world are sensitive to contrasts in the human condition ('the eternal polarities of the human condition') such as being beautiful versus being ugly, being rich versus being poor, and that people seek the more pleasant polar extreme.[24] The pleasant polar extremes represent a fairly universal system of values though different societies will weight them differently. Leymore goes on to argue that the relative effectiveness of advertising depends on the extent to which an ad establishes an *association* between the product being advertised and the highest level of values in society.

One criticism of this argument is that the values to which advertising should appeal are, more correctly, the *specific* values of the subculture to which the target audience belongs. Western cultures spawn subcultures with a consequent plurality of belief and behaviour. Each subculture seeks 'self-legitimation' of its lifestyle, allied to a belief that it alone shows how life should be lived. Attaching to the brand the values of the subculture to which the target audience belongs arouses emotional support for it.[25] An important part of this process is using the language and vocabulary of the subculture (including the slang) since this is part of how its members differentiate themselves. This does not mean advertising should support the norms and values of all cultures and subcultures. Unfortunately, just saying something is a cultural norm has prevented justified criticism of behaviour which would otherwise be condemned. These norms should not be affirmed in advertising.[26]

Appeals to subculture values by advertisers need to recognize there can be value conflicts within the subculture. For example, in Britain one young entrepreneur launched a new brand of cigarettes called Death, with a skull logo. The aim was to appeal to alienated youth by its open honesty. By mocking the earnest health warnings of the government, the product's greatest negative was satirically turned into a unique selling appeal. Though the brand name, logo and packaging generated immense free publicity, corresponding sales were not forthcoming: potential buyers appreciated the macabre humour but not the constant reminder of death being the end result.

At the beginning of the twentieth century, advertising focused more on the reliability and efficiency of a product in the performance of its core function. Today consumer advertising is more likely to associate the product or brand with attractive images reflecting a lifestyle, on the ground that lifestyle rather than functional utility is where consumer interest lies. As products converge on a similar set of performance standards and specifications, product imagery becomes more important as the source of differentiation: the result is that the corporation can become a domestic marketing core, with manufacturing consigned to remote locations in foreign lands.

Advertising does not necessarily always uphold the cultural values of a society but may differentiate a brand through symbols of cultural opposition, as when ghetto images or the image of the hoodlum are attached to it. The attraction of such images is the association with power; wearing the clothes of the hoodlum allows the fantasy that some of the power to create fear rubs off on the wearer. Advertising may set out to offend those who are not members of its target audience, not uncommonly ridiculing the values of others, like Pepsi's spoof of traditional values. The ads for Diesel's 'ultra-hip gear' use obese models to ridicule the ultra slim line of glamorous models used elsewhere. They mask their international reach to present a front of catering to individuality and non-conformity. Breaking all the rules in the book has contributed to their success as in this way they ally themselves with their target audience in a sort of joint protest against some other group. This is consistent with the thesis of Mary Douglas discussed below.

Psychographics

Advertising tied to lifestyle or psychographics appeals to values. Of the many different psychographic systems, VALS 2 is the one most often mentioned.[27]

Lifestyle marketing, as Solomon says, is premised on the assumption that consumers sort themselves into groups on the basis of the things they like to do, how they spend their time and how they choose to spend their money.[28] Advertising based on lifestyle differentiates a brand by depicting a lifestyle that reflects a set of values. It says, in effect, if this lifestyle or set of values resonates with you, then our product or brand is the one for you. Psychographic research can be product specific or non-specific and can be combined with demographic data for advertising purposes. The best-known system of non-specific psychographics is VALS (Values and Lifestyles), developed by SRI (formerly the Stanford Research Institute). The initial VALS system was criticized from many points of view and SRI brought out VALS 2 which is claimed to be a better predictor of purchase decisions. VALS 2 classifies consumers into eight segments along just two dimensions: (a) self-orientation; and (b) resources available to sustain the self-orientation.

Self-orientation

SRI from its research identified three primary self-orientations:

- *principle-orientation*, where individuals look within themselves to make choices rather than just reacting to physical experience or social pressure; that is, the individual is inclined to base his or her decisions on strongly held principles, following established codes of family, church or nation;
- *status-orientation*, where individuals make choices guided by the opinions, actions and anticipated reaction of reference groups. Such individuals seek a secure social position and act accordingly;
- *action-orientation*, where individuals make choices guided by a desire for physical and social activity, variety and risk taking.

These three orientations are meant to be suggestive of the type of motives likely to be pursued in buying.

Resources the consumer can draw on to sustain the self-orientation

Such resources include education, income, health, energy level, self-confidence, interpersonal skills, inventiveness and intelligence.

The self-orientation and resources available combine to form eight segments within the three primary self-orientations.

The *principle*-oriented can be either (a) *fulfilled* or (b) *believer*, the fulfilled having more resources. The fulfilled as a segment are reasonably active in community and politics but their leisure really centres on the home. Values relate to education, travel, health and tolerance. The believers are a segment with fewer resources, who respect authority figures and societal rules. They socialize within family and other established groups and are conservative in politics though fairly well informed.

The *status*-oriented can be what are called (c) *actualizers*, (d) *achievers*, (e) *strivers* or (f) *strugglers*, with the actualizers having the most resources and the strugglers the fewest. The actualizers as a segment are highly social and apt to be politically active. They are well informed and value personal growth, education, intellect and varied leisure activities. The achievers as a segment are politically conservative, with lives centring on career and family, with formal social relationships. Strivers as a segment are politically apathetic and look to their peer group for motivation and approval while being easily bored, with narrow interests, not including health and nutrition. The strugglers as a segment are conservative and tied to organized religion. With limited interests, their values centre on safety and security while they are often burdened by health problems.

The *action*-oriented are either (g) *experiencers* or (h) *makers*, the experiencers having most resources. Experiencers as a segment are politically apathetic, value wealth, power and fame and the new, risky and offbeat. They like exercise and sports, and although concerned about image, they are non-conforming. Finally, the eighth category, the makers, distrust politicians and avoid joining organizations except unions. They value the outdoors and 'hands on' activities, also spending time with family and close friends.

VALS measures relate somewhat to product ownership and media use. One claim is that VALS 2 will point to one or more of the eight categories most associated with a product class and it will then be up to advertisers to design category-relevant appeals for a particular brand. As this is the major psychographic system in the United States with imitators in other countries, it deserves some comment.

The self-orientations are motivational categories in that they concern dispositions to seek certain goals:

1 The principle-oriented already hold beliefs about what rules (principles) ought to be followed in many areas of life and also believe they should follow these principles. But how predictive will this be of their buying since doubts are likely to arise as to what principles to apply?
2 The actions of status-oriented consumers will depend on what purchases they consider will enhance status or social acceptance. Can it just be assumed that there will be a general consensus on what products or brands symbolize status?
3 Action-oriented consumers do not seem likely to be pre-programmed in any way. They will vary, in line with their individual beliefs about what fits best with their desire for activity, variety and risk taking.

While the VALS categories seem to be describing distinct personalities, how people are grouped into them depends on who passes what mark on a scale as the categories of self-orientation are not discrete but continuous. The categories would suggest that the segments are not mutually exclusive. We often exhibit different lifestyle behaviours in different situations, including buying. Thus in buying books and newspapers, I might behave like an actualizer but in buying clothes I might behave like an achiever. One final comment should be made on where the richness in the segment descriptions came from since it cannot just be deduced from the relevant basic dimensions. Inferences from these dimensions could not result in all this richness of description.

VALS 2 seems to be based on a one-factor theory of motivation, namely self-esteem. Self-esteem is important since it relates to the emotions of self-assessment like pride, guilt and shame. But it is not the only motive at work in buying though no doubt it is a major one when nothing distinguishes brands in the market beyond their image. But it is not clear that VALS 2 does distinguish categories of consumers with distinct orientations and it ignores household decision making altogether.[29]

The Mary Douglas thesis

A recent addition to the literature on lifestyles and consumer decision making is that offered by Mary Douglas, a distinguished anthropologist. It should be of interest to every advertiser. Douglas claims her *Cultural Value Bias Approach* is founded in cultural theory.[30] She sets out to explain in terms of cultural bias why different consumers make different purchases. If what Douglas has to say is valid, it is of central interest to the question of what values have the potential to be most emotionally arousing. In other words, advertising is given definite directions in making value appeals.

In an earlier book, *The World of Goods* (which includes a section on economics by Baron Isherwood)[31] Mary Douglas argued that individual purchases are always *coordinated* with other purchases, as goods assembled in ownership present a set of meanings, more or less coherent, more or less intentional. Douglas now suggests that the coordinating principle in all consumer purchases is *protest* against other competing ways of life. For her, the most basic choice that a rational person has to make is about the kind of society to live in or, if you like, about his or her preferred lifestyle. The perspective is of people continuously trying to bring about their ideal form of community life. In other words, the superordinate value for any person is his or her ideal form of community and it is the emotional attachment to this ideal which dominates as a concern in making product choices. The choice of ideal community life is the major determining influence on all product choices and the products selected reflect the rejection of the other lifestyles or communities.

71

According to Douglas, people do not so much know what they want as know what they do not want: standardized hates are more persistent and more enlightening than studying expressed desires. *This is because the things we hate are more emotionally arousing.* For Douglas, choosing 'for' is a choice 'against': to choose any product is a *protest*, with each choice a declaration of defiance against alternative lifestyles. It is this *protest* that gives coherence to purchases. In the eighteenth century the English Quaker chocolate firms (Fry, Cadbury, Rowntree and Terry) got over the image of chocolate as a symbol of Catholic immoderation in self-indulgent Europe by promoting chocolate as morally healthy, allowing the working man to keep on his feet all day; but, most important, it was an alternative to the pub and so stopped the working man turning to drink: chocolate was a protest against drinking in pubs.[32]

A good deal of comparative advertising can be interpreted as a protest. Comparative advertising is generally a tactic for new entrants with a strong competitive advantage who want to make an impact quickly. It is also used to regain market position, as witness Maxwell House in its aggressive attacks on P&G's Folgers brand of coffee. Comparative ads are banned in many parts of Europe. Though they are ostensibly permitted in the European Union, restrictions are so severe as to ban them in practice. This contrasts with the United States where about 30 per cent of ads shown on network television are comparative. But comparative claims are getting risky; legal suits against them are becoming ever more common.

While comparative advertising has been found to enhance purchase intentions, the advertising profession as a whole has not been enthusiastic. In the first place, it seems to require no creativity to protest the competition by bad-mouthing it. Second, when competitors respond, a shouting match develops that lowers the credibility of both advertisers and perhaps advertising in general. Consumers can also be put off by strident and offensive advertising claims. Why? Because many comparisons have nothing to do with the reasons for a particular choice of brand: in other words, the superior features being claimed do not enter into the consumer's choice criteria. Thus one advertisement contrasted 'our' brand's fresh ingredients with the dry ingredients of the major rival's brand. In actual fact the dried ingredients were what made the taste so good.

Protest is a fundamental cultural stance as, for example, the protest of the young against the older generation. It could be argued, for example, that some of the emotion over the tragic death of Diana, Princess of Wales, was a protest against the 'stuffiness' of the rest of the royal family but we suspect identification with the personality, charitable actions and 'victim' history of Diana herself were also involved. In the 1998 Congressional elections some of the support for President Clinton, in spite of his behaviour, was a protest against Kenneth Starr's 'witch hunt' and against the suspect motives of Clinton's Congressional opponents. One pollster and political consultant, Patrick Cadell, has based his whole approach to politics on an alienation thesis – how politicians can exploit the myriad resentments of the powerless. The word 'populism' links with this philosophy.

Cultural conflict among lifestyles is Douglas's explanation of the choices made by the consumer. For instance, people who show a strong preference for holistic medicine are likely to be antagonistic to lifestyles in which other kinds of medicine are preferred: their preference results from that antagonism to these other lifestyles. But the choice of holistic medicine will not be an isolated preference uncoordinated with other purchases and values. Personal identity, on the Douglas account, is defined in terms of what we hate, and what we hate is signalled by the culture with which we identify. This view of personal identity contrasts with the view, as expressed by Dittmar, that the symbolic nature of material objects plays a key role for the owner's social and personal identity.[33] It also contrasts with Flanagan for whom self-identity reflects the whole narrative of our lives.[34] But the Douglas view is consistent with the view of self-identity put forward by Maalouf who claims that our personal identity is often formed in relation to our enemy or the groups we fear or resent.[35]

Douglas posits four cultural lifestyles, claiming the consumer's choice coheres with just one of these, and that this choice is a protest against the others. Each of the four lifestyles is set up in opposition to the others and it is their mutual hostility that accounts for their stability. The four lifestyles persist as they are tied to conflicting organizational principles, and there is constant pressure to define allegiance to one or another. Each of the four cultures is a way of organizing, reflecting attitudes to authority, leadership and competition. These four cultures are:

1   conservative hierarchical social structure;
2   individualistic social structure or active individualism;
3   egalitarian social structures constituting 'dissident enclaves';
4   backwater isolation where structure is rejected altogether.

If the Douglas thesis is valid, advertisers should determine which actual lifestyle their target audience fits. Then attach to the brand the valued symbols of that lifestyle.

Conservative hierarchical social structure

This way of life or culture is the most complex, being based on a *hierarchical community* supportive of formality, where power is backed by authority coming from a hierarchical establishment espousing traditional cultural values and constraints. In the hierarchical home, there is a strict division of labour with the man doing the heavy work while the woman cooks, washes up, cleans and makes the beds and so on. (Sometimes advertising may parody this way of life when promoting an opposing lifestyle, using role reversal to show it is the woman who is off on the business trip today!) This conservative hierarchical way of organizing is carried over into other areas of life and is reflected in what is bought by those preferring this lifestyle. Purchases reflect socially endorsed rules and display. This lifestyle is 'driving in the slow lane' as it is defined by a hierarchical system, adherence to established traditions and institutions and maintaining a network of family and old friends. There is a preference for collaboration within a rationally integrated society.

Individualistic social structure or active individualism

This way of organizing is based on the culture of competitive individualism with weak structure and wide room for personal initiative in making choices. This is because the individualist chooses products adapted to personal uses. In the individualist home, the husband and wife are both involved in shopping, washing up, etc. The values are the competitive values of the market, and power comes not from some traditional establishment but from influence and wealth in the market. It is a culture that is acquisitive, aggressive and action-oriented. Treasured objects will have to demonstrate their value individually, without support from the rest of some series of purchases, and they will be impressively durable, heavy or large. Gifts are given not just on seasonal occasions but throughout the year since they are apt to be more like tokens supportive of alliances and loyalties. The individualist lifestyle is one of 'driving in the fast lane', enjoying high-tech products, sporty, arty, risky styles of entertainment and the desire to be free to change commitments. This lifestyle is sometimes captured in advertising where home and office interiors are utterly contemporary, portraying a sort of individualistic planet where there are fast cars, luxury meals out and the newest smart clothes. It is very cosmopolitan but rootless, with no patina of time, context or tradition. Like the conservative hierarchical structure, the individualistic social structure accepts authority, leadership and domination though the source is not tradition but the market.

Egalitarian social structures constituting 'dissident enclaves'

This way of organizing a community is in the nature of a protest against those who would want to domineer and is based on stressing equality while favouring spontaneity and free negotiation. The focus is on what is egalitarian. With the egalitarian being committed to the group, choices are standardized in line with group norms or agreement. Sometimes advertising makes direct reference to the egalitarian lifestyle and values to tap anti-materialist feelings, for example, in the promotion of 'green' consumer goods. Club Med, whether through historical accident or design, has placed great emphasis on the egalitarian lifestyle in its holiday communities and, as a consequence, appeals to those favouring such a lifestyle. It also involves rejection both of the inequalities of the complex hierarchical lifestyle and of the vulgar display of personal power associated with the individualistic social structure. The egalitarian lifestyle of such dissident enclaves is a rejection of products that reflect formality, pomp and artifice, as it is opposed to authoritarian structures and prefers simplicity, frankness, intimate friendships and 'spiritual' values.

Backwater isolation where structure is rejected altogether

This way of organizing is for a society in which an individual has the right to be left alone, without any desire to negotiate for power. This is a protest against the oppressive control of the other forms of social life, whether societal, market or group based. Like Greta Garbo, the individuals here want to be left alone, introverted and reclusive. Even if rich, people falling into this category are not ostentatious in their purchases: their possessions are not for display, or to bring status and visibility. Tastes are apt to be eclectic since, of all the cultures, this one is less antagonistic to the others, based simply on a desire to be left alone. Nonetheless, the isolated position shares with the egalitarian its protest about the use of power. An example would be the so-called down-shifters, people who move away from high-pressure city jobs to a simpler, poorer, rurally based lifestyle.

Douglas argues that in many contexts, objects and conduct are implicitly ranked on a scale ranging from the 'materialistic' to the 'spiritual', which can take in related forms of contrasts between vulgar/refined, harsh/gentle, mechanical/personal and so on. She argues that the isolates and the 'egalitarian enclavists' are towards the gentle/spiritual end of the continuum while the reverse is true of the two other cultures.

For Douglas, every choice can be construed in terms of the culture it expresses and, in consequence, the cultural positions it protests against. Douglas's theory of culture assumes we are predominantly interested in the kind of society or community we want to live in and any choice is an act of protest against undesired models of society. According to this *cultural theory*, when the consumer chooses, she chooses a flag to wave and knows whom she is waving against. All choices are symbolically badges of allegiance. All four cultures coexist in a state of mutual antagonism at all times. No person can belong to more than one culture for long as the contradiction would be too great to live with. The most basic choice is not between products but between kinds of society. Once the cultural lifestyle has been chosen, it becomes a goal, so it is rational that consumption should be engaged to serve it, and that conscience be invoked to uphold the pattern. These implications of 'cultural theory' are said to apply everywhere throughout the world. Ultimately this politicizes all consumer choice; what I wear becomes where I stand and what I believe – and what I oppose. The thesis assumes that wants, goals, beliefs and values group uniformly into separate ideological packages.

In practice, things are never quite this neat. The Douglas categories are essentially the same as those of Aaron Wildavsky, a political scientist who spoke of four *political* cultures, all of which he regarded as necessary for political order. Berger neatly summarizes the Wildavsky categories as comprising: (a) hierarchical elitists who believe in stratification and in the responsibility of those at the top to look after those below them; (b) competitive individualists primarily interested in themselves who want the freedom to compete fairly, protected by the government; (c) egalitarians who stress that people are equal in terms of their needs and that differences between them are social, not natural, and should be played down (egalitarians are critics of the hierarchical elitists and the competitive individualists who form the backbone of democratic societies); (d) the fatalists who believe in luck and opt out of the political system.[36] The Douglas/Wildavsky categories have a certain family resemblance to Riesman's three types of American character: (a) the tradition-directed; (b) the inner-directed; and (c) the other-directed.[37]

The thesis demands more support than Douglas offers. Would we consider personal identity to consist of nothing more than a sense of the things we hate or a sense of belonging to a certain protest group? Also it is doubtful that our choices, whether brand, product form or product category, would be predictable by simply knowing what cultures we disapprove of and which we approve. This is because cultural community preference would seldom be specific enough to allow deduction of situational rules sufficient to determine product/brand choices. When rules are very general, they have very little applicability to the individual case. That said, there have been studies showing a significant correlation between political attitudes and brand loyalty.[38] Thus 84 per cent of Campbell soup consumers were pro-impeachment of President Clinton as opposed to only 20 per cent of those loyal to Burger King.

If Douglas is right, we would expect people to be absorbed in politics since its distinctive subject matter is 'the proper arrangement of the communities in which we live', with Aristotle in Book 1 of *The Politics* asserting that human identity is bound up with being a citizen or part of the polis.[39] Yet it does not seem to be the case that politics is the most salient thing in people's lives. Moreover, if the Douglas thesis were correct, much successful advertising would be grounded in ideology since all consumption would be part of a political expression of personality. It is by no means certain that this is so. In fact, many ads go out of their way (through such devices as paralanguage) to make the ideology of the ad open to negotiation.

Douglas's thesis suggests the causal chain: *different ideological positions on community life → mould perceptions/attitudes → mould buyer behaviour.* Something similar to this has been suggested as occurring in voting behaviour: ideological identifications of voters → moulds their perceptions of candidates → moulds their voting behaviour.[40] However, it is easier to classify people into one of the four cultures than to say what products cohere with each of the cultures. The four cultures are essentially 'ideal types'. An ideal type is an abstraction rooted in plausible assumptions suggested by experience. It may or may not closely correspond to the real world but is assumed to represent core features like the economist's concept of pure competition. But we suspect Douglas regards the four cultures as something more than ideal types, rather representing value constellations. Yet whether consumers' dislike of three of the cultures spells out specific rules determining the choices they make must remain a matter of empirical inquiry. It would appear more likely that people seek consistency of basic values than consistency of beliefs on specific matters of buying while basic values, reflected in the four cultures, are more likely to proscribe than fully prescribe a specific product or brand.

Douglas argues that *cultural* preference is the strongest predictor of preferences in a wide variety of fields. *This suggests that knowledge on attitudes to the four cultural forms would be predictive of differences in buying.* The thesis takes no account of the ambivalence, the confusion and uncertainty that is common in a good deal of buying. It is this uncertainty that can be exploited by persuasive appeals. An example of the confusion over values is illustrated by one reviewer of Patti Reagan's book about her father, President Reagan. The reviewer pointed out that what Patti wanted was both the convenience of modern metropolitan America and the fecund warmth of a French peasant family in Burgundy.

The major evidence quoted by Douglas in support of her thesis is an unpublished study commissioned by Unilever entitled 'The Creation of Household Cultures' by Gerald and Valerie Mars. They found the four ways of organizing to be linked to four distinct sets of values, attitudes and cosmology. They then took an *extreme* example of each type of cultural adherent and studied them in detail in relation to choice of toiletries, foods and methods of preparing them. They established that cultural preferences and *product* choices were related at least in these 'extreme' examples. Douglas also quotes a study by Wildavsky and Dake[41] but this offers only weak support of her thesis since it is concerned with connecting attitudes to risk and political preferences. Of course, it could be argued that the real evidence lies in cultural theory itself, viewing consumer buying as simply one of its applications. However, even Douglas admits that, at present, cultural theory is short on empirical support.

We suspect earlier periods in history might be more congenial to the Douglas thesis in that consumers (and voters) today seem to be quite happy with less than a coherent package of choices tied to cultural lifestyles. People do not seemingly find a problem in being, say, pro-hunting and pro-gun yet at the same time be seen as advocating animal rights. Douglas assumes a fairly stable and coherent sense of identity. Today people seem much more flexible. It is a matter of common experience in marketing that consumers will endorse some general rule or principle, such as the need to buy products that are environmentally 'friendly', yet fail to follow the rule in some specific context. Principles are rules but rules that are more general than specific. Principles and policy preferences would thus appear to be only weakly related. As Levitin and Miller show, there tends to be only a weak relationship between self-proclaimed ideological positions and preferences on specific issues.[42] We suspect it is the same in respect to products. Sniderman *et al.* point out that, in determining a preference, people take account of a number of considerations and beliefs which interrelate and cohere only to varying degrees.[43] To view the forming of a preference as merely making some implicit deduction from an overarching general principle or lifestyle position presupposes a considerable coherence in beliefs. The deliberation in decision making is apt to take account of many beliefs and many values. When there appears to be inconsistency, it may be the result of some non-expressed value being rated more highly than some value or principle previously endorsed.

Even if we accept that people implicitly adopt one culture and oppose the others and that this guides their behaviour, how determining would these be? (This is also the problem in evaluating VALS 2.) Any rules of action following from one's cultural position would work as follows: if we want to promote *the conservative hierarchical social structure*, we must do X. However, doing X to promote a cultural preference rests on beliefs. Yet beliefs as to the best means of achieving X may be many and varied, while being equally defensible in terms of cultural preference. It would seem more likely that Douglas's cultural categories would be more dominant as people get older and more experienced in making choices; young people are less likely to be so firmly attached to a cultural position, except as reflected in their social groups.

Douglas believes that acting in line with the preferred culture is indicative of rationality though it would seem to be more rational to amend the rules when we cannot accept the actions the rules demand. An alternative (more rational) interplay between norms (rules) and action is what Rawls calls *reflective equilibrium* which allows 'principles' to be tested against experience.[44] (In *A Theory of Justice* Rawls sets out to establish a rational basis for the personal and civil liberties which are held to be inviolable rights by twentieth-century liberals.) There is also the implicit assumption in Douglas that the four cultures are hermetically sealed when in fact they are social entities that constantly influence each other whenever their members interact socially.

What Douglas has to say is nonetheless stimulating and important. We must not throw away the baby with the bathwater. Consumers do not determine their preferences in an entirely *ad hoc* way but start with some general perspective and this could be some vision of what their ideal community would be. The inference could be *affective* (emotional) with little cognitive input, going from 'This is what has most intrinsic appeal for me' to 'This is the one I prefer'.

The claim is made by Douglas that we are surer of what we hate than what we like, and that choices are in the nature of protests. This has appeal. In a social world where possessions are perceived as influencing how others see us, we may deliberately eschew buying the most popular brand, or in fact any brand with a designer label. *It is a way of protesting.* This is what seems to have occurred in the sales of Porsches in Britain when the car became closely identified with the greed, aggression and conspicuous consumption attributed to the financial institutions in the City of London.

We are all familiar with the power of negative advertising in politics which highlights what people are likely to dislike about the opponent. Similarly a brand image can be rapidly established by a sharp contrast with what it is not (e.g. the un-cola). Midas, the auto repair chain, attracts customers by ridiculing the proprietors of independent garages as overweight, incompetent slobs. The ad campaign for the Infiniti car (no car is actually shown, only a country scene, emblem and logo) was an implicit protest against the jazzy images of most car ads. The Energizer battery's successful Bunny ad campaign fastened on to the dislike of stale, maddening TV ads. An Esprit ad promised its jeans offered 'elegance' that was both anti-fashion and also anti-luxury. An article in the *Washington Post National Weekly Edition* points out that commercials on Scottish television use brazenly anti-English imagery to sell their products to Scottish consumers.[45] Even a name can be declaratory of its opposition, like the toothpaste called Fluoride Free. Such ads succeed by tapping the pet hates of the target audience, so bonding them with the advertiser by shared dislikes. When advertising appears to be 'revealing all' in exposing and opposing the pretences and pretensions of advertising, it is a tactic to gain credibility, by in effect saying they agree with the audience so the audience can trust them. In one American ad exposing the gross exaggeration used in advertising, the salesman selling the car (the Isuzu car) has his sales spiel ridiculed as silly and dishonest by a superimposed commentary. All this may be good for the advertiser but it is undermining advertising in general. Similarly, highly negative political advertising discourages voter participation in the democratic process as it shrinks and polarizes the electorate.

A dramatic example that supports the Douglas thesis about appealing to hates is Nike's phenomenal success with its *initial* entry into running shoes. Nike's campaign depended for its success, not on saying anything about the product itself (the attributes of the product itself were ignored), but on an advertising campaign that assumed that there was a target segment that wished to protest against professional sport and focus on the *egalitarianism* of running for pure enjoyment, for healthy exercise. For this market segment, extrinsic rewards from running diminished the satisfaction by stressing the instrumentality of running to achieve material reward. Those in the segment wished to signal opposition to this professional running. The Nike running shoe plus its promoted image communicated an individual who was defining himself or herself in terms of what they opposed. (Since these early days Nike has happily appealed to the values of the professional runner.)

ASSOCIATIONS TIED TO A FEELING OF SOLIDARITY WITH OTHERS

Persuasive advertising based on solidarity appeals are those that call upon group loyalties, suggesting a commonality of interests between those doing the persuading and the target audience. Solidarity appeals may on occasion incorporate the Douglas notion of a protest. The rhetoric of solidarity has always been the stock-in-trade of trade unions as they remind workers of their common interests and need to protect themselves against employer exploitation. It is also the rhetoric of the new Far Right in the United States, based on solidarity appeals against minorities like gays, Jews and blacks: it is a shared hatred that holds members together. Curbing such hate groups presents a real dilemma to any democratic government in that it means strengthening the state which can easily undermine liberal freedoms.[46]

Whatever is advocated is claimed to be for the good of the group and something to be supported in the interests of group solidarity. A recent Canadian ad for Molson beer caused a stir when it rallied the Canadians to a sense of solidarity by stressing what distinguished them and how they differed from their US neighbours. Here we have Jeff Douglas saying: 'I can proudly sew my country's flag on my backpack. I believe in peacekeeping, not policing; diversity not assimilation. And the beaver is a truly proud and noble animal. A toque is a hat, a chesterfield is a couch. And it's pronounced zed. Not zee. Zed.' It ends in a final shout: 'My name is Joe. And I am Canadian'.

A French entrepreneur, Mr Mathlouthi, launched Mecca Cola, which, as he openly admits, was designed to take advantage of anti-American sentiment around the world. (We have the exploitation of hate here.) Zamzam Cola, an Iranian drink named after a holy spring in Mecca, has already been a success in the Middle East where there is outrage against the United States over its 'one-sided' support for Israel, leading in the first three months of 2002 to a decline by more than 40 per cent in US exports to Saudi Arabia. As long as people love to hate and have a defensible target for that hate, solidarity appeals will be effective though this is not to suggest that such appeals are always built on something to hate, even if these are the most effective; the focus can be on what a group has in common that distinguishes it in a positive way from other groups.

Margalit makes a distinction between 'shared' memory and 'common' memory.[47] A shared memory does not just aggregate the individual memories of the group – this is a common memory – but, through communication, integrates and calibrates the different perspectives on some event or episode into one version. It is the shared memories that operate in solidarity appeals and nostalgia, so the advertiser must first establish that the memory is in fact shared. Margalit, an Israeli, points out that the chief bond of solidarity for many nations is based on hatred of others, usually neighbours, often fostered by myths about ancestry. This suggests shared memories need to have sustained emotional resonance: when feelings fade away, so does the solidarity.

Sennett sees fewer bonds of solidarity in the United States today which may explain the poverty of the welfare services for the disadvantaged, with over 40 million with no health insurance.[48] The wealthy do not feel they sink or swim together with the labouring classes, while ethnic divisions make common cause more difficult. President George W. Bush used the persuasive appeal of solidarity as he sought approval for war against Iraq, trying to give a coherence and a cement to the need for solidarity by arousing fear that Iraq has or can acquire weapons of mass destruction that could be sent (postage paid) to the United States. Creating a sense of fear can be an effective solidarity appeal since it is the catastrophe that dominates the mind and not its likelihood. In international relations it is less mentally taxing for a dominant country just to use the stick and carrot, neglecting diplomacy and persuasion. But coercion (the stick) results in minimal compliance while material incentives (the carrot) simply rent allegiance only for as long as the rent is paid.

Myths exploited in advertising do *not* need a base in reality to hold a target audience's attention and interest, and characters can be completely fictional and yet grab the emotions. What matters is how the story or characters come across. The target audience must understand what is going on, both from the outside looking on and from the inside as if participating. Different weightings of the same facts, different interpretations of the same events can be crucial in acceptance or rejection of any assertions made.

Mayhew claims that if persuasion is to be effective, it presupposes that the persuader and the target audience share a common interest or concern; not all interests need be in common, only the interest relevant to the appeal.[49] For Mayhew, group membership is part of everyone's identity and explains why social interests reflecting group membership dominate political appeals. In politics, the rhetoric of 'public interest' is a condition for any successful appeal, even if 'public interest' has a narrow agenda. As with Douglas, the common interest may be what the target audience has in common in opposing another group. As an example, Lupia shows that the 'uninformed' among Californian voters regard any endorsements by those viewed as opposed to their interests as negative symbols to guide their voting behaviour.[50]

For Mayhew, an attempt to persuade is an offer of affiliation and its acceptance an act of affiliation. This is an insightful and refreshing viewpoint. It is true regardless of whether the persuader is a professional adviser like a doctor, a politician, a family member, a friend or a co-worker. *In the offer of affiliation, the persuader must not come across too strong as this would border on coercion. Enthusiasm, though, counts.* In accepting an offer of affiliation, people feel a glow of satisfaction in going along with an advocated position when it affirms what they believe. This explains the 'cultist' feel attached to some brands: the sense in buying and using the brand that you are part of a movement of discerning people, a sense that advertising can cultivate.

The need for emotional affiliation is strong. Just treating people as if they had some basis for acting together, may be all that is required to get them to see themselves that way. This is the *granfalloon technique* discussed in Chapter 2, the word 'granfalloon' referring to a meaningless association.[51] The categorization of others as being like oneself produces shared expectations of agreement, in this case of wanting a product that claims to cater to one's group specifically.

As Mayhew says, while shared interests may not currently form the basis for 'solidaristic' identification they can become so through rhetorical appeals. Hence, the number of clubs that have been formed for different makes of car and so on. Knowing the appeal of belonging to an 'in group' is one reason why some companies build a sense of group sharing or community not only among the firm's customers but among employees, suppliers and distributors. This strategy is very much under-exploited.

The principle of reciprocity is at work throughout all social relationships. Even in saying 'thank you' or returning a 'good morning' we are reciprocating while at the same time adhering to social norms and making ourselves more attractive. Ingratiating ourselves with powerful figures offers the hope of their doing us a favour and so reciprocating our admiration and devotion. Marcel Mauss (1872–1950) claimed that gift exchange was a major way of drawing people together and creating solidarity. Aristotle viewed society as bound together by the reciprocal exchange of benefits which went beyond gifts associated with births, baptism, marriage and funerals. Social bonding is very much tied to mutual obligations to give, receive and repay. For Mauss the giving of gifts is simultaneously generous and self-serving. If communal solidarity necessitates a rule of reciprocity with a threefold obligation, namely to give, to receive and repay, there is a case for arguing that gift giving is no different from any other kind of exchange.

Social relationships in history have been cemented by the symbolism of gifts, service and gratitude. In sixteenth-century France, the exchange of gifts was a major social lubricant making for solidarity: gifts between equals made for friendship while gifts involving superiors reduced the psychological distance imposed by hierarchy though it is also true that gift giving often imposed an intolerable obligation.[52] Davis even argues that the Reformation in Europe could be interpreted as being about gift giving in that the basic argument was whether human beings could reciprocate God's gifts and whether God could be put under some obligation. Ambassadors at the time, while presenting gifts from their monarch to foreign rulers, commonly sought to avoid receiving gifts in exchange; thus the obligation to reciprocate would remain with the foreign ruler until support was needed.

Although we stressed the significance of reciprocity in social solidarity, the principle also applies to the reciprocation of an injury, not just benefits. The principle of reciprocity here undermines solidarity as it involves tit-for-tat retaliatory actions. It undermines between-group solidarity even though it may enhance within-group solidarity.

ASSOCIATIONS TIED TO STATUS AND PRESTIGE

A persuasive appeal can be linked to prestige, which Mayhew views as drawing on the 'influence of hierarchy'. If this is the case, those consumers in Douglas's egalitarian and isolation categories would have little interest. However, in general, those higher in the social hierarchy, celebrity hierarchy or knowledge hierarchy have an advantage in persuasion. While there may be some questioning, compliance is often driven by a desire to identify with the prestige group or person. While respect is something demanded by everyone, prestige is something bestowed and, being associated with those on whom it has been bestowed, gives rise to a vicarious satisfaction. This is why all organizations concerned with persuasion look for prestigious spokespersons to endorse their position and thus endow it with something of their own prestige. People seek social approval from all others, but it is more valued when it comes from those higher up the social scale since it is less likely to be self-serving and is considered more perceptive.

Plate 3.2 *Celebrity sophistication: Omega*

Source: Courtesy of Omega

Plate 3.3 *Nostalgia: Panerai*

Source: Courtesy of Panerai

Case study:
THE OXO FAMILY

The Oxo Family and their rituals became one of the most celebrated institutions in British television advertising. In September 1955 Oxo was advertised on television for the first time, featuring Harry Corbett and Sooty, a bear glove-puppet. In 1957 the Oxo Family were introduced, and for eighteen years the polished, upper-middle-class 'Katie' and 'Philip' evangelized Oxo. Then, in 1983, an entire young family was introduced, presided over by a tough long-suffering matriarch, and set in English suburbia.

This family might be seen as an ideal type, and the persuasive force of the advertising is explained via associationism, that is solidarity with others and links to the social norms of the target group, its values and valued images; and there is an activation of the likeability heuristic. The rites of passage of middle-class, middle-English family life, such as the children going off to university, and its rituals and familiar types were closely observed and gave the series a popular following. Normality was celebrated humorously: the family is depicted as a matriarchy, with a sheepish father who commits occasional acts of rebellion, a precocious daughter and a son with attitude; the family is self-parodic, their greed, for example, contrasted with the self-sacrifice of the mother (with whom women in particular identified) who remarks 'That good?' after returning home from work, lifting the casserole lid and finding it all gone. There are elements here of a universal type: we recognize in these playlets a sociology of our own families. Sales of Oxo rose by 10 per cent after the introduction of this family, and for the next sixteen years advertisements portrayed their trials and trivialities as they sat down together for dinner. While these did celebrate the resilience of 'family values', they were also updated, with the mother going out to work, etc.

The soap opera format created permanent novelty rather than boredom, since an evolving narrative is a text that is constantly renewed. There is a power in narrative and in its accumulation: we watch this family mature, and each new advertisement reminds us of its predecessors. The appeal of the advertising could be seen as nostalgic – many families were no longer like that – but it also worked through familiarity which induces liking, so that the Oxo Family became part of the viewer's family, as happens with soap operas.

But it is awkward for advertisers to negotiate changing social trends. In this case, the result was a decision to pension off the Family, and in September 1999 the last advertisement in this series was aired. A final dinner, and they were gone. After this, Oxo introduced a radically different style of domestic relationships, claiming that the formal family dinner was an anachronism for today's generation with their solitary eating and microwave suppers.

The new advertisements showcased contemporary couples and flat-sharing younger men with brash enthusiasms for beer and football. Instead of the soap opera of Linda, Michael and their two children, Oxo promised to 'focus on family life as it is lived today with interchangeable characters who will strike a chord with every viewer'. Younger couples ate meals together in London homes, in one case demonstrating 'what happens when the power of love overtakes hunger'. In another, the four 'laddish' lager-swilling young men are watching football and one is delegated to do the cooking at half-time. A further advertisement featured an Essex council house family who were shown consuming spaghetti bolognese rather than the sort of traditional Sunday roast favoured by the earlier Oxo Family (www.news.bbc.co.uk).

However, the new series caused protests from consumers. In December 2001 Campbell's, the new owner of the Oxo brand, promised that a recognizably traditional Oxo family would now return (www.media.guardian.co.uk).

Did Oxo make a serious error in deviating from their tradition? The case illuminates how advertisers try to reflect social trends, and the problems they have in attempting to interpret their meanings: in this case, execution was followed by resurrection. Social values and institutions do change, but this does not mean that all advertisements should try to give an authentic account of contemporary mores. Consumers look for symbols of stability in their lives, and they may be vulnerable to feelings of nostalgia for an imagined past: we may even be embarrassed at being reminded of how we live now. In this case, some of the new types such as the 'lager lads' could be seen as negative reference groups for much of the target market, which is probably not in the 25–35 age group. Being contemporary is a strategy rather than *the strategy*, and this abrupt shift from the static suburban domesticity of an earlier time into today's culture could be seen as a misunderstanding and therefore mismanagement of the imagistic capital of the product Oxo. People had expectations of what this brand signified, and these were undermined by the new and modish style. There is a love of, and comfort in, the familiar. Advertisers often fear social conservatism, which they equate with an image of dowdiness, but their radical instincts are not always right. Nuclear families have not ceased to exist, many like the idea of their continuity and their rituals, and some aspire to be in such a family even when they are not. Oxo correctly diagnosed a social change, the demise of the institution of the family mealtime, but they should have asked deeper questions about the meaning of social rituals and the imagistic heritage of their product.

References

www.browneyedsheep.com
'Oxo puts sex on the menu', www.news.bbc.co.uk, 20 December 1999.
'Oxo Family returns to dinner table', www.media.guardian.co.uk, 11 December 2001.

Case study:
MECCA COLA

This is a 'conviction' product created by French entrepreneur, Tawfik Mathlouthi, and it represents a new type of social protest using the system of commercial product market signification. It would appear to embody in an extreme form the ideas of Mary Douglas about products and purchases functioning as a kind of social protest; that is, we have a more clearly formed idea of our dislikes – what we are against – than our likes, and the products we buy reproduce this idea. Like Death Cigarettes, Mecca Cola could be merely a fad, a one-time purchase, or it could signify a permanent trend and a harbinger of more, such as Muslim Up, or the promised Halal Fried Chicken. Indeed, many iconic American products could be given the Mecca make-over, by which Mecca, the name of the holiest city in Islam, is being appropriated as a commercial brand. Mathlouthi conceives his brand as entirely political in inspiration, claiming it is about combating 'America's imperialism and Zionism by providing a substitute for American goods and increasing the blockade of countries boycotting American goods'. Coca-Cola accuse him of exploiting the sensitivities of the Middle East for commercial ends. He blames the US government: 'It is not my problem, it is the problem of the US administration. If they want to change anti-US sentiment they must change their policies and their double standards on human rights and politics' (www.news.bbc.co.uk).

The entire, and brief, history of Mecca Cola is an exercise in symbolism. Coca-Cola itself is of course the ultimate symbol of Americana, banned by Dr Salazar in Portugal, and following the US army around the world as bottling plants were established to pep up troop morale during the Second World War. But Coke also has content created by generations of advertising, meanings connected with ideas such as freedom, youthful hedonism and the unity of all peoples under the Coke banner ('I'd Like to Teach the World to Sing'). It is therefore ironic that such a resonant symbol should be stolen and its signification reversed (though such hijacks are common in propaganda, as, for example, in the British General Election of 1997, when the Labour Party annexed that old symbol of high Tory England, the bulldog). As Mathlouthi says, 'We are taking the best in American culture and we are fighting them with that.' We may admire the imagination or the irreverence by which the meaning of a universal symbol is reversed in the service of a politicized entrepreneurship, exploiting a market niche for consumption that is also a social and political protest.

Beyond this, it is actually quite difficult to 'read' the real message of the protest. It could be interpreted as a gesture of rejection, but, also, as a symbol of inclusion, one that is not overtly hostile. It may of course be seen as endorsing anti-US Islamic terrorism or just support for the Palestinians, or not even that. Mecca Cola is not as alienating as might first appear, since the message is actually that we like your culture (its modernity), we simply reject aspects of your politics. It fuses rather than separates Muslim identity, and in particular neatly articulates the identity ambivalence of Europe's Muslims, of whom there are four million in France. While there is a social symbolism in this purchase – to buy it is to make public expression of adherence to a cause – it is also an imprecise expression: the purchase could be read as a perverse endorsement of the American culture and values, or simply as an affirmation of Islam. The subtext is more ambiguous than it might appear on the surface, the product representing a political rather than a cultural antagonism to the United States. The fit with Islamic perspectives is helped by the assimilation effect: when views are close to our own, we believe them to be even more so, and vagueness is useful here (www.news.bbc.co.uk).

But Mecca Cola is already beginning to make an impact in the marketplace, following on from the success of the Iranian drink Zamzan Cola and such related phenomena as the 40 per cent drop in US exports to Saudi Arabia in the first quarter of 2002. The drink is exported to the Middle East and to five European countries and retails in their supermarkets: at the time of writing fourteen million bottles have been sold with orders for many more (two million for the UK).

The psychology of association might help to illuminate the character of the market for this product, since the degree to which associations are effective may depend among other things on exploitation of feelings of solidarity with others. This product does so visibly: in buying Mecca Cola, you create a special, public connection with all its other consumers. You remind yourself, and those from the non-Mecca public, of your collective power. You contribute to the sustenance of your cause every time you drink it. In fact 10 per cent of profits go to charities in Palestinian lands (though in goods, not cash) and 10 per cent to European NGOs. Consistency theory (see Chapter 5) may also explain the phenomenon of Mecca Cola; the explicit message of the product is: if you feel this way, why don't you do something about it? The message is expressed in the slogans: 'No more drinking stupid, drink with commitment' and 'Don't shake me, shake your conscience' (www.cnsnews.com) It is at least a solution, at the symbolic level, to our need to reconcile beliefs with behaviour.

References

Murphy, Verity, 'Mecca Cola Challenges U.S. Rival', www.news.bbc.co.uk, 8 January 2003.
Cahen, Eva, 'Soft Drink Politics: Mecca Co' Takes off in France', www.cnsnews.com, 30 April 2003.

KEY ASSERTIONS

■ If new associations are attached to it, a brand is placed in a new context which conjures up different meanings for it. Whatever is associated with a brand has the potential to affect its image. A brand is condensed meaning, as messages and associations are poured into it by advertising to articulate and define its symbolic meaning for the consumer. But the meaning or significance of a brand is the result of all the behaviours of the company (not just advertising): the brand with its associations becomes a sort of symbolic theatre over and above its utilitarian function. Brand purchase is an identity-building activity as brands become part of the consumer's social identity.

■ If marketing management aims to develop a favourable brand image, it may have to overcome some aspects of the existing image resulting from country of origin or unfortunate publicity.

■ If marketing management is successful in attaching favourable associations to the brand, first-time buyers may come to regard it as their implicit favourite and proceed in subsequent deliberation to select evidence that 'proves' that it is the right choice.

■ If marketing management succeeds in making its brand the best-known, that is, the most familiar, it is easily available in the memory and more likely to be recalled first.

■ If marketing management is to protect brand image, it must protect it from negative publicity, negative associations and negative word-of-mouth since negative information is more persuasive than positive information, other things remaining equal.

■ If marketing management is to attach favourable images to its brand, this means exploiting one or more of the following:

● linkage to values and valued symbols: link the brand to the target group's subcultural values and valued symbols since these resonate emotionally. One element of this linkage is ensuring you are using the same language as the target group. The fusing of esteemed values and symbols with the brand can outweigh rational reasons for buying. The target group responds more emotionally to value associations than to arguments based on tangible benefits. Avoid simply attaching favourable images to a brand without ensuring they cohere in signalling what the brand stands for. In any case, any cultural image can become debased through misuse;

- the repeated exposure effect: a brand becomes more popular purely as the result of mere repetition of (pleasing?) advertising;

- lifestyle advertising which in effect says: if this lifestyle or set of values resonates with you, then our brand is for you. There are many categories of lifestyle segmentation. Perhaps the most serious limitation is that values, without corresponding beliefs about means to achieve them, may be too broad for predictive purposes though the question is still open. Mary Douglas is right in arguing that consumers know better what they do not want than what they want; and that knowledge of what they oppose (hate) is a guide to how they will behave. Buying can be a protest vote;

- representing a brand as a means to group solidarity: the brand may be advertised as something through which to foster a sense of solidarity with others. This approach focuses directly on the offer of affiliation which, if
accepted, gives a sense of group backing that is a boost to individual self-esteem. This is facilitated by the 'granfalloon technique' in that people treated as having a common interest (e.g. a specific cologne for lorry drivers) will come to think of themselves that way;

- link to prestige: any linking of the brand to those higher in the social hierarchy, celebrity hierarchy or knowledge hierarchy makes persuasion easier since agreement is often driven by a desire to identify with the prestige position.

Chapter 4

Persuasive advertising appeals, 2

- Associations tied to the mental modes of seeking excitement and experiencing relaxation (reversal theory)
- Associations tied to positive or negative reinforcements (behaviourism/conditioning)

REVERSAL THEORY

Reversal theory, as developed by Apter, offers another insight into why associations are effective, in this case associations tied to excitement and relaxation.[1] Reversal theory is a branch of *structural phenomenology*. Phenomenological psychology seeks to understand the significance or meaning of social phenomena from the perspective of the individual. In phenomenology, the reality of interest is what people perceive it to be. *To give a phenomenological account of Y is to say how Y is experienced by some person or group.* Structural phenomenology accepts as a given that subjective experience does not consist of a 'blooming, buzzing mass' of unrelated items and events but forms a meaningful, coherent *structure* for thinking, feeling and doing. In structural phenomenology, the interest lies in the ways in which experience can be structured and how the structuring of that experience changes over time.

Reversal theory employs structural phenomenology in explicating the mental structures lying behind motivation and emotion. It contrasts with mainstream cognitive psychology which takes the rational processes for granted and neglects emotion and motivation. Cognitive psychology typically focuses on rational (cognitive) decision processes, ignoring the fact that important decisions are often stressful with the decision maker anxious, worried, embarrassed or excited. This omission is not surprising, given that the basic model for cognitive psychology is the computer.

The basic assertion in reversal theory is that, as arousal increases, it becomes either increasingly pleasant or increasingly unpleasant. When high arousal is pleasant there is *excitement*, and when high arousal is unpleasant there is *anxiety*, both excitement and anxiety being emotional states. Similarly, when low arousal is unpleasant there is *boredom*, and when low arousal is pleasant we have *relaxation*.

Plate 4.1 *Excitement – the paratelic mode: Oliver Sweeney*

Source: Courtesy of Oliver Sweeney, © Oliver Sweeney Ltd

Anxiety and boredom create emotional tension: in anxiety because the arousal is too high and in boredom because it is too low. *In an anxiety-avoidance mental mode, we seek to avoid anxiety and to experience relaxation. In an excitement-seeking mental mode, we seek excitement to avoid boredom.*

The theory is called *reversal theory* because there is a frequent reversal or switching between the two modes, a person either being motivated to seek the high emotional arousal of excitement or motivated to avoid the high emotional arousal of anxiety. If bored, we seek excitement. If anxious, we seek relaxation. Harré supports the claim that the physiological aspects of an emotion need not be specific to it by quoting reversal theory, a central tenet of which is that people who are highly aroused may switch rapidly between the two modes.[2]

Reversal theory speaks of 'modes', the anxiety-avoidance mode or the excitement-seeking mode, with the word 'state' being reserved for particular values of the modes. The two modes of high arousal/excitement and high arousal/anxiety are mutually exclusive in that people can be in either one mode or the other but not both at the same time. They are also exhaustive in that people are always in one or the other of the two general modes. This accounts for the use of the term 'mode' rather than the term 'mood'; it emphasizes the need to be in one mode or the other.

Reversal theory claims not only that people are motivated to reduce or increase arousal intensity (depending on their mode), but that the motivation has a directional tendency. But the theory is not claiming that motives alone determine the action taken (since this generally depends also on beliefs). It simply maintains that, at any one time, motivation must be concerned either with goal achievement or, alternatively, with excitement. In a *telic* mode achieving the goal is the *primary* motivation; but, in a *paratelic* mode, achieving the goal will be secondary to carrying out the activity itself. Thus in amateur sports, the goal of winning may be secondary to enjoying the game itself. In a telic mode, satisfaction is tied to making progress towards goal achievement but in a paratelic mode, satisfaction comes from being involved with the activity itself, and is intrinsic, not instrumental.

If in a telic mode, the focus is on goal achievement whereby means (activities) change as beliefs change as to the best means for goal achievement. In a paratelic mode, the focus is on means (activities), so that goals can change to ensure the continuation of the enjoyment. *The telic mode is tied to a disposition to avoid the high arousal emotion of anxiety while the paratelic mode is tied to a disposition to seek the high arousal of excitement.*

Reversal theory claims that while there will always be some feelings of anxiety or relaxation in the telic mode, this is never so in the paratelic mode. Similarly, there will always be some excitement or boredom in the paratelic mode but never in the telic mode. This may sound counter-intuitive, in that we might expect both relaxation and anxiety to occur in the paratelic mode. But relaxation, as the opposite of anxiety, is always *pleasant* low arousal, not the unpleasant low arousal of boredom.

Why does anxiety not occur in a paratelic mode? The reason is because the paratelic mode provides protection against anxiety:

- in the paratelic mode there is the protection of *feeling confident* about dealing with any problems that come along;
- in the paratelic mode enjoying the *activity* is so *absorbing* that a person acts as if in a safety zone that is free of risk;
- in the paratelic mode there is a sense of *detachment* from others even in threatening situations.

Reversal theory refers to these three protections as *protection frames*, claiming that they (particularly the detachment frame) allow us to enjoy *all* emotions when in the paratelic mode. This is reversal theory's explanation of our enjoyment of horror films.

The telic and paratelic modes can be related to Thayer's work on moods.[3] Moods are important in buying and also in reacting to whether a message is loss-framed or gain-framed.[4] When spirits flag, consumers hold back from buying. As reflected in consumer confidence measures, mood is a better indicator of downturns than the stock market. In the summer of 1981, even though the economy was growing at 4 per cent per annum, confidence measures suggested the subsequent dip.[5]

Thayer argues that the central components of what we experience as moods are *energy* and *tension* and identifies four mood states arising from these two arousal continuums:

1 calm-energy. This is the optimal mood. It is equivalent to the paratelic mode where there is an absence of anxiety. It is probably the mode we most admire in others when we view them as playing it 'cool';
2 calm-tiredness. This is also a paratelic mode. There is no stress, only a pleasant sense of calm-tiredness;
3 tense-energy. This is a telic mode. There is low-level anxiety, in preparation for a flight/fight response;
4 tense-tiredness. This is also a telic mode. Fatigue is mixed with nervousness, tension and anxiety, without relaxation. This is the mood that underlies depression with negative thoughts about oneself, leading to low self-esteem.

Apter points out that there are people who get locked into one state or the other. Those who get locked into a telic mode are constantly anxious about achievement. With a tense-energy mood in a telic mode, there is slight anxiety allied with energy. This mental state is probably common among high achievers. But a tense-tiredness mood in a telic mode is dysfunctional to both achievement and health. If we were permanently in a telic mode we would miss all the fun. On the other hand, while the paratelic mode embracing the mood of calm energy makes us feel good, what we are doing must be intrinsically absorbing if goals are to be achieved. In this mood consumers judge things more positively and so are more susceptible to being persuaded. In a positive mood people think less and can be influenced more by an invalid argument than a valid one.[6] The paratelic mode in a calm-tiredness mood is the one to be in for a good night's sleep. To be locked completely into a paratelic mode implies a somewhat hedonistic lifestyle. A paratelic mode favours spending because there is less risk aversion. Thus people spend more freely on holiday as they are likely to be in a paratelic mode.

Because a product sampled on holiday can arouse emotional memories when recalled, companies promote heavily in *destination marketing* in prime holiday areas. Beck's North America, the US division of the German brewery firm, has been one of the leaders in destination marketing, believing that if heavy promotion induces people to sample Beck's while on holiday, they will continue to buy it when back home because they will associate it with pleasant times. If a newspaper is more likely to be read in a telic mode (at breakfast or on the way to work) and an entertaining magazine in a paratelic mode (at weekends and so on), this is something advertisers need to keep in mind.

If being in one mode rather than the other is important to sales, how can modes be changed? Whenever a change of mode is induced, it changes the *perceptions* of *ambiguous* events: threatening to those in a telic mode and pleasurably intriguing to those in a paratelic mode. This is because the telic and paratelic modes can be regarded as distinct ways of interpreting experience. A telic mode allows little 'tolerance for ambiguity' because a person in this mode dislikes conflicting ways of interpreting a situation. Reversal theory quotes three conditions that induce a switch from a telic to a paratelic mode and vice versa.

1 The first condition is *satiation* which builds up after a time to bring about a switch from one mode to another.
2 The second condition occurs when trying to act in one of the modes leads to *frustration*. Thus those in a telic mode who are unable to pursue their goal may just 'switch off' and fantasize or those in a paratelic mode who are frustrated in their excitement seeking can be thrust into a telic mode. It would seem there are many sufferers from goal frustration who are given relief by fantasizing, helped by advertising.
3 The third condition is some *environmental happening* that inserts or removes one or more of the protective frames. 'When the going gets tough, the tough go shopping:' luxury shopping can be a highly

97

pleasurable experience for those with a large disposable income as it is one way of changing from a telic to a paratelic mode. Similarly, entering a place of entertainment can induce a paratelic mode while any loud sudden noise or just entering one's place of work can induce a telic mode. This relates to another concept of reversal theory, namely the concept of 'cognitive synergy'.

Cognitive synergy is the experience of recognizing incompatible attributes in something. There are 'reversal synergies' and 'identity synergies'. In both cases synergistic effects are produced in that something appears to be X, yet more than X. *Reversal synergy* occurs when the incompatible attributes *follow* each other as in the TV advertisement when a man starts to walk up a wall and along the ceiling. *Identity synergy* occurs when some item, person or thing exhibits incompatible properties *at one and the same time*, as in an advertisement when a cheap, delicate-looking watch 'takes a licking and keeps on ticking'. Both synergies are (unknowingly?) but commonly exploited in advertising for attention getting by creating puzzlement. For those in a paratelic mode, synergies are enjoyed. For those in a telic mode, the synergies just irritate. This needs to be noted by advertisers who tend to assume their ads are going to be pleasant and attention getting, regardless of the viewer's mental state.

Not everyone switches easily from one mode to the other, even when a change in conditions occurs. Switching is more difficult for some, so that one mode dominates. An operational measure of the degree to which one mode or the other dominates is provided by the Telic Dominance Scale mentioned by Apter in his book *Reversal Theory*, mentioned above. *Where the paratelic mode is dominant, people describe their experiences in an evaluative way while those in a telic mode are more factually descriptive.* Teenagers are much more likely to be paratelic dominant, indulging in a wide variety of pursuits in a more spontaneous way, while those who are telic dominant are more likely to be older married people, engaging in more planned activities as they seek to achieve their goals.

Is the buying of our product conducted in a telic or a paratelic mode? It is useful to know since when in a telic mode consumers are just interested in efficiently conducting business and not in being entertained. When in a paratelic mode, consumers are seeking excitement, with boredom the chief sin. Thus consider the marketing of services. There are two types of pure services: (a) those like banking and plumbing that are instrumental to utilitarian goals; and (b) those that are used, bought or consumed just for enjoyment, like a visit to Disneyland or the opera. Where the service is instrumental, customers are likely to shop in a telic mode, focused on efficiency and the satisfaction that comes from a feeling of progress being made towards achieving goals. What the customer wants is to avoid apprehensions, anxieties, fears, discourtesies and frustrations that might arise in the process of rendering the service. The customer wants the service provider to 'just get the job done' without fanfare or panoply. Any ambiguity is frustrating and distracting as the customer is just interested in goal achievement. Thus consumers are usually in a telic mode in a bank or pharmacy. What we term a business-like atmosphere is sought where the consumer perceives the service provider as reliable, competent and responsive to special needs, and the sales personnel as courteous and accessible. When the service is to provide enjoyment (e.g. Disneyland), customer satisfaction comes from excitement and the avoidance of boredom. Whereas providing an exciting atmosphere in a bank would be out of keeping with that type of service, the atmosphere of any place of entertainment needs to be concerned with stimulating intrinsic liking and enjoyment. While the essentials of good service are customization and personalized execution, there is a need to take account of whether customers are likely to be in a telic or paratelic mode. Many television 'instruction' programmes, like programmes on cooking, would benefit from knowing this. It can be very irritating to those watching the programme because they want to learn to cook if the instructor is trying to be a comic.

Employing association tends to go with the soft-sell approach as the aim is deftly to fuse the associations with the product even if they just evoke a fantasy of sharing. Yet it would be wrong to assume that effective persuasion amounts to nothing more than selecting the right things with which to associate a brand. While this can be crucial and decisive where brands are otherwise undifferentiated, elsewhere substance can be decisive. In fact the opposing view was expressed by Heidegger in his *Being and Time*, that how things function and how we can work out how to use them is the major concern as we go about our lives, not the perceptual properties of things.[7]

ASSOCIATION WITH POSITIVE OR NEGATIVE REINFORCEMENTS (BEHAVIOURISM/CONDITIONING)

Behaviourism was the first system of psychology to influence marketing, particularly its promotional strategies. Though now overshadowed by cognitive psychology, it is still a viable system. Although there are several forms of behaviourism, all subscribe to the thesis that behaviour is caused by external environmental factors that condition the individual to respond in certain ways. While the *methodological* behaviourism of J.B. Watson (1878–1958) regarded cognitive experiences such as thinking and feeling as having no role to play in behaviour, the *radical* behaviourism of B.F. Skinner (1904–90) viewed private (covert) events like thinking and feeling as mental events, and part of behaviour, thus to be explained by reference to environmental factors. Skinner sought to explain even the most complex human behaviour as a series of conditioned responses to outside determinants but he denied the usefulness of hypothesizing about unobservable mental events and eschewed any form of formal theory (though he somehow managed to do a fair amount of speculation).

Behaviourism argues that psychology should focus on relating environmental factors (the independent variables) to behavioural responses (the dependent variables) and not be concerned with mental processes. Although behaviourism has had an impact on sociology, political science and economics, its main influence has been as a movement within psychology itself. This is because the behaviourists' concentration on laboratory research with animals has made generalization to humans controversial. There are at least three forms of behaviourism:

1 Pavlovian conditioning, sometimes called 'classical conditioning' or the 'contiguity model';
2 operant conditioning, pre-eminently associated with B.F. Skinner;
3 Tolman's behaviourism. This particular form of behaviourism introduced by E.C. Tolman departs in major ways from the other forms in claiming that learning can arise from making stimulus/stimulus connections and not just from making stimulus/response connections. Tolman incorporated into his theory the idea of behaviour being 'purposive', with learning involving changes in people's *expectations*. These differences are so fundamental that it would be misleading to classify the Tolman system as behaviourism were it not for the fact that he used the term himself.

Pavlovian conditioning

Pavlovian or classical conditioning is known as the 'contiguity model'. It is the behaviourism of J.B. Watson whose job (after an academic career) with the advertising agency of J. Walter Thompson ensured the visibility of classical conditioning as a major theory for advertising. Because classical conditioning is the earliest form of behaviourism, Watson is credited with being the founder of behaviourism in psychology though it was Pavlov who pioneered the first experiments in 'classical' conditioning.

In classical conditioning there is an understood connection between some stimulus and a true reflex reaction, e.g. between the stimulus of food and the dog's reflex reaction of salivation. The dog reacts to the *un*conditioned stimulus of food by the *un*conditioned response of salivation. If a bell is sounded simultaneously with, prior to, or just subsequent to the unconditioned stimulus of the food, this gives *contiguity* to the food stimulus and the bell stimulus. After a repeated contiguity of the two sets of stimuli (food and bell sound), salivation will follow the bell sound alone. Once this has happened, the sound of the bell becomes a *conditioned stimulus* and the salivation a *conditioned response*. Watson claimed that our physiological reflexes were the only behaviour we inherit, all other behaviour being the result of learning via Pavlovian conditioning. He saw Pavlovian conditioning as a way to construct a purely mechanistic theory of human behaviour. Watson's methodological stance was 'physicalism' which claims that all descriptive terms in science must designate only the observable properties of things. This was very much in line with the doctrine of positivism which had a dominant influence at the time. Psychological laws must be translatable into observable, physical language to ensure the laws can be tested. Watson's views were so dominant that even today criticisms of behaviourism are often just criticism of his particular version.

Classical conditioning is an explanation in the form of Stimulus (S) $\rightarrow$ Response (R), with the stimulus being the cause and the response the effect. There has been a revival of interest in classical conditioning with the development of the distinction between central and peripheral routes to persuasion in (say) viewing an ad on TV (see Chapter 5). The alleged influence of peripheral cues, like humour or celebrity sponsorship where involvement with the product is low, is explained as the result of classical conditioning. Similarly, the relationship between A_{ad} (attitude towards the ad) and its impact on A_b (attitude towards the brand) is typically explained as the result of classical conditioning. It is assumed that if some unconditioned stimulus like a beautiful girl or valued lifestyle or attractive image is associated with a brand, it will become a conditioned stimulus, bringing forth a favourable attitude towards the brand advertised. But classical conditioning was not meant to be just a matter of establishing associations. Classical conditioning was in fact meant to replace the 'associationist psychology' of the nineteenth century by providing a physiological basis for the behaviour observed in terms of involuntary reflexes. Classical conditioning presupposes the existence of involuntary reflexes as it is these that are said to make the associations compelling. In the absence of the relevant reflexes, the power of association must be justified in some other way as, for example, in the explanations discussed in Chapter 3.

Conditioning was once assumed to be unconscious learning. However, Allen and Janiszewski (and others) claim, on the basis of experiments, that conditioning without awareness 'need not follow from the Pavlovian position'.[8] They claim that their work 'does not corroborate the view that conditioned learning comes about through a non-cognitive process and it is difficult to demonstrate conditioning in humans without subjects' awareness'. The assumption of non-cognitive conditioning meant that the advertiser needed merely to expose the viewer to a series of pairings of unconditioned and conditioned stimuli for attitudes to be affected. In contrast, the assumption that a cognitive process is at work means that attempted conditioning must promote recognition both of the unconditioned stimulus (e.g. a beautiful woman in an ad directed at men) and of the conditioned stimulus (the brand being advertised) since the attention given to brand may otherwise be ephemeral.

101

Operant conditioning

Pavlovian conditioning is dependent on the existence of a true reflex that can be stimulated (e.g. the salivary gland). This dependence limits the scope of any mechanistic psychology built on it since not much behaviour is mediated by Pavlovian reflexes. A more embracing concept of conditioning emerges in the form of *operant conditioning*. The central idea is that all living organisms are spontaneously 'emitting' behaviour and whenever this behaviour is reinforced, the chances they will repeat the behaviour are increased. Although B.F. Skinner[9] is most closely identified with operant conditioning, its basis is to be found in the work of Bechterev, a Russian physiologist, while the explanatory principle lying behind it is 'law of effect'. The law of effect states that acts that are followed by positive consequences are repeated, while acts followed by negative consequences are not. More formally, the law states that any emitted behaviour that continues to be reinforced will be repeated with greater frequency, intensity and duration. This is the basic premise behind operant conditioning which, unlike Pavlovian conditioning, assumes neither a true reflex nor some initial stimulus to start the process.

Pavlovian conditioning is an S $\rightarrow$ R (stimulus $\rightarrow$ response) psychology. Operant conditioning is different. The father of operant conditioning was B.F. Skinner (1953). Skinner's operant conditioning, however, is not a stimulus $\rightarrow$ response model since it views behaviour as acquired, shaped and maintained by stimuli *following* responses, not preceding responses. Skinner viewed operant conditioning as not only subsuming classical conditioning but as an advance over classical (Pavlovian) conditioning, because it came to grips with the two problems to be overcome for any psychology to be considered successful. The first problem is to account for human creativity (novelty in behaviour) and the second is to account for the fact that people are motivated by future goals. Skinner felt operant conditioning got over both these problems.

Foxall views operant conditioning as part of the experimental analysis of behaviour (EAB).[10] EAB, as a system of behaviourism, is based on operant conditioning with its denial of the causal significance of mental events such as attitudes or motives. In addition, it explains behaviour purely by reference to its environmental consequences regardless of whether it is reinforced or not. For EAB, mental events are an epiphenomenon, meaning that they are caused and not causal in any way. An analogy is often used to illustrate this: just as the body causes its shadow and that shadow has no causal effect upon the body or even upon other shadows, so the brain causes consciousness and mental events but these cannot affect the brain since the causal process is just one-way.

In operant conditioning, we wait for the behaviour to be 'emitted' by the subject. Thus, Bechterev waited for his dog to lift its paw. If the dog is given food as a consequence of lifting its paw, then the dog's lifting its paw is a *response* that acts on the environment to produce consequences (food provided) and hence is termed an 'operant response'. Responses are only termed operant responses if their rate of emission is affected by their consequences. The dog is *conditioned* to perform the act of lifting its paw and has *learned as a result of reinforcement*. All consequences like the provision of food to a dog that increase the rate of emission of a response (e.g. the dog lifting its paw) in the same or similar circumstances are called 'reinforcers'. But since the dog's response is instrumental to producing the reinforcement, operant conditioning gives rise to 'instrumental learning'.

Thus according to operant conditioning, all behaviour is contingent on being reinforced. Whenever the consumer buys *XYZ* and the result is pleasant, we talk of *positive* reinforcement which encourages a repetition of the buying action. A favourable brand image is created by associating the brand with reinforcers. Unless a response is reinforced, it faces extinction. Reinforcement is simply any external (environmental) happening that increases the probability of emitted behaviour, and a reinforcer is anything that increases the probability of the occurrence of a given *class* of responses. The term 'reinforcer' is distinguished from 'reward' in that what might normally be considered a reward may not in fact work to strengthen the emitted behaviour. If a pigeon pecks a key and receives food and the key pecking increases, the food is termed a reinforcer. If pecking does not increase, the food (normally viewed as a reward) is not a reinforcer in this instance. This makes it difficult to say in advance what will be a reinforcer in a particular context.

Behaviourism focuses on the reinforcement of behaviour and eschews punishment. In fact what is termed *negative reinforcement* is not a punishment but simply the withdrawal of a punisher and is therefore reinforcement. Positive reinforcement is direct while negative reinforcement comes as a consequence of removing some adverse stimulus: stopping the torture would be negative reinforcement. Responses with the same consequences are regarded as examples of the same 'operant'. Thus an operant is a class of responses defined in terms of their consequences. If these consequences are an increase in the rate of response then the consequences are 'reinforcers', but if the rate of subsequent response drops off, the consequences are termed 'punishers'.

Operant conditioning controls behaviour by manipulating reinforcement, so the 'stimulus' is the whole set of conditions under which reinforcement takes place. Operant conditioning uses the term *discriminative* stimulus to cover any stimulus in the presence of which responses are reinforced and in the absence of which responses are not reinforced. As Foxall says, discriminative stimuli do not elicit behaviour as in classical conditioning's stimulus → response methodology but set the occasion for its performance by signalling the consequence it is likely to have.[11] Whatever it is about conditions that communicates the likelihood of negative or positive reinforcement constitute *discriminative stimuli*: these are those elements of the situation (e.g. brand name or package) which signal the opportunity for reinforcement (or punishment though this is downplayed in behaviourism).

Although the discriminative stimuli can control behaviour in the sense of signalling an opportunity, Skinner claims that any class of behaviour is explained (caused) exclusively by its consequences. This is because, in the absence of reinforcement, the behaviour may remain for a time under the control of the discriminative stimuli but it will eventually not be emitted because of the absence of reinforcement. Discriminative stimuli in marketing might take some form of promise, such as advertising the beneficial consequences of buying. This, however, will only exert a partial control over behaviour since it is the consequences (experiencing the benefits themselves) that are important. Yet if constantly paired with reinforcers, discriminative stimuli can become conditioned reinforcers themselves. This is the process known as 'chaining'. In any case, it is the specific reinforcement history of the consumer that determines what constitutes discriminative stimuli.

Behaviourism is a psychology of learning, claiming that we learn that which we have been reinforced to learn. Learning occurs most quickly when the reinforcers continue as when a customer continues to get good service or satisfaction from a purchase. This probably explains the success of serial or *episodic advertising* campaigns like the original one for Nestlé coffee where the viewer experiences 'the magical, mystical moments of courtship, of possibility'. Serials become soap operas, allowing the characters to develop their own personalities with which the viewer can identify. Each episode tells a story that builds on the previous one, so reinforcement is continued. This contrasts with the usual commercial, each of which enacts the same routine.

There is quick cessation of the behaviour when reinforcers stop as, for example, when a patient ceases to patronize a doctor after one bad experience though previous service had been satisfactory. Learning via conditioning is not the only way of learning. In fact, many psychologists regard this as the most trivial type of learning. There is *incidental* learning or learning that occurs without reward, effort or purpose which can happen through, say, watching television. There is the learning that arises from *imitation*, from observing and 'imitating' others, as when consumers copy some celebrity in buying a particular brand of perfume. *Extinction* is the process of eliminating the occurrence of a conditioned response, typically by withholding the reinforcer (e.g. a discounted price) that initiated its acquisition.

According to behaviourism, whether a consumer tries a product or brand is intimately related to past experience, while repeat buying is tied to the past consequences of purchase. Because operant conditioning focuses on reinforcement in moulding behaviour, messages signalling untried benefits might have limited appeal. Hence those advocating operant conditioning are apt to downplay the role of advertising in promoting new-to-the-world products. Under operant conditioning, complex new behaviours may be explained as emerging after a succession of preceding acts, each reinforced in turn, that together constitute successive approximations leading finally to the behaviour observed. This process is referred to as 'shaping'.

Reinforcement may not occur every time the behaviour is emitted; that is, there may not be continuous reinforcement. Reinforcement instead may be intermittent in the sense of being at fixed or variable intervals. This influences the rate of learning and the rate at which extinction of the behaviour takes place. Where every response is reinforced (the continuous reinforcement schedule) learning occurs rapidly but the behaviour is also most likely to cease when reinforcement stops. Where responses are only periodically reinforced (the intermittent reinforcement schedule) learning is slower but drops off more slowly when reinforcement ceases. Both reinforcement schedules result in learning by what behaviourists call 'shaping' (see above) which is the reinforcement of a *succession* of acts to guide behaviour to making the desired response.

If the consumer receives reinforcement of one response and, as a consequence, responds favourably to similar stimuli, then the behaviourist speaks of *response generalization*. In other words, if I am pleased with the brand I have bought, there is the likelihood of my buying other products of that brand. This is the assumption behind brand and line extensions. If the reinforcement of the response in one situation leads to the same response in like situations, there is '*stimuli* generalization'. If I am pleased with the products I have bought in one Wal-Mart store, I may buy at other Wal-Mart stores.

Skinner claims that operant conditioning replaces and incorporates classical conditioning. But, unlike Watson, Skinner argues that unobservable thoughts and feelings can be scientifically studied if these thoughts and feelings are viewed as conditioned responses, not causes of behaviour. He classifies thinking as covert behaviour and verbal communication as overt behaviour, both of which are conditioned since all behaviour (except certain innate reflexes) he regards as explainable by conditioning. Conditioning is assumed to act automatically irrespective of whether the subject is aware of what is happening. Conditioning occurs automatically or not at all. It is probably this view of conditioning which gives rise to so many charges of manipulation by advertising.

Skinner views operant conditioning as a scientific methodology for studying the precise effects of different schedules of reinforcement. But it is probably his explanation of superstitious behaviour (e.g. wearing a certain scarf) and reward (e.g. safe return from a bombing mission) that gave him most visibility outside academia. Every prospective purchase is accompanied by potentially reinforcing consequences (product benefits) and punishing consequences (cost and effort spent in obtaining the product). Hence the probability of purchase depends on the difference between the two sets of consequences. Advertising can always downplay the costs and dramatize the benefits.

Like Freud and today's cognitive psychologists, Skinner was of the opinion that there are limits to self-knowledge. But, for Skinner, the reason for this has to do with language in that a necessary condition for knowledge of one's thinking (private events) is to have competence in a language of private events. This is controversial as some psychologists claim that people are born knowing a pre-verbal language in which thought is couched before being clothed in words, whether English, Chinese or Apache.[12]

Skinner rejected almost all previous psychology and his text *Science and Human Behaviour* contains no references and no bibliography. While initially denying the existence of subjective entities, Skinner later spoke of behaviour being both overt (public) and covert (private) with all thoughts being regarded as covert (private) events. However, he always eschewed looking at mental events as a stage in some causal chain of S → O → R (stimulus → organism → response) on the ground that if the 'mental way station' itself fails to divert attention from the first stage (the stimulus), it would surely divert attention from the last stage (the response). Skinner was right to point to the problems in the use of mental constructs like motive and attitude, but ignoring cognitive processes altogether reduces radical behaviourism to ignoring many basic questions about human behaviour. Today most psychologists would wish to link the environment (the external stimulus) to behaviour (response) through mental constructs like attitude, beliefs, emotion and motives.

Criticism of operant conditioning

At the time of his defence of his Ph.D. thesis, Skinner was asked what deficiencies there were in the theory. The story goes that he could not think of any. Since then operant conditioning has become a favourite whipping boy of both philosophers and social scientists though none has succeeded in relegating it to historical oblivion. This is because behaviourism explains some aspects of behaviour in a more *useful* way than other approaches but also because it is doubtful whether behaviourism can be empirically shown to be absolutely false. After all, to be able to check predictions about an individual's behaviour presupposes knowing his or her *total* reinforcement history.

The following are the major criticisms of behaviourism. Those employing it in advertising need to make up their own minds as to the validity of the criticism for the application they have in mind:

1 explanatory 'emptiness';
2 neglect of innate capacities and thinking;
3 conflict with people's own experience;
4 simplistic assumptions, interpretations and extrapolations.

EXPLANATORY 'EMPTINESS'

Operant conditioning is a technique which some critics claim is bereft of any theoretical underpinnings except for a simple hedonistic view of human motivation as expressed in the law of effect. Unless there is a specification of what a reinforcer is, independent of its effect on the probability of response, the law of effect seems devoid of empirical content, simply saying that whatever it is that increases the probability of behaviour tends to increase the probability of behaviour.[13]

Skinner sees no need to explain what makes reinforcers reinforcing. He does not deny that people talk of having motives, but in his view, a motive refers to some property by which a stimulus gains control over the resulting behaviour. Operant conditioning makes no distinction between behavioural responses in general and intentional action. A behavioural response in the form of an arm movement is different from a voluntary (intentional) action. An involuntary blink must be distinguished from the voluntary wink. Operant conditioning assumes that people behave, not out of any conscious deliberation on anticipated consequences, but because of the consequences that followed similar behaviour in the past: they look back rather than reason forward.

NEGLECT OF INNATE CAPACITIES AND THINKING

Skinner's work focused on showing how factors in the external environment (as opposed to internal wants and beliefs) can change animal behaviour. But ethnologists have shown that much animal behaviour *outside the laboratory* depends on an innately determined neural programme. They argue that what is really distinctive about much of animal behaviour is that it is fixed (hard-wired) and cannot be eliminated or altered by the environment. To account for the existence of such instinctive behaviour, ethnologists inquire about its survival value.

Garcia and Koelling challenge the whole Skinnerian thesis by showing that while rats have no problem learning to associate a noise and light with an electric shock, they fail, for example, to learn the connection between a novel flavour and an electric shock.[14] It seemed some types of association were just too implausible to consider or beyond what their survival programmes were designed to accept.

Behaviourism claims that the direction taken by behaviour is a function of stimulus/response connections that are either innate or have been built up through learning. The probability of a given type of response is deemed to be a function of previous conditioning and the state of deprivation. This answer can be shown to have some validity in many simple cases but to accept that it applies to all behaviour amounts to an act of faith. As Humphrey says, behaviourism is hopelessly inadequate to the task of modelling the subtleties of real behaviour.[15] He suggests that if a rat's knowledge of other rats were limited to what behaviourists have discovered about rats to date, the rat would show so little understanding of its fellows that it would bungle disastrously in every social interaction in which it engaged. (Humphrey at the time was an experimental psychologist at Cambridge University specializing in animal behaviour.)

CONFLICT WITH PEOPLE'S OWN EXPERIENCE

It is a common observation that people continue many activities (like betting) when there is no positive reinforcement (periodic wins) and cease the activity when they do receive positive reinforcement (e.g. a big win). Behaviourist assumptions seem to be in conflict with what we know about ourselves. The inner debates, appraisals and evaluations that go on in our minds in making a decision can never be adequately accounted for in the behaviourist sequence of Sd $\rightarrow$ R $\rightarrow$ Sr connections where Sd means a class of discriminative stimuli, R a class of responses, and Sr a class of reinforcing stimuli. *Intentional* actions appear to be mediated by meanings and considerations of consequences. Behaviourism does not see people (as we see ourselves) as strategically rational actors who are constantly adjusting their plans to cope with change.

Behaviourism belittles reason yet reasoning is what distinguishes human beings from other forms of life. This does not mean going to the other extreme and assuming, like the existentialists, that all important human behaviour is the result of human decision (so that even one's sadness is the result of choosing to be sad). But people can and do reflect on past experiences and immediate stimuli. They do not learn from trial and error alone but reason from general principles, imagined circumstances and imitating others.

Malcolm points out that the statements people make about their intentions, wants, feelings, etc., are the most important source of information about them.[16] Yet such self-testimony cannot be checked by simply looking for relevant external influences; self-testimony is not replaceable even in principle by observations of functional relationships between physical variables. He further argues that the reasons that lie behind intentions and action cannot be shown to be functionally related to anything; that is, a reason cannot be shown to be some dependent variable resulting from independent variables operating in the environment. Elster argues that many social situations have little regularity and too much noise for reinforcement really to shape behaviour in a finely tuned way.[17] He argues that the human capacity for conscious choice and the sheer complexity of human affairs reduce the importance of purely mechanical reinforcement in explaining behaviour.

SIMPLISTIC ASSUMPTIONS, INTERPRETATIONS AND EXTRAPOLATIONS

Watson viewed habits as the result of a long chain of conditioned reflexes. However, Hilgard and Marquis show that simple chaining of conditioned responses will not account for the characteristics of complex habits.[18] Skinner assumes operant conditioning is conditioned behaviour and as such is automatic learning.

Opposing this is the view that a person's response may be made knowingly in order to get a reward.

The behaviourist assumes that generalizations from experiments on animals are transferable to humans. While it is easy to tabulate the reinforcement or conditioning history of a pigeon to predict its behaviour, the conditioning histories of people are just not available. Hence, explanations of people's behaviour in terms of their history must rest more on faith than on the evidence available. Also, while there may be something approaching a uniform rat or a uniform pigeon, humans in different cultures show a wide variation in behaviour under similar circumstances. The most fundamental criticism of generalizing from animal behaviour is that animals do not think conceptually: they cannot use their non-verbal language to suggest abstractions that cannot be directly perceived through the senses. Signs for animals are only meaningful when tied to some physical object.

Even someone as sympathetic to behaviourism as Foxall regards it as naive to extrapolate from animal experiments to humans.[19] Thus human subjects react differently from animals to different schedules of reinforcement (whether continuous or intermittent). He agrees with those researchers who attribute this to the human capacity to determine their own rules of conduct through reasoning about its likely consequences. But, in any case, there are many operational problems in identifying what constitutes the operant responses and discriminative stimuli as well as over the extent to which responses must be similar to belong to the same operant.

Foxall claims that only dogma prevented Skinner from ascribing causal significance to discriminative stimuli.[20] Such discriminative stimuli can be thoughts and feelings, and not just factors in the environment. Somewhat related to Foxall's point is the claim that humans, in their ability to reflect on what others are doing, can just imitate others in similar circumstances as well as anticipate to some extent the consequences of their behaviour and take appropriate action.

Dennett (1986) argues that while behaviourists claim their predictions are in terms of bodily responses to physical stimuli, the responses could be interpreted as appropriate rational action, given the circumstances.[21] Behaviourists are able to 'sell' their interpretation by conducting highly artificial experiments designed to ensure that only one bodily response (e.g. eating) is available that is appropriate to the circumstances. Dennett points out that behaviourists naively believe they are dealing only with the brute facts of behaviour, failing to recognize that facts are not given but interpreted as facts. To designate something as a fact is already to pass an interpretative judgement on it.

Goldman claims Skinnerian events cause behaviour only by first causing wants and beliefs which in turn cause the behaviour.[22] In other words, Goldman rejects the phenomenalism of behaviourism and maintains that the 'law of effect' and concepts like 'response', 'stimulus' and 'response generalization' make sense in terms of the reason-giving explanation which focuses on wants, beliefs, intention and action. For many writers, the law of effect, etc. are just folk psychology dressed up in new obscure jargon to sound scientific. Rosenberg, while acknowledging that behaviourism has had success in animal experiments, claims that it has been no more successful in predicting human action than approaches based on the reason-giving model.[23] Behaviourists attribute this defect in prediction to there being no universals to go on, given that people have different reinforcement histories. This leads behaviourists to downplay the influence of advertising, *except* for its effect of retaining existing customers by reinforcing their satisfaction with a particular brand.

It is not easy to predict the consequences of conditioning when behaviourism is not linked to any larger theory. Early behaviourists believed that mothers who responded warmly to a baby's cries would produce excessively dependent adults, unable to function in modern society. This view had a profound influence on both parental behaviour and government policies for national institutions like orphanages which were encouraged to minimize contact between carers and children. It was the work of Harry Harlow, showing the essential need of young baboons to have 'contact comfort' with their mothers that led to research showing the same could be said for children.[24]

Hull's drive reduction theory

Behaviourists have sought explanatory mechanisms to account for conditioning. Hull's drive reduction theory is the best known.[25] The theory assumes a state of homeostasis: an organism is in a state of equilibrium until some internal metabolic deficiency or chemical imbalance becomes a (causal) 'drive', sending the organism into a state of tension and trial-and-error learning until equilibrium is restored. Hull sought a physiological foundation to behaviourism. Only a few biological 'drives' (like hunger, thirst and sex) were thought necessary to account for all behaviour on the grounds that other 'motives' were derivative and acquired through these basic drives. The 'drive state' at any one time depends on the extent to which the organism is deprived. (Hull's drive reduction theory does not use terms like 'wants' though, according to the theory, a person would only want something to the extent that it had led in the past to drive reduction.)

CRITICISM OF HULL'S THEORY

Criticism of Hull's drive reduction theory has come from several sources. Harlow showed that monkeys find problem solving self-rewarding, so continue on such tasks even without reinforcement. This curiosity motive is difficult to reconcile with the homeostatic assumption lying behind drive theory.[26] Hebb has also challenged the homeostasis assumption.[27] In studies on sensory deprivation, it was shown that a certain level of arousal is necessary for the optimal functioning of the central nervous system. If deprived of such arousal, the organism seeks stimulation.

As Robinson says, if we take satiety as the equivalence of physiological equilibrium, many of life's goals (e.g. friendship, power) are not things with which we become satiated, unlike the biological examples Hull considers.[28] Drive reduction theories do not say where in the system and in what manner equilibrium states reveal themselves. Any stimulation results in disequilibrium from a resting state so that a resting state is not any more normal than a state of arousal.

Dretske makes the point that while a drive can be the cause of movement, unlike a desire, it is not *for* anything: a desire for some product is not the same as a drive for equilibrium.[29] We cannot explain behaviour by an appeal to drives in the same way that we can explain actions by an appeal to wants and beliefs. The concept of drives lacks the intentional properties of reasons for action.

Positives about behaviourism

One thing that behaviourism (conditioning) has taught us is the strong desire for instant gratification: such pleasures are immediate while long-term consequences seem remote. Hence, talk about long-term consequences is less effective than stressing immediate (felt) consequences, e.g. the more immediate effect on facial appearance of smoking cigarettes. Advertising that promises instant gratification, either in using a product or through immediate delivery by telephone ordering after watching a TV commercial, increases its effectiveness.

Positive emotions arise when the benefit is greater or the relief is faster than expected. Negative emotions arise when the benefit or relief is less than expected. This suggests that whatever is promised in an ad should, in the follow-up of buying, pleasantly surprise the consumer and certainly not disappoint her. Hence the old advice to 'build in something extra so as to surprise and delight'. It also suggests that advertising should not build up consumer expectations beyond what can be met. After all, consumers are only disappointed to the extent to which their expectations have been let down. Unexpected 'extras' become important when key benefits are the same for all the rival brands and much, like quality, is taken for granted. In the automobile industry, when even air bags have started to become universal, comparatively minor things like electronic navigation maps assume significance.

Of interest to advertisers is the behaviourist concept of *partial reinforcement* and its effect on extinguishing a response. If behaviour is reinforced every time it is emitted, it is likely to cease when the reinforcement is withdrawn. But if reinforcement is partial, only occurring sometimes when the behaviour is emitted (e.g. periodically finding a bargain in a certain store), the behaviour may persist longer (e.g. the customer will still visit the shop in hope of a bargain). Thus with the intermittent schedule, learning takes longer but also lasts longer. But when it comes to people as opposed to pigeons (the typical subject used by Skinner), much also depends on the information possessed (beliefs) in that I may know there are going to be no more bargains. Advertising that periodically offers some bargain can be partial reinforcement in that the customer pays attention to each and every ad for that brand in the hope of finding a repeat of the bargain offer.

Behaviourism offers insights for marketing and some marketing academics have made serious attempts to expand it and moderate its dogmatic rejection of all reference to mental happenings.[30] But for many marketers, operant conditioning has serious defects, such as its assumption that buyers do not adopt new and appropriate behaviours in new situations, or that the extinction of non-rewarding behaviour is as slow as is suggested. Also it seems crass to believe that new behaviour in new environments does not occur unless present behaviour is linked to it by a continuous chain of reinforcement. It could be argued that in classical conditioning, subjects, whether dogs or people, are simply demonstrating their capacity to recognize signals. Similarly, so-called 'extinction' is not a cessation of learning, as is suggested, but an instance of new learning.

Tolman's behaviourism

Tolman's behaviourism is the third category of behaviourism. It consists of *relational* behaviourism and *purposive* behaviourism. Tolman's work anticipated later work in cognitive psychology.[31] Whereas with the contiguity (classical conditioning) and the reinforcement (operant conditioning) models, people are said to learn and act through stimulus/response connections, in the case of *relational* behaviourism, learning and action arise through stimulus/stimulus connections, i.e. the relation between the stimuli themselves. Tolman's *latent learning* is an example. He showed that rats learned a maze merely as a result of moving around in it, even though no response was reinforced directly. He used the term 'cognitive map' to account for the animal's ability to improve by mere exposure: the rat forms a map of the environment.

Tolman saw no incompatibility between behaviourism and purposive explanations, and regarded reference to purpose as necessary to understanding. He argued that what organisms learnt was 'expectancy': a belief (cognition) that a particular response (R) in the presence of a particular situation (S) leads to the recurrence of some event (E). For Tolman, learning involves changes in expectations. Expectations always reflect probabilities about courses of action leading to desirable consequences. Tolman was willing to include the organism's expectancy as part of the explanation of behaviour. Tolman named his system *purposive behaviourism*.

In introducing the concept of expectations in relation to the likelihood of achieving goals, Tolman was moving to an explanation based on assumed mental events and processes. The concept of expectations has found its way into economics, decision theory and modern cognitive psychology. Expectations are commonly regarded as a cause or part of the cause of actions though, for the traditional behaviourist, expectations would be regarded simply as an epiphenomenon, the result of environmental factors but with no independent causal role to play in behaviour. The aim of marketing is not just to satisfy buyers (since competitors might go further and please them) but to match or exceed *customer expectations* which are based on what has been promised, what appears reasonable, what has to be given in exchange and, most important of all, what competition is known to be offering.

What buyers seek, when they seek it, where they seek it, from whom they seek it, and how they go about buying, are all influenced by expectations. Action is a function of expectations much more than of the 'objective' facts though, as a cognition or belief, expectations are just one determinant of action since they do not incorporate the want itself.

The concept of expectations is frequently cited in marketing to explain behaviour. Lattin and Bucklin, as an example, argue that to use price discounting effectively, managers must understand the link between their pricing and the consumer expectations used as a reference point[32] and based on past pricing of the brand. A response to an unexpected price decrease (i.e. below the consumer reference price) can signal a special opportunity, resulting in a greater response than to an expected price decrease. It follows that by increasing expectations too much, price discounting can dampen consumer response to a decrease.

Tolman's behaviourism eschews the physiological or mechanistic explanations sought by other behaviourists, arguing that explanations of behaviour should involve the use of psychological as opposed to physiological concepts. For Tolman, each person's stream of behaviour is segmented into a variety of purposive acts and it is essential to include a reference to the goal towards which an action is directed for it to be understood. Tolman regarded the hallmark of purposiveness in behaviour as characterized by its 'persistence until' aspect. However, not all human behaviour is purposive.[33] Unconscious causes, not the pursuit of goals, account for behaviour such as doodling, nail biting, whistling and so on though such exceptions are unlikely to be relevant to those interested in intentional buying. We will return to the notion of unconscious motivation in Chapter 6.

We have argued that behaviourism seeks causal explanations. In the case of the contiguity model, the conditioned stimulus is regarded as the cause of the conditioned response. In the case of operant conditioning the cause or stimulus of the conditioned response is the whole set of conditions associated with reinforcement. On the other hand, in Hull's drive theory (once a favourite for writers of marketing textbooks) the cause is the deprived drive state that leads to a conditioned response to seek drive reduction; the deprived drive state triggers actions which in the past have led to drive reduction. In the case of Tolman's relational behaviourism, the cause is the pattern of connections emanating from stimulus/stimulus relations,

113

leading to a conditioned response based on indirect reinforcement. Finally, Tolman's purposive behaviourism views the cause as some pattern of connections which leads to a conditioned response, depending on the individual's expectancy that a certain response will in fact lead to whatever is sought.

CONCLUSION

In spite of all the criticism levelled against behaviourism, it does dramatize the importance of reinforcement so that we come to see that even the withdrawal of a reward can act like a punisher. In any case, operant conditioning has an impressive record of success in behaviour therapy where deviant behaviour is assumed to be the result of maladaptive learning. A major way of learning is by positive or negative reinforcement. The whole process of socialization is marked by behaviour that is shaped this way.

If any support is needed, conditioning supports the case for customer orientation. Products that live up to expectations give positive reinforcement while products that do not give no reinforcement. Researchers like Skinner distinguished themselves, not by demonstrating that behaviour which is reinforced tends to be repeated, but in devising techniques for ensuring that reinforcement takes place. There has been no corresponding creativity among marketing academics though the success of the various 'frequent flyer' programmes can be interpreted as an application of operant conditioning imaginatively applied by management.

Case study:
DEATH CIGARETTES

This product worked by confronting directly what all cigarette advertising avoids: the knowledge that the product kills you. Turning this into a joke – and the product is a sick joke – may grab attention and press interest but it makes the product a fad. It cannot last, and it did not. People can buy the idea once, but they cannot live with it.

Death Cigarettes were the concept of British entrepreneur B.J. Cunningham who started his Enlightened Tobacco company in 1991. The products were contained in black packets with a death's head on the front; there were also white packets called Death Lights. This corporate identity was created by Denison Design, which deliberately conceived the packet to look like a coffin: Death Cigarettes were finalists at the London Advertising Awards. There are also rumours about coffin-shaped vending machines in pubs and clubs.

Cunningham's motive lay partly in his recognition of the expressive meaning of products. He recognized that such a product would be a signifier of bravado – brutal wit, irony, recklessness. These are the social characteristics that consumers would exhibit by buying the product. As Cunningham explained:

> When you'd take a packet of cigarettes out of your top pocket and put it on the bar in front of you, you're making a statement about yourself, exactly as you do with the clothes you wear, the music you like, and the newspaper you read. You're saying, these cigarettes are part of me. So if you take out a packet of Benson and Hedges, you're saying, I'm classy – gold packet – part of high-society. If you take out a packet of Marlboro, you're saying, I'm an outdoor type, I like wearing a cowboy hat and riding horses . . . Now, if you produce a packet of Death Cigarettes, what you're saying is . . .
>
> www.zurismokefree.ch

The use of the media to promote this product made it a legend, but achieved one-off sales and not customers. As a joke, it can be consumed only once, it is incapable of sustaining the situation beyond a first reading when boredom and, alternatively, disgust set in. This is gallows humour, which implicitly flatters the purchaser's courage in confronting the great unmentionable, their own mortality, and the fact that this ghoulish product helps to take you to that destination. But this is not a convincing reason to buy. Once everyone knows that joke, why repurchase? So Death Cigarettes petered out, though in America entrepreneurs later revived the title.

Cunningham's motivation was also candour, a crusading antagonism. He argued that Death Cigarettes were 'for the smoker who wants to say, yes I'm kidding myself, but at least I know it, and I smoke a brand which doesn't try to hide the fact'. Cunningham claimed that he wanted to expose the hypocrisy behind the tobacco industry: governments cannot afford to ban smoking because they receive huge amounts of money from it in tax; tobacco companies try to sanitize their image by sponsoring sports events such as motor racing, rugby, football, cricket and tennis, at vast expense.

But those such as Cunningham who would strip us of our delusions and make us confront realities can never enjoy long-term popularity. By the end, Death Cigarettes were losing about £1 million per year: it could not afford to advertise on the same scale as larger companies and had to depend on media-generated publicity. Ultimately, this bizarre product illuminates our massive need for illusion. Few are willing to confront the fact of their mortality. Marlboro, for example, gives off an implicit message that cigarettes are healthy, and we become partners in our self-deceit, co-conspirators in a fantasy. While other cigarette advertisements might on occasion have flirted with the idea of death and the hereafter, they have done so in immensely subtle, abstracted and symbolic ways.

Cunningham's further objective was to protest against interfering, paternalistic authority. He argues that Death Cigarettes say, 'don't you dare tell me to stop', that it gives him a chance to 'attack the anti-smoking killjoys. Those puritans who will try to control our lives. You just can't have laws which control every aspect of the way people live.' Thus this curious experiment could be viewed as a case of consumption as protest. Buying the product becomes a political act rich in symbolism, and this may be regarded as part of a new trend where the processes of mass consumption are exploited by those with a political message to articulate. At this level there is a connection with Mecca Cola.

This 'product as protest' may be an extant illustration of the Mary Douglas thesis (and some explanation may also be sought in consistency theory, where we seek to reconcile beliefs and behaviour). But reversal theory is a particularly useful approach to understanding both the appeal of this product and its demise. The appeal is to novelty — the excitement of the paratelic mode — to experience the consumption of a symbol that is both outrageous and unique. This is an offer of a fantasy where we can look death in the face and laugh at it. But the truth is, we can't. This novelty stimulated the wide publicity, but to stress not merely the association with ill-health but the causal connection with death was just too extreme.

References

www.denison.co.uk.
Andrews, David, 'Death Cigarettes: you must be joking!', www.zurismokefree.ch.

KEY ASSERTIONS

Reversal theory

■ Consumers seek excitement and avoid boredom or, alternatively, seek to avoid anxiety and experience relaxation. If bored, people seek excitement and, if anxious, seek relaxation. Advertising should favour ads that excite through novelty, are never boring and use fear appeals only to demonstrate that people can relax because the brand advertised solves the problem.

■ An ad that can arouse excitement for a brand provides the emotional energy for the reader or viewer to seek out the brand. In arousing excitement, there is a move away from boredom through the novelty of the ad or the product advertised.

■ If the accompanying TV programme suggests viewers will be in a paratelic mode, an exciting ad is required. If the accompanying TV programme (like a documentary) suggests viewers will be in a telic mode, the ad should focus on being informative in an efficient and businesslike way. In a paratelic mode, goal achievement is secondary to activity that is exciting (avoids boredom) while in a telic mode goal achievement is paramount to avoid anxiety and feel a sense of relaxation.

- In a paratelic mode consumers feel confident about dealing with any problems that come along, and this confidence makes them more susceptible to non-rational appeals

- If the central components of mood are energy and tension, paratelic modes embrace two moods of calm-energy and calm-tiredness. In neither mood is there anxiety, so the target audience is at their most reasonable from the point of view of persuasion. A paratelic mode is best for spending as it means less risk aversion.

- The telic mode embraces tense-energy and tense-tiredness. Tense-energy means a low level of anxiety associated with goal achievement, so advertising should focus on showing a brand as the most rational means for the applications or functions envisaged. For viewers in a tense-tiredness mood, advertising needs to reassure to help dispel anxiety.

- Assuming consumers are in a paratelic mode on holiday, they will associate brands bought during their holiday with that pleasant state. This will induce buying of those brands at other times. Such is the thinking behind destination marketing.

- If a newspaper is read in a telic mode (e.g. on the way to work) and an entertaining magazine in a paratelic mode (at weekends), ads should help relaxation when reading newspapers, while promoting exciting ads in magazines.

- Vagueness and ambiguity should be avoided in ads aimed at people likely to be in a telic mode as they could then appear threatening (look at accompanying programmes or reading material carrying the ad). On the other hand, ambiguity in ads can be intriguing to those in a paratelic mode.

- Advertising can help the consumer to switch from a telic to a paratelic mode and vice versa, since serious ads are suited to a telic mode while light-hearted ads could induce a paratelic mode providing the environment is suitable.

- Cognitive synergies, whether reversal or identity synergies, are commonly exploited in advertising. These synergies are enjoyed by those in a paratelic mode, but they merely irritate those in a telic mode.

Behaviourism

- Attaching an unconditioned stimulus (e.g. a beautiful girl or valued lifestyle) to an ad can make the advertised brand the conditioned stimulus

cont.

to evoke the same feelings towards the brand as were evoked by the unconditioned stimulus.

- A consumer who emits the behaviour of looking at an ad will only continue to do so or look at it again if there is reinforcement, that is if it is worth looking at again because it grabs attention. What reinforcement is being offered by ads for the brand?

- Reinforcement can be maintained by episodic advertising.

- Advertisers should seek the discriminative stimuli in the firm's offering (product, price, promotion and distribution) which signal to the target audience the opportunity for reinforcement. An ad can centre on these discriminative stimuli by enhancing its attractions.

- Ads can exploit partial reinforcement by periodically offering some 'bargain' so that consumers are likely to single out repeats of the ad in the hope of further 'bargains', so becoming subject to the repeated exposure effect.

- Where a brand is successful, the firm may advertise related brands with it to exploit response generalization.

- Advertising should seek ways of offering instant gratification before any focus on long-term benefits.

- The more additional sources of reinforcement a brand provides for consumers, the more dependent they are on it. Advertising needs to retain these customers by reminding them and reassuring them of these additional satisfactions.

- Condition the target customer group by associating the brand with reinforcers; in particular, sometimes give more than was promised or expected since something extra gives surprise and delight and so becomes part of emotional memory. On the other hand, never disappoint by underachieving since negative evaluations arouse negative emotions which become tightly etched into the emotional memory.

- The less satisfied consumer A is with brand B, the less likely he or she is to continue to buy it as more brands become available. Advertising needs to retain such customers by showing the disadvantages of brand switching while describing the upgradings that are taking place.

- The more advantages in terms of reinforcement are offered by brand B compared with its rivals, the more additional buyers it will attract. Advertising can accelerate this process of attracting new buyers by demonstrating both the product's additional advantages and its popularity since brand popularity can be a reinforcer.

- Consumers buy whatever brands yield the most for the least cost. This assumes that they can and do make such calculations. Whether in order to retain existing customers, attract new ones, convert from rivals, or increase sales per customer, advertising can change the perceptions of costs and benefits by an enhanced description of the product or by taking account of costs not normally considered, e.g. lifecycle cost or savings stemming from better service.

- Consumers repeat-buy whatever has proved a reinforcer in the past, other things remaining equal. If advertising needs to *convert* in such a market situation it needs to appeal to curiosity and desire for novelty so as to tempt consumers to break a habit.

- A brand associated with past reinforcement is likely to be bought again. This is why advertising that has been successful in the past may need no more than updating to continue to be successful.

- Repeat-buying only continues as long as the reinforcement. This may have resulted from the images attached to the brand from past advertising. When advertising changes dramatically, and uses different images, repeat-buying may no longer be reinforced.

- Consumers display emotion if actions (e.g. looking for a favourite brand) which have previously been rewarded are suddenly not rewarded (e.g. store runs out of stock). If advertising directs consumers to where the product can be obtained, it is essential that these outlets have adequate stock.

Chapter 5

Persuasive advertising appeals, 3: cognitive approaches

- Hierarchy of effects models
- The elaboration likelihood model
- The persuasive communication approach
- Consistency theory

Persuasive appeals are not confined to creating associations suited to the target audience. This chapter covers cognitive approaches to persuasion. Marketing texts have highlighted learning theory in the form of *hierarchy of effects models* and the *elaboration likelihood model of persuasion*. Another approach discussed in this chapter is the *persuasive communication process*, as proposed by psychologists, which takes account of the receiver of the information, the source of the information and the content and presentation of the message. Finally, the chapter considers the contribution of *consistency theory* to persuasive communication. The approach to persuasive appeals through the persuasive communication process is the one that holds up best to criticism and that we believe has most to offer. While the other approaches have something to teach us about persuasive communications, they have fundamental flaws which need to be considered. We discuss them in detail so that the reader can make up his or her mind as to what can be salvaged and what criticism is worth noting.

COGNITIVE PSYCHOLOGY

Mainstream cognitive psychology sees the mind as computer software with the brain itself corresponding to the computer's hardware. In this view, the psychologist's job is not to programme the brain but to work backwards to identify the mental programmes that cause behaviour. In seeing people as information-processing machines, the cognitive psychologist takes account of the input of information (sensory impressions), the internal processing of this information (thinking) and the output of information (verbalization of thought).[1]

Little ebony number

If you love slipping into a little black number then imagine slipping into a sexy one-off, the special edition Ford Focus Ebony. Imagine being wrapped in its panther black metallic pearls and midnight black leather trim. The thrill of showing off the alloy wheels, chrome exhaust and grille. The fun of flaunting the 6xCD player, parking sensor, air conditioning and remote central locking with boot release. Turn up anywhere in this little black number and everyone will see green. And its yours for £13,495. Call 08457 111 888 or visit www.ford.co.uk/focusebony. Life's better when you take control.

FordFocus Ebony

Designed for living. Engineered to last.

Ford

The official fuel consumption figures in mpg (l/100km) for the vehicle shown are: urban 30.9 (9.4), extra urban 51.4 (5.5) and combined 40.9 (6.9). The official CO₂ emission is 165g/km.   Metal pearlescent only (used in available.

A learning theory approach: hierarchy of effects models

It was Carl Hovland and his colleagues at Yale who brought together learning theory and persuasion, claiming that persuasion requires that the message be first learned and then accepted by the target audience.[2] The target audience are assumed to go through certain mental stages: (a) awareness/attention; (b) comprehending the message; (c) coming to accept the message as true; (d) acting on this learned knowledge when there is an incentive to do so. This approach (with variations) is known in marketing as the *hierarchy of effects model*. The aim of advertising is to move the target audience through these mental stages, to accelerate the movement of attitudes in the direction favoured by the advertiser.

Plato in *The Republic* saw the mind as having three parts: a reasoning part, an emotive part and a desiring part. Psychology, too, until recently, viewed the mind as having three parts: cognition, affect and conation. These psychological categories were not very different from those posited by Plato: 'cognition' embraces Plato's reasoning and other forms of thinking; 'affect' covers Plato's emotive category; and, in being a disposition to action, 'conation' implicitly involves Plato's desiring. Such tripartite divisions of the mental faculties have now lost their appeal in psychology. The reason for this is the recognition that cognition, affect and conation are interdependent aspects of the brain and cannot be properly understood as independent entities. In life as it is lived, the emotive invades the cognitive and the cognitive influences the emotive while both cognition and affect sway the conative. That said, this tripartite system is still echoed in hierarchy of effects models in marketing which focus on the alleged mental stages in attitude formation.

In hierarchy of effects models, attitude towards buying is conceptualized as having the three components of cognition, affect and conation. The earliest of these models was put forward by Colley.[3] It shows the cognition stage as 'awareness and comprehension', the affective stage as 'conviction' and the conative stage as 'action'. If, in mainstream psychology, cognition, affect and conation are regarded as so interdependent and commingled as to defy treatment as independent faculties, it seems erroneous to treat them as such in marketing. These mental stages no more form a development process than stones assembled in

▓ ***Plate 5.1*** *Creating metaphor: Ford Focus*

Source: Courtesy of Ford Motor Company and Ogilvy and Mather. Photography by Tif Hunter

If you love slipping into a little black number then imagine sliding into a sexy one-off, the special edition Ford Focus Ebony. Imagine being wrapped in its panther black metallic paint and midnight black leather trim. The thrill of showing off the alloy wheels, chrome exhaust and grille. The fun of flaunting the 6×CD player, parking sensor, air conditioning and remote central locking with boot release . . . Turn up anywhere in this little black number and everyone will see green. And it's yours for £13,495. Call 08457 111 888 or visit www.ford.co.uk/focusebony. **Life's better when you take control.**

Designed for living. Engineered to last.

ascending order of magnitude form an evolutionary order; both simply show an order that is logical. While hierarchy of effects models are worth discussing as conceptually interesting and educational, they cannot be taken as representing the mental processes through which consumers must go in forming attitudes.

Zajonc speaks of the *primacy of affect* over cognition.[4] By this he means that we experience emotion (affect) before conscious appraisal of the triggering stimuli has occurred, though beliefs about the triggering stimuli can form in parallel, or even as a direct result of, the emotion. According to this theory, an attitude may arise through a simple reflex process: there is no need for any three stages. The work of neurologists like Damasio[5] and LeDoux[6] demonstrates that our initial appraisals are non-conscious and can be at variance with the more reflective (conscious) appraisal of events, actions or attributes that occurs subsequently. Goleman[7] neatly summarizes Damasio's position:

> Damasio's conclusion was that our minds are not designed like a computer, to give us a neat printout of the rational arguments for and against a decision in life based on all the previous times we've faced a similar situation. Instead the mind does something much more elegant: it weighs the emotional bottom line from those previous experiences and delivers the answer to us in a hunch, a gut feeling. We could have no preferences, unless feelings enter into the pros and cons to establish the relative weight of each.

Stimuli reaching the conscious mind are not *neutral* perceptions that people later evaluate but have a value already tacked onto them by the brain's processing mechanisms. The non-conscious appraisals occurring in the first microsecond may prevail. In the absence of further reflection, the initial non-conscious appraisals can be final, meaning we are likely to choose or reject on this basis. In other words, we follow the *likeability heuristic*. With matters that concern us, we form instant attitudes which stay put, other things remaining equal. This rules out the idea that attitudes always start with a cognition stage like awareness and comprehension. The very idea of attitude as a tripartite sequence of cognitive, evaluative and conative steps or some mix of these three is unsound. If the stimulus is emotionally charged, an immediate reaction of like/dislike follows as, within milliseconds of our perceiving anything at all, we unconsciously assess (divorced from sober, rational reflection) whether we like it or not.

Even if there were a developmental process along the lines suggested by hierarchy of effects models, there would still be crippling deficiencies in what is suggested. These models would, at best, only be able to tell us where we are and where to go but not how to get there, as no mechanisms are given for moving from one stage to the next. The standard sequence of learn → feel → do (representing the stages of cognition, affect and conation) assumes a very rational approach to attitude formation and high involvement with the purchase; if a product has high involvement for a purchaser, the purchase has high meaning for her, with high meaning implying the purchase is of *central importance* for the function for which it is being bought and there is *perceived risk* (financial or social) attached to buying it. There is also the assumption that the three processes are separate, distinct mental processing steps. But just because we can separate the steps conceptually as logical stages does not mean these are separate, distinct mental stages.

Are all the stages necessary and is the standard sequence invariable? The answer to both questions is 'no'. Additional hierarchies have been suggested to replace the single process view.[8] If we interpret cognition as 'learning'; affect as 'feeling' and conation as 'doing', we have Ray's additional sequences:

1 standard view: learn → feel → do;
2 dissonance/attribution view: do → feel → learn;
3 low involvement view: learn → do → feel.

The other three possibilities, which Ray does not discuss, could just as easily have been put forward and defended. Again, the obvious questions arise. Do we really learn without first forming an instant affective response? Can we not just go from feel to do? Advertising is not always interested in moving along any hierarchy, for the goal might simply be to retain current customers. Also, if different members of the target segment are at different stages in the hierarchy or at different stages of different hierarchies, different campaigns may be necessary.

One prominent advertising agency that has promoted the hierarchy view classifies learn → feel → do and the feel → learn → do as operating in conditions of high involvement, with the first sequence being attributed to the consumer as 'thinker' and the second to the consumer as 'feeler'. Do → learn → feel and the do → feel → learn are seen as operating in conditions of low involvement, with the first sequence being attributed to the consumer as 'doer' and the second to the consumer as 'reactor'. The claims made are based not on any hard evidence but on the ground that they just sound right, given a belief in a hierarchy of mental stages. The trouble with this sort of speculation is that it forms a framework for so much else; one that remains unquestioned through *ad hoc* rescue hypotheses when things do not go according to 'theory'.

In sum, hierarchy of effects models are weak theoretically: (a) the logical steps assumed need not be the actual mental steps that occur; (b) all the steps need not occur for a message to be persuasive; (c) different sequences of the steps are equally plausible; (d) there is an unjustified assumption of uniformity in the choice process; (e) even if the hierarchy of effects model had validity, it may tell us where we are now but *not* how to get to where we want to go since the time-stages themselves are not forcing variables: what is missing are the motivational mechanisms. However, we should not throw out the baby with the bathwater.

125

What made the hierarchy of effects appealing in the first place was the recognition that there is usually some learning to do; that attaching feelings to a brand aids favourable evaluation while there is often a need to trigger action. Hence advertisers need to ask themselves whether there is an educational job to be done, whether they can develop an ad that promotes favourable feelings towards a brand and whether there are appropriate sales promotions for triggering buying.

Elaboration likelihood model of persuasion

The elaboration likelihood model of persuasion is associated with Petty and Cacioppo.[9] This cognitive model is concerned not with the development of attitudes where none exist, as is the case with hierarchy of effects models, but with *changing* the direction of attitudes through persuasion, a more difficult task. The authors posit two routes to attitude change:

- the *peripheral route* where persuasion is a form of short-term acceptance based on affective cues, or what is most socially acceptable;
- the *central route* where persuasion is long lasting. Attitude change here comes about through thoughtful reflection on information received. This central route leads not just to outward compliance (mere behaviour change) but to a change in beliefs (private acceptance). The choice of the central route assumes: (a) the target audience have the motivation to process the information because of high personal relevance; (b) the target audience have the ability to process the information.

Central route persuasion comes about through careful consideration of the merits of the evidence while persuasion via the peripheral route emanates from affective cues or social conformity. Much of what we say in Chapter 3 about associating the brand with attractive images and values would presumably come under the peripheral route. *What would be argued in this model is that, to ensure long-term belief in a product, ads must have high personal relevance for the target audience but be simple enough to be understood, their appeals being grounded in solid facts and arguments for buying.*

This distinction between the central and peripheral routes mirrors the distinction between *informational* conformity (where we are convinced by the information presented) and *social* conformity (where we are persuaded by social pressures). Many in academia welcomed the elaboration likelihood model of persuasion as a rebuff to the claims of postmodernists that we are persuaded not by rational argument but by the quality of rhetoric, shorn of substance. However, there are criticisms of this model.

What determines which route is taken? According to the authors, it is the ability and the motivation to reflect on the message. This is not helpful as it is simply a truism. It is like saying that if we want and can, we will choose the central route but not otherwise. The model views validity as an *objective* property of information instead of as a function of the *perceptions* of the recipient. Validity is not an objective property of information itself, but something subjective, and, as such, a function of the perceptions of the recipient. If regarding information as valid is a matter of consumer perception (what the consumer perceives as valid), then it is not independent of social norms, conventions and affective considerations, as such perceptions are influenced by social attachments.

The Petty/Cacioppo model separates the rational from the emotional as if being deeply convinced were purely a rational matter rather than being related to values and emotions. This separation echoes the Enlightenment in eighteenth-century Europe which sought to establish the autonomy of reason by divorcing it from custom and tradition.[10] Led by Immanuel Kant (1724–1804), the Enlightenment took the motto 'Dare to know', and a dominant strand of its beliefs concerned the possibility that pure reason could control human life.

Does the evangelist Billy Graham, for example, convince via the central route? He certainly can and does convince, though Roland Barthes argues that he 'shrinks from logic', his message being simply an outburst of discontinuous affirmations with no content that is not tautological: all his material belongs to the music-hall hypnotist.[11] Both the historian Laurence Moore in his *Selling God*[12] and the psychiatrist Marc Galanter in his *Cults*[13] give all the evidence that is needed to show that people can internalize a message (that is, be convinced) based solely on the fact that it is socially and emotionally satisfying. People have an extraordinary faith in things, faith that is based on trust without any real understanding. A good deal of the exhortation found in books on management and marketing depends on the 'departure lounge school' of writing in a cheer-leader style, packed with anecdote and hyperbole but no real evidence. It is pure rhetoric. People may believe the absurd when in an emotional state. Thus German newsreels in September 1939 claimed (and were believed) that the Polish forces were actually trying to invade them. Support for the Petty/Cacioppo model might, however, be found in a study of religious *conversions*. Mary Jo Neitz's analysis claims people undergoing religious conversion do engage in a rational process.[14] In other words, conversion is not the unexpected metamorphosis associated with Paul on the road to Damascus. But what is meant by rational? What she terms 'rational' is simply engaging in a process of trying to make sense of things. But this is insufficient for rationality since the process could be vacuous in the absence of data embracing the right concepts and perspective. Hers is a phenomenological view. But Polanyi and Prosch are probably correct in their view that if we are to be converted to a new position, a new perspective, a new theory or idea, it must offer the possibility of attaining richer meanings than the views it displaces.[15] Polanyi and Prosch demonstrate that hard experimental evidence however well established, does not convince in science if explanations seem to lack credibility. Ramachandran, a neuroscientist, claims that an absolute conviction regarding 'Truth' derives from the limbic structures concerned with the emotions and not from the thinking and rational parts of the brain whose function it is to discern truth from falsehood.[16]

In a test of the elaboration likelihood model, undertaken by Petty, Cacioppo and Goldman, source expertise was used, defined as what the experimenter believed would be perceived as a source of high expertise as a peripheral cue.[17] As predicted, the results showed that in the low-relevance conditions where an issue was not important to the subjects, source expertise influenced their attitudes and argument quality did not. On the other hand, in high-relevance conditions, source expertise had no impact on attitude whereas the quality of the argument did.

The question is how good was this study that has not been corroborated by others? Subjects are likely to accept any source of designated expertise when they are indifferent to an issue (since thinking takes time and effort). However, it does not follow that, just because apparent expertise is ignored when an issue is highly relevant to the subjects, they ignore social factors and focused hard thinking on hard arguments. In the first place, it was the experimenter who designated the source as one of expertise. But for a source to be credible, it must be *perceived* as both expert and trustworthy. There is no evidence that this was established. The acceptance of the expert source might have reflected nothing more than its being the only opinion available, subjects having no reason to generate their own. On the other hand, the rejection of the expert source in the issue-relevant situation might simply mean that it was not, on reflection, perceived as trustworthy and so not perceived as credible. It certainly does not mean that social and affective contextual factors were irrelevant. Even if the experiment had been well conducted and corroborated the hypothesis, the model would still be highly suspect as its explanatory content is so deficient. *The Petty/Cacioppo model confuses the way real knowledge is acquired with the means by which we are persuaded; persuasion can be convincing and long lasting without our having to acquire real depth in knowledge.*

Irrational and firmly held convictions can simply result from social group membership. We may join a political party for all sorts of reasons but, after membership, conviction quickly follows. In groups where uncertainty prevails (e.g. the acting profession and professional sports), members are often convinced believers in superstitions.[18] Consider the number of prominent actors enlisted in the ranks of Scientology. The emphasis is on uncertainty. The cultural anthropologist Bronislaw Malinowski (1884–1942) claimed that 'primitives' never resorted to magic if they possessed the means to achieve their goals directly. They never resort to magic to look after their herds: 'people do not exchange with the Gods when a more efficient alternative is known and available'.

We cannot ignore the power of dogmatic assertion in convincing people. TV evangelists of all religious persuasions use it all the time and manage to convince. The whole purpose of assertive rhetoric is to endow what are essentially value judgements with the status of fact. There is no reason, contrary to the Petty/ Cacioppo model, why such rhetoric should not be convincing, given that people are often happy to let others do their thinking for them. This happens in politics all the time, with many people prepared to believe the rationally indefensible if uttered by their 'leaders'.

More surprising is the focus in the model on the individual. As Herbert Simon says, some people regard individuals as Leibnizian monads (little hard spheres of some sort), each with a consistent utility function that is independent of the utility functions of others, interacting with others through knowledge of market prices.[19] Petty and Cacioppo seem to view individuals in this way. Simon goes on to say that most of our beliefs gain their credibility not from direct experience and experiment but as a result of their acceptance by credible and legitimate sources within society. What has been described as the *law of social impact* claims that the individual is more likely to be persuaded by:

- several people rather than just one;
- nearby people rather than faraway people;
- concentrated (but not coercive) pressure rather than non-intense pressure.

Advertising frequently stresses how many within the consumer's social milieu buy a brand, at the same time using concentrated and intense pressure.

Acceptance of a source of information as credible and convincing can rest on nothing more than that it appeals emotionally. As Stuart Sutherland says, to the dog-loving target audience, the advertiser says, 'Dogs are just like people'. The appeal of this truth, well recognized by dog lovers, opens the way for the dog owner to accept the other claims in the ad.[20] Statements can be true but not credible or credible but not true.

In the promotion of new products, visibility must be gained and credibility quickly established. How claims are presented is always a factor in both visibility and credibility. It is the same in interviews. Although psychologists talk of personality tests revealing 'real' character traits, we assess each other's personality largely on the basis of appearances, treating it as mainly physical and assessed by gut (emotional) reaction. It is not so much what people say but how they say it that is important. The few valid personality tests that are available are concerned with what are essentially emotional characteristics. While all sorts of characteristics have been included in personality inventories, according to one study only four basic dimensions have emerged from over fifty years of research.[21] These are: (a) extroversion (being sociable, open, outward-looking) versus introversion

129

(being inward-looking, aloof, inhibited); (b) neuroticism (the tendency to worry and be anxious); (c) psychoticism (tough-mindedness, sensation-seeking, cruelty); (d) obsessionality (including neatness, control, pedantry, rigidity). These are all emotional factors.

The debate over central versus peripheral routes to persuasion is not just academic. At least one national campaign against drug taking by children focuses on the central route, avoiding 'purely emotional and social appeals'. It is doubtful if any campaign to prevent young people taking drugs can be effective without making the immediate consequences highly emotional. This is recognized in the history of anti-drug advertising. However, just the one style of campaign would find it difficult to be effective both in preventing people from taking drugs in the first place and in getting them off drugs. This is because it is difficult to persuade people not to take drugs without painting a vivid unflattering picture of the drug taker. What has helped to make the anti-smoking campaign a reasonable success in the United States has been the claim that passive smoking is injurious to others. We may not respond to appeals about our own health being adversely affected, but the emotional impact of strong social norms against being seen to be injuring others has made smoking in public taboo.

While we reject the notion that affective and social influences cannot convince someone sufficiently to bring about lasting attitude change, the elaboration likelihood model does remind us that persuasion relies not necessarily on information and logic alone but also on social and affective factors. One weakness of the rational choice model in economics is that it ignores the social aspect of decision making, how social factors influence opinions and choices.

The persuasive communication approach

We think of communication as the exchange of new information but we communicate all the time in exchanges that do not contain, and are not expected to contain, new information. The traditional model of the communication process ignores this fact as it sees the communicator encoding and the receiver of the communication decoding the message. As Sperber and Wilson emphasize, this code model of communication is simplistic: human communication cannot be fully examined or explained in terms of such a model.[22] This is because communication achieves some 'unparaphrasable' effects: more is communicated than is actually encoded and receivers (the target audience) extract more (or less) from an ad than is encoded.

The persuasive communication approach has a long history and, from our point of view, has much to offer. The approach sees persuasion as dependent on:

- the individual receiver of the communication;
- the communication/information source;
- the content/presentation of the message.

This approach can be viewed as focusing on the 'acceptance' stage in the hierarchy model, though with no commitment to any hierarchy of effects.

The three headings listed above allow us to pull together many more findings and ideas about persuasion than are normally discussed in these contexts.

The individual receiver of the communication

There is intended content in any communication but individual receivers may get a little more or a little less than intended: a little more because any interpretation of a communication, whether visual or verbal or both, requires some conjecture to fill in the gaps; a little less in that the meaning that the source intended will not be completely taken in by the individual receiver. Some of the things to consider are now studied.

GAINING ATTENTION

As attention must necessarily be selective, gaining it presents a challenge. Attention has to be selective not only because there is just too much around us to take in but also because we see and look out for what we have been taught to see and look out for and what concerns us. When consumers learn a set of new concepts in respect to a product, they see things they would not do otherwise. A trained car mechanic will see and look out for things in a used car that others will not see. The biologist sees under the microscope what eludes the layperson or the biologist of a hundred years ago. Getting attention is a necessary condition for persuasion and, concomitantly, a sufficient condition for failure. However, too many ads are focused solely on getting attention, forgetting that they must also have persuasive content.

REPETITION OF THE MESSAGE

Repetition of a message is important when it has to compete for attention. But what also needs to be acknowledged is that high repetition of a message and acceptance of the message are related. The sequence is: high repetition of a message → (leads to) growth of audience familiarity with the message → (leads to) acceptance of the message as true because it is then absorbed and familiar.

Old beliefs are not erased completely but buried to be resurrected in more favourable circumstances. Thompson's *rubbish theory* has relevance here.[23] In this theory, people who do not carry forward some relevant belief to the next stage of some plan of action are regarded as 'throwing away' the belief. But it may stay 'hidden' in the mind either in a distorted form or as part of a system of *default* beliefs. The ideas or beliefs that are thrown away can sneak back into one's thoughts to reverse some action plan. The consumer whose opinion of a service becomes more positive can find her original opinions are resurrected when things go wrong. Many 'findings' linger on in social science after being discredited and

131

thrown away. They continue to come back to haunt the scientific community, to become what Thompson calls 'excluded monsters'. Thus, although Max Weber's thesis on the relationship between Protestantism and early capitalism has been demolished, many sociologists and historians still treat it as gospel.

DISTRACTION

Distraction (e.g. music in the background of an ad) of the audience interferes with the development of counter-arguments — just as it is difficult to count when people are talking nearby. Humour, often used in an advertisement to get attention, acts as a distraction, disarming possible criticism. When the British government was preparing to privatize electricity, it faced public hostility and fears from potential investors about hidden costs, including the cost of decommissioning nuclear reactors. So a series of ads were created featuring the domestic life of Frank N. Stein, an electricity-powered monster, to distract and defuse the situation and disarm criticism. It was judged effective.

COGNITIVE AND EMOTIONAL BACKGROUND

Social attachments (culture, reference groups, social class, emotionally grounded experiences) and individual perspectives (beliefs and values) are always relevant in developing persuasive communications. However, existing preferences and mood cannot be ignored. Messages that (a) conflict with strongly held social attachments; (b) deviate too much from existing preferences; (c) are communicated when the audience is in a bad mood; are unlikely to be accepted. Taking these into account should be part of any screening pretest for proposed ads.

ASSIMILATION AND CONTRAST EFFECTS

Hovland *et al.* showed that when a target audience have views that are similar to those expressed in the message, they minimize what little difference there is; that is, they interpret the communicator's view as closer to their own than is actually the case.[24] This is the *assimilation effect*. On the other hand, when the communicator's expressed views are obviously in conflict with those of the target audience, they exaggerate the discrepancy; that is, they interpret the communicator's views as being much more opposed to their own than is actually the case. This is the *contrast effect*, well demonstrated among Christian denominations that tend to exaggerate differences to retain or expand market share.

You cannot *make* people believe, even if church and state have often thought otherwise. However, people may want to believe and may even feel they believe if it is a matter of life and death. As Susan Haack says: 'while, to be sure, one cannot believe at will, wishful and fearful thinking are a problem precisely because the will *can* get in the way of our judgment of evidence'.[25] We always want to believe that to which we are emotionally committed. Beliefs are adopted because they are perceived as true. In any case, much can be done to facilitate adoption of a set of beliefs. The function of a proselytizing organization such as the Mormons is to convince its own members by having them convince others. But acceptance is tied to the target audience's preconceptions embodied in their perspective. As Proctor shows, even scientists' assessments of environmental hazards are influenced by their preconceptions of whether nature is benign or already full of potential hazards when undisturbed by human intervention.[26]

ANCHOR POINTS

Consumers have anchor points, standards for comparison on which they rely to form an opinion of the brand they have bought, what competing products are available and what is reasonable in respect to price. These anchors affect consumer expectations and consequently customer satisfaction. Anchor points involve latitudes of rejection, acceptance and lack of commitment. The latitude of *rejection* is that domain within which options (brands) are rejected. Thus the consumer may reject the lowest-priced brand when choosing in the supermarket. The latitude of *acceptance* is that domain which consists of the alternatives (options) from which the consumer would choose. Thus the consumer's latitude of acceptance may include only well-known brands so as to minimize risk. The latitude of lack of commitment is that domain which falls between the latitudes of acceptance and rejection, the domain where there is still a willingness to consider the pros and cons of buying a particular brand. These three latitudes are rarely, if ever, fixed in stone as people change with circumstances.

It is common to demonstrate anchor points by dividing a class into two separate sections. One section of the class is asked whether the average textbook costs, say, around 100 (in local currency) and the other section of the class is asked whether the average textbook costs around 10. Both prices will be rejected as extreme but, when the two sections are asked what they think is the average price, the first will estimate nearer 100 than 10 and the second will estimate nearer 10 than 100. This shows how anchor points influence expectations.

Negotiators try to establish anchor points by making higher demands than they can reasonably expect. In this way they hope to change anchor point expectations. The original price of any sale item can be viewed as constituting the anchor point, suggesting to the buyer the extent of the bargain. Anchor points exploit the *contrast effect* in that there is a contrast between, say, the original (anchor) price and the sale price. Estate agents are apt to exploit anchor points by showing buyers a poor value-for-money house to establish an anchor point and make them more appreciative of the other houses they are shown.

EGO INVOLVEMENT

Ego involvement is a factor in persuasion. There are several meanings that attach to the word 'ego'. It originated from the Latin 'I' or self and was initially conceptualized as simply the central core of personality around which all psychic activities revolve. There is also the use Freud made of the term which will be discussed in the next chapter. The meaning of ego as popularly conceived is the core self with which the individual is crucially concerned, and which serves as a psychological touchstone for sensing one's interests. This is the meaning of ego when used in terms like egoistic, egocentric and egotistical. When we speak of ego involvement we draw on this meaning as ego involvement concerns the task, goal or whatever is important to one's ego. Ego involvement has the potential to be emotionally arousing. In the Cuban missile crisis, it appears that what drove Khrushchev, as much as anything else, was fear of humiliation.[27] Kennedy's strategy took account of the need to save face by promising to withdraw the US missiles from Turkey, which was no loss to the United States. In recognition of the importance of boosting the ego, much advertising that formerly emphasized the avoidance of embarrassment has adopted the more positive (and generally more applicable) approach of implicitly claiming the product helps consumers feel better or think better of themselves. Yet embarrassment, too, can be very ego deflating and for many people, embarrassing situations are to be avoided at all costs.

The wish to avoid embarrassment helps to enforce the *principle of reciprocity*, this constituting a social norm whose violation results in embarrassment. The principle of reciprocity operates in book clubs which offer a number of books at some nominal cost to new members, 'at no obligation to buy any future books'. The anticipation of embarrassment influences people to go on buying. It operates in the giving of samples and in giving 'little' gifts to customers or clients at Christmas time. In fact all small courtesies like saying 'Good morning', providing coffee and so on create corresponding minor obligations. It is the compelling nature of the principle of reciprocity that makes politicians' acceptance of gifts from lobbyists tantamount to bribery. There is no way the reciprocity obligation can be ignored.

INDUCING SELF-PERSUASION

Self-persuasion is generally accomplished by advertising evoking the experience (feelings) of using a product; shaping the consumers' experience of the product; telling consumers what it would be like (really like) to have the emotional experience of possessing/using the product. This is the essence of *transformational advertising* which aims at associating buying, possessing, using or consuming a brand with values and experiences that are highly desirable. The problem, as we have seen in Chapter 3, lies in making the association compelling since not all juxtapositions of images in an advertisement come to be associated in the buyer's mind. Self-persuasion is easy if it simply amounts to being given an excuse to justify what would otherwise be unconscionable. This relates to Smart's comment on terrorism:[28]

Thus I suspect that terrorists who contend that their terrorism is merely an unfortunately necessary means to a good ideological end may well be deluding themselves, and that in many cases what they particularly enjoy is the mayhem of terrorism itself, and that any ideology that seemed to provide an excuse for it would thereby gain in attractiveness.

INTERPRETATION PROBLEMS

The interpretation of a message or ad is tied to culture, social experience and education. There is an open texture in ads in that there is no final, fixed interpretation. Historians reinterpret the 'facts' of a given historical period in accordance with their own period's prevailing social ideologies and political obsessions. Viewers and listeners do the same with ads. Aberrant decoding is common in advertising since the same ad may have one meaning in one context for one set of people, and an entirely different meaning in another context. There is also aberrant encoding when the advertiser fails to recognize that different cultures or subcultures are likely to interpret a message differently. A film featuring police and gangsters was shown in a hostel for the homeless in New York: the street people cheered when the police were losing, reversing the ideology of the film.

What is encoded is not necessarily what is decoded (if for our purposes we accept the coding metaphor). Much advertising is atmospheric or impressionistic so as to avoid such problems. Advertising is sometimes deliberately designed for multiple (favourable) interpretations, so consumers can read into it the most desirable interpretation. This is facilitated when the interpretation depends not on words but pictures, music and other forms of non-verbal communication.

Too much logic often enters into comments by critics on ads which simply ask their audience to share a fantasy, and not to make literal interpretations. The meaning of an ad as extracted by an expert is often far removed from how it will be interpreted in the context in which it is normally viewed, read or heard. 'Experts' often assume a literalness of meaning, ignoring stylistic and rhetorical devices and the related complexities of satire, spoof, parody and self-parody. For example, Schwarzenegger movies have been read as emblematic of anti-feminist reaction and appealing to dumb, nihilistic youth, but their self-parody elements make this kind of precise classification difficult. Similarly, some critics read the 1960s series *Get Smart* as propaganda for US imperialism, whereas it is full of parody, allowing the viewers to appropriate meanings from multiple, indeterminate and floating meanings. The end result is co-production between audience and producer. Satire and irony in particular create problems for those who seek to bring analytic rigour to media analysis. Thus people can (and some critics did) easily miss the satiric in, for example, Noel Coward's song 'Please Don't Be Beastly to the Germans'. As Richards says, in literature, in contrast to science, the multiplicity of meaning, allusion and verbal play is meant to be enjoyed;

135

and, in nearly all poetry, the sound and feel of words impact first, and the senses in which the words are later more explicitly taken are subtly influenced by this fact.[29]

Propaganda can on occasion be viewed as an invitation to share a fantasy, with allegations too lurid in themselves to be taken seriously, like the Serb claim that Christian boys were being kidnapped by Muslims to serve as 'janissaries' (soldier-slaves), or the journalistic claims in the First World War that the Germans melted down human bodies for fat. A common attraction of propaganda is emotional indulgence: at the rational level we know that claims are exaggerated or fabricated, but we enjoy imagining that they are true as they feed our hatreds.

NEED FOR RELEVANT PERSPECTIVE

As stated in Chapter 1, good arguments are only good if the target audience already holds the relevant perspective. Doing a rain dance to end a drought only makes sense to those who assume that the weather is the gift of the gods.[30] Learning new concepts often goes hand-in-hand with a change in perspective. Concepts mediate between the mind and the world: they are tied to the world by representing it and are linked to the mind by being constituents of it.

In a sense, all persuasion is tied to altering perspectives, however minimal, as all persuasion seeks to alter the target audience's definition of a problem or situation in such a way that they see the proposed action as in their best interests. Concepts are important since learning new concepts results in seeing new classes of objects or ideas that can change perspectives. It takes time to learn to recognize important differences and words have the major role here.

Social science concepts do duty as *sensitizing concepts*. We may miss a phenomenon if we do not have a word for it (e.g. demand curve). The adoption of new words or concepts trains us to see things in a different way. Hence the demand that we become sensitive to the words we use, and, for example, abandon 'idiot' for 'intellectually challenged'. This is good even though when the reality remains unchanged, the old connotations return with time. Words may be chosen to inhibit seeing something important; for example, the words 'collateral damage' hide the human cost of a bombing campaign. Like scientific models, language systems are a way of seeing and also of not seeing. In marketing we speak of 'channel intermediaries', a term which conjures up an image of retailers acting purely in a liaison role although they are capable of taking on a far wider marketing role in stimulating demand.

As the consumer adds concepts to her repertoire, perceptions are apt to change, just as being introduced to the concepts applicable to the Internet alters perception of the technology. Advertising, by introducing some (however simple) new concept to the field, can restructure perceptions. Thus in describing a pair of trousers as having a 'relaxed fit', perceptions are structured towards feelings of comfort, diverting attention away from the fact that such trousers are apt to make the wearer look fat. The frequent need to restructure perceptions makes it difficult to use logic alone, and ignore emotion.

Persuasive appeals are made within some frame, perspective, paradigm, model or conceptual lens, so having the right perspective and the 'right' perceptions follows. Those putting forward the case for genetically modified crops talk about there being a 'compelling moral imperative' to develop them to help combat world hunger and poverty. This is more likely to resonate emotionally with the public than talk about such crops being cheaper. One element in changing perspectives involves promoting the acceptance and usage of our own label for our campaign, so that supporting the right to abortion is called pro-choice by everyone, or, alternatively, not supporting it is called pro-life by everyone. Some words like 'vulgar' and 'common' drop out of usage because they come to be socially inappropriate, e.g. because they carry the elitist tone of an earlier age.

No target audiences are merely passive when receiving a message but interpret it against some background of 'reality out there', striving to maintain their own view of that reality. Thus the top people in Russia are the same individuals as under communism and it is doubtful that their perspectives have completely changed even if those in international diplomacy act (wrongly) as if they had. Consumers, like people generally, must be on the right wavelength to accept a message. If sellers have exactly the same perspective as their audience, then they should use 'rational' arguments, given that, if we agree premises, logic has a strong role to play. But if sellers have to change fundamentally the way people look at an issue, so as to induce the right perspective in the first place, then *indirect* means of persuasion via rhetoric are needed as a more direct approach will be resisted.

In order to change perspectives, it is better not to attempt to debate the logic of a position but simply to suggest a more appealing perspective. Thus consumers are asked to look at an issue in a different way, through a different frame. For instance, it was claimed that changes in Medicare in the United States were introduced not to save money but to guarantee the solvency of Medicare in the long term. *With imagination, an alternative narrative or 'spin' can always be put on an issue.* The concept of 'spin' is that of fixing an interpretation onto a fluid situation in the hope that opinion will converge on it, with bandwagon effects. Perhaps the ultimate spin was devised by Churchill at Dunkirk, successfully turning appalling defeat into a seeming triumph. The problem of Ronald Reagan's political ignorance, when he first ran for Governor of California, was dealt with by positioning him as a 'citizen politician' whose blunders were excusable. Almost any position can be retrieved by this kind of ingenuity.

RHETORIC AND CHANGING PERSPECTIVES

What the above suggests is that changing perspectives is where rhetoric comes into its own. Often rhetoric creates realities rather than the other way round; it

137

is, as Walter Lippmann once observed, not the event but the received image of the event that counts.

There has been a strong revival of the study of rhetoric largely due to the work of Chaim Perelman[31] and Brian Vickers[32] in recognizing its importance in changing perspectives. Plato made a sharp distinction between philosophical thinking and what he regarded as its bogus counterpart, rhetoric. While the sophist Gorgias claimed rhetoric or persuasive speech making to be an academic discipline, Plato viewed rhetoric as something cultivated by the 'con artist', commonly working through flattery. It was not a form of knowledge as it involved no evaluation of received opinions, put no statement to the test, and did not attempt to separate the true from the false. Success in persuasion was its only goal and raison d'être.[33] But we now realize that persuasion is needed in every field of endeavour. For Gadamer, all science which aims to have practical usefulness needs rhetoric to support it.[34]

The current interest in rhetoric results from the recognition that people have widely differing views and perspectives, and are not merely detached information processors. Rhetorical use of tropes (figures of speech, analogies and metaphors) are inevitable whenever we consider persuading an audience to take a different point of view. There is also the rhetorical use of pseudo-science like the use of the Laffer curve in the Reagan years. But a perspective (or Kuhn's concept of a *paradigm* when applied to science) is not easy to change. Advertisers, like politicians, prefer to intensify a perspective rather than attempt to change one.

Political advertising in the United States, more than in any other country, understands that rhetoric is of key importance in changing perspectives and perceptions. Think of terms that in the right context are highly emotive, like 'sweat equity' and 'urban renewal'. But, more typically, advocates express 'cause' in terms of the audience's existing ideology. The 'trickle-down effect' of Reaganite economics was satirized in a Democratic commercial with the pictorial metaphor of champagne spilling down from one glass onto another, with finally a few drops falling onto a tin can, and the words: 'You must wonder how much has been trickling down to you lately'. The entirety of Martin Luther King's 'I have a dream' speech is framed in terms of classic American values. For example, the plea that men may be judged not by the colour of their skin but by the content of their character is an appeal to meritocracy, a strong societal value in America.

A perspective acts as a set of values and beliefs to which we are emotionally attached, and with which the trade-offs made in reaching a decision fall in line. In the social sciences, academics are pressured into adopting one particular perspective, usually that of their supervisor. As all perspectives have their successes and failures, they cannot give rise to crucial experiments by which they could be falsified. All this is not to suggest that decisions are predictable from knowledge of perspectives alone (otherwise they would not be decisions) but knowledge of perspectives certainly helps.

138

The use of rhetoric has grown in the last twenty years because old certainties have been undermined. With everything becoming questionable, indirect means of persuasion are needed, so the metaphor rather than logic becomes more relevant. John Locke (1632–1704), the empiricist philosopher, condemned all rhetoric, yet his basic model used metaphor, viewing the mind as an empty cabinet, blank sheet of paper, wax tablet. Thomas Hobbes (1588–1679), another philosopher, regarded it as an abuse of speech to use words metaphorically, yet his famous book was called *The Leviathan*, using the powerful aquatic animal from Scripture as a metaphor for the state. Persuasion would be lost without metaphors. This explains why metaphor is particularly common in the marketing of causes or ideas. Metaphorical language can be exploited in emotional appeals. Thus, in education, advocates of the new mathematics attack what they called 'drill and kill' memorizing; or the cry of American feminists, 'Get your rosaries off our ovaries'. Unlike reasoning by analogy which uses a comparison from a related domain, the metaphor comes from an entirely different domain.

In Colombia, an election poster for one of the opposition parties depicted, in striking black and yellow, a lavatory shown to be blocked, below which was written 'the country' and next to it was a plunger captioned 'your vote'. This *symbolic metaphor* had its effect on voter perspectives.[35] An advertisement for Senator Jesse Helms featured a pair of white hands tearing up a rejection slip. The Senator himself never appeared in the ad. It is hard to imagine a more appropriate comment to help change perspectives on the Falklands/Malvinas war than the Argentine writer Jorge Luis Borges's metaphor that it amounted to 'two bald men fighting over a comb'. But although this may be the realistic perspective, it ignores what the conflict symbolized for the two sides. In one union election campaign, the metaphor was three pigs eating dollar bills with the comment: 'They're feasting on your dues'. This proved to be highly persuasive.

In the marketing of people and causes, the use of symbols is paramount. With Nixon there were the ringing red telephone, the lie detector and the weather vane. An anti-Spiro Agnew ad simply featured the slogan 'Agnew for vice-president' and loud laughter. The metaphor involves the hearer in that he or she is expected to amplify and adjust the metaphor.[36]

Metaphors, in affecting what we see and how we interpret it, influence not only thinking but emotional reactions. As Klein says, metaphor structures our thinking and conditions our sympathies and emotional reactions.[37] In structuring our thinking, the metaphor can mislead. A possible example is our earlier discussion about the mind 'encoding' and 'decoding' since such metaphors may in no way capture the processes at work. Every new technology saturates the language with a new wave of metaphors – 'hard wired', 'software of the mind' and so on. The English language is full of metaphors drawn from the technologies of the twentieth century (e.g. 'switched on') and from major historical events like the phrase 'over the top', a reference to the trench warfare of the First World

War. In fact it has been persuasively argued that conscious thought itself is mainly figurative in being normally metaphoric, metonymic and ironic.[38] Master orators are adept at using metaphor. From John Bright's pacifist eloquence in 1854 ('The angel of death has wandered the land, and few have not heard the beating of his wings') to Hitler's exhortation to German youth ('Be swift as greyhounds, hard as Krupp steel'), the power of persuasion has been seen to lie partly in the power of metaphor.

Great rhetoric is primarily metaphorical: for example, the Pericles funeral oration, Lincoln at Gettysburg – the latter address was in fact scarcely audible to its audience and made more impact in the two world wars. Roosevelt loved personification like 'a day that will live in infamy' or 'rendezvous with destiny' and so on. In fact the defining moments in a nation's life are typically expressed in metaphors, like Reagan's eulogy on the Challenger disaster when he spoke of touching the face of God. Although the use of metaphors is less striking in consumer advertising, every magazine is full of advertising exploiting the metaphor. Not surprisingly, as Stephen Brown points out (while lending support to those who claim that tropes are central to the way we understand the world), marketing is replete with metaphors like the product life cycle, marketing myopia, channels of distribution and so on.[39] Metaphors need not be verbal and some of the most effective are visual. Thus EMC ('the storage architects') draw attention to their software storage systems with the image of two contrasting stomachs, one a protruding 'beer belly' and the other sleek and ready for action. One right-wing pressure group in the United States invited people to return one of two choices in the mail shot – a 'white flag of surrender' or the 'stars and stripes'.

Rhetorical devices are employed to get the reader or listener to contemplate something through a certain interpretative schema or conceptual lens so that judgements cohere with the schema and make sense according to its standards. Thus copywriters in advertising agencies often refer to the managerial cadre as 'suits' to emphasize their grey conformity and substitutability, just as generals once dismissed politicians and civil servants as 'frocks' (frock-coats). Different metaphors lie behind different social science approaches: man as a developed ape; man as a puppet on a string (social forces); man as a supercomputer and so on. In early stages, metaphors are commonly used to direct inquiry ('the mind is a computer') in, as yet, unexplored directions.

Everyday discourse is festooned with metaphors: we are back seat drivers, couch potatoes, night owls, early birds, white socks. The English language is full of metaphors of capitalism: we 'invest' in education, exploit our assets, seek a return, etc. And casual discourse in academia betrays attitudes in referring to non-quantitative subjects as 'soft' in contrast with 'hard' subjects that are usually quantitative. The metaphorical structures often contain implicit ideologies; for example, when we speak of the march of progress or being backward looking, we are articulating a view of progress, not always shared by, say, environmentalists. Rhetoric is important to persuasion in wartime because governments are trying to get people to kill, so particularly powerful metaphors are needed if killing is not to be deeply repugnant to those being called upon to do it. Hitler likened his race enemies to a bacillus and his race discourse is saturated with metaphors of purity and pollution. A metaphor:[40]

- compares different things which do not appear related, so presenting an anomaly that whets curiosity;
- provides the possibility of resolving the anomaly;
- typically uses colourful language as well as raising ambiguity, enticing us to explore what is felt only dimly. Charles Dickens constantly used anthropomorphism, a category of metaphor, to satirize or render sinister some position. Thus in *Hard Times* the term for an industrial worker ('hands') takes on a new meaning as Dickens offers a surreal vision of thousands of mobile, disembodied hands;
- in bringing together different terms, creates broader conceptual wholes;
- is basic to thinking within any discipline since metaphors can translate into models as a way to view the discipline. Any inquiry in science needs a strong metaphor to drive it (e.g. black holes). Even when, as in quantum mechanics, there can be no physical representations, scientists still attempt to employ imagistic public language, since few laypeople can grapple with the professional language of mathematics. (It was this attempt to provide physical representations of phenomena which can only be talked about in mathematical terms that led to Susan Stebbing's brilliant attack on the whole attempt to explain quantum physics in physical terms.[41])

Rhetorical arguments are designed to induce a certain perspective from which the persuader's arguments or claims will be viewed favourably. Rhetoric is thus inseparable from persuasion. When one senior scholar says that young university academics are encouraged by the system to produce yards of garbage rather than inches of value,[42] many academics are moved to cheer. Rhetorical phrases enshrine cultural myths and articulate a nation's sense of self-hood. For example, such phrases as 'too clever by half' or 'it's not what you know but who you know' tell us something about how English people believe their society really works.

Metaphors impart a good deal of emotional symbolism. When Iranian President Khomeini called the United States the great Satan, it was to get his own people to view the US as a great tempter of the righteous from the paths of virtue. We condemn others for 'wanting to turn the clock back'. This is a common rhetorical tactic which implies the inevitability of progress through time, so tomorrow must be better than today. This is by no means always true but it is a strongly entrenched cultural myth which can be exploited in argument. The word 'time' is itself interesting. We speak of time being wasted, invested or spent and it seems almost impossible to think about time without the use of metaphor.

Much rhetoric works by tapping into cultural myths. Thus when US journalists described an early paramour of Bill Clinton as 'a sleazy woman with big hair from a trailer park', they were consciously producing a stock-in-trade figure from a thousand soap operas and Hollywood movies. Metaphors construct reality for many people. Lakoff and Johnson suggest that early physical sensations of warmth and hunger become reference points to which the developing mind compares its perceptions, and in the process creates metaphors linking world and body.[43] We speak of having a 'close' friend because physical proximity is associated with intimacy. Even abstract concepts are described using physical metaphors ('weighed down with obligations', 'we are heading for a fall'). Attacks on those advocating the manipulation of interest rates 'to cool down the economy', suggest that high interest rates are akin to the eighteenth-century medical practice of bleeding patients to try to cure disease. Someone else in the same reference says: 'as Government regulations grow slowly, we become used to the harness'.

Visual metaphors are used all the time in advertising. What many investors might consider an appropriate one is that used by BNP Paribas, the French bank, to revive relationship banking and put a gulf between them and their competitors.[44] The ad shows a locust in a business suit against a ravaged field of corn with the caption: 'What do you want, a banker or a locust?' Another ad features the mayfly, recognized for its short life, with the caption: 'We will be here today and we will be here tomorrow.' Both these ads are likely to resonate with 'burnt' investors though the question remains as to whether they will perceive BNP Paribas as a credible alternative.

In *The Embodied Mind*, Lakoff and Johnson claim that we are no more aware of the bodily origins of our modes of thought than we are conscious of being influenced by our genetic code. But could it not be that the metaphors arise, not from bodily experience, but simply out of shared perceptions of a reality outside our bodies? In any case, whatever the evolutionary origins, metaphors have an adhesive quality and smoulder in the mind. It was Marshall McLuhan who argued that media can change our way of thinking about the world, as he illustrated with the telegraph which made people see it was possible to communicate across long distances, thus 'destroying' space.[45]

McCloskey shows how economists use rhetoric to influence other economists.[46] As he says, economics claims to be a science and to be non-normative but it tells stories as part of its rhetoric and all stories have morals, so economics is not a science in the positive sense. The very language of economics — indifference curves, maximize utility, rational choice — is both rhetorical and ideological, assuming a particular model of man and the human condition.

Mason reminds us that the traditional distinction made between rhetoric and philosophy – that rhetoric aims to please while philosophy aims at truth – is meant to illustrate the distinction between ornament and substance.[47] Yet Plato's Socrates is the master of rhetorical techniques as rhetorical images (usually emotional) are needed to explode previous moulds of thought. Mason uses a metaphor to illuminate the metaphor by claiming that a live metaphor is one in which the 'switchboard is hopping with signals. . . . Connections are made all over the place. . . . But once they have been made and everyone is familiar with the relations involved, the metaphor dies and loses interest.'[48] He points out that there is no single rhetorical method but simply a set of rhetorical strategies. Mason regards J.L. Austin's concept of the *perlocutionary* speech act as a help in understanding the nature of persuasion because it is associated with indirect means of persuasion. Austin, a philosopher, pointed out that the function of language is not simply to communicate beliefs from one person to another. While what he called 'constative' sayings can be either true or false, 'performatives' or *performance* utterances are those about which it makes no sense to ask whether they are true or false.[49] Thus when Disraeli called Gladstone 'a sophisticated rhetorician, inebriated with the sheer exuberance of his own verbosity', he was enacting a performance utterance, not asserting something that was true or false. This is because performance utterances are not concerned with truth or falsity but with effect. While the sharp distinction between constatives and performatives is not the clear division assumed by Austin, his classification of performance utterances has proved useful. He distinguishes: (a) the *locutionary* speech act, where the inherent meaning of a statement arises from its being syntactically and semantically correct (e.g. 'I will be there' means simply I promise to be there); (b) the *illocutionary* speech act, in which the speaker can be said to do something like praying or making an utterance that *entails* the execution of a socially recognized form of action (e.g. 'I pronounce you man and wife'). More broadly, illocutionary acts rely on words like promise, guarantee, command, complain and apologize. Mere utterances become illocutionary acts through cultural meaning. Harré argues that, from a social constructionist view, displays of emotion commonly have illocutionary force as social acts so that, say, the person to whom anger is directed is rebuked by the act of anger itself.[50] Finally, (c) the *perlocutionary* speech act is one which produces certain effects by its words, for example obtaining compliance, and so is concerned with its effects on the hearer or addressee (e.g. 'I am tired', interpreted, and acted on, as in effect saying 'Let's go home'). While illocutionary speech acts are essentially intentional, perlocutionary acts may or may not be intentional: perlocutionary acts may bring about effects other than the recognition of an intention. It is the perlocutionary speech act that Mason regards as relevant to persuasion in that persuasion is concerned with creating an effect on an audience.

143

Every ad is trying to evoke some effect. But perlocutionary persuasive speech acts in advertising should *not* be *transparent*. If they are to be successful, the audience must not realize the speech act is trying to manipulate them. (Hence to say to someone: 'You are quite a salesman', is really to imply he or she is trying too hard.) Audiences need to feel autonomous in their decision making, so the best rhetoric is that which leads them without their perceiving the advertiser's persuasive strategy, for example the use of questioning as in Mark Antony's funeral oration for Caesar. Another device is to make a questionable assertion sound like a truism: 'We all know that multifunction products are like jacks of all trades, masters of none.' The persuasiveness of an argument is enhanced when the source of the communication seems not to be forcing his or her views onto the audience but to be making an offer of affiliation. Commonly, the persuasive perlocutionary act uses *indirect* means like appeals to greed and gullibility or, more typically, emotional appeals to self-image. As Mason says, the perlocutionary speech act involves the notion of what someone does *by* saying something, not like the illocutionary speech act *in* saying something.

The indirect approach to persuasion in advertising involves rhetoric with vivid imagery, using a good metaphor that sticks in the mind to challenge an existing perspective. Roosevelt was the past master of this, using every form of metaphoric strategy from the biblical ('We have thrown out the money changers from their high seats in the temple') to the homely, as when he compared lend lease to helping your neighbour when his house was on fire. An outstanding example of metaphor advertising was that undertaken in the Apple Macintosh launch at the 1983 Super Bowl. To demonstrate the user-friendly advantage of the new computer, the commercial showed a single lone female athlete shattering the culture of Big Brother and DOS with a precise throw of the hammer.

The English language is full of metaphors that are so concealed it is forgotten that they are metaphors, e.g. 'firm' intention, 'fervent' belief, 'burning' desire and so on. *Metaphors* (like our favourite example: 'the mind is a computer') *defamiliarize the familiar to reorient thinking*. There is now a public treasury of metaphors from which people choose when making apologies. We are 'stressed', our opponents are 'in denial', and our children tell us they are 'latch key' children and so on.

Minor shifts in perspectives occur just by *redefining a situation* (e.g. 'you should regard this as an investment not a payment'). Thus the jurors in the O.J. Simpson trial were invited to see him as the victim of a racist conspiracy and a symbol of an oppressed group. Philip Morris has consistently sought to have the cigarette issue defined as one of freedom of choice: no more, no less.

ASKING QUESTIONS

Asking questions is a way of redirecting thoughts and bringing about minor changes in perspectives, e.g. 'Do you want more government interference?' or the classic opening of the encyclopedia salesperson, 'Are you interested in education, madam?' The choice of words conjures up a fresh perspective but may also be designed to give a certain tone, say, of professionalism by the use of Latin or scientific jargon as occurs in advertising medicines to establish credibility. In his 'I have a dream' speech, Martin Luther King, to create the right impression, did not shrink from language which would have sounded elevated even before an audience of university graduates. He refers, for example, to the Governor of Alabama, 'his lips dripping with the words of interposition and nullification'. Martin Luther King flattered his underprivileged audience by using a Latin-laden rhetoric more associated with academic discourse. In any case, without the right choice of words to fit the audience or the profession, the message is undermined from the start.

Rhetoric is especially important when uncertainty surrounds a decision. Uncertainty is an endemic feature of life which excites some but which most people seek to reduce. Where there is uncertainty, metaphorical emotional symbolism counts. While a scientific law may operate with *practical* certainty (never *logical* certainty), elsewhere there is no cast-iron certainty but a great deal of risk. Consumers, like people in other aspects of their lives, seek to reduce uncertainty and risk. Hence the liking for 'package deals' to avoid hidden costs and the nuisance of buying each part of the whole (needed to fulfil the overall function) separately. But risks in buying are not just financial but also social. It follows that much marketing imagery is devoted to reducing the perception of risk, whether through the use of an honest seeming salesperson or by anticipating objections.

The communication/information source

The *credibility* and *attractiveness* of the communication source are key elements in persuasion. When the cost of reliable information is prohibitive and its sources have to be discovered and evaluated, someone who is perceived as credible and attractive has a huge advantage. Where buying involves social or financial risk, it is commonly assumed that information search will be extensive but this presupposes the ability, motivation and opportunity with time pressures absent. This is not often the case and the collection and evaluation of information may be a task the consumer delegates to others as beyond his or her capabilities. We may not even know how to assess the 'evidence' if it is technical. As Mayhew says, a

> realistic account of how influence works cannot ignore the fact that people regularly accept on faith, without independent verification, the pronouncements of others. Confidence in reputation and prestige, in perceived common interests, and in the good faith of others is a pervasive background force in daily life.[51]

145

Whenever consumers act on advice without independently checking, they are said to be *decisively* influenced. Retailers complain that consumers exploit their knowledge about products and choose on the basis of that advice – but buy on the Internet. Acting on advice is unavoidable in many cases for no consumer or indeed anyone has the time or capability to do otherwise. Consumers seek summary information and the evaluations of others and this means relying on their credibility. If they had to weigh and evaluate every minor decision, life would be impossible. It is this very reliance on the views of others that offers the possibility of manipulating agreement.

A *credible source* is perceived as trustworthy and as possessing relevant technical expertise. A good reputation brings with it perceptions of trustworthiness and honesty while a lack of perceived credibility brings with it a lack of trust and more risk for the buyer. The influence of perceived trustworthiness and technical expertise (credibility) lies in the appeal to *values*, so the message is *internalized*. In any case, perceptions of credibility are tied to a source's reputation, so the source's *reputational capital* is a valued asset. Of course, the law itself can be a credible persuasive symbol because it defines what should be regarded as legitimate. Majority opinion has credibility but, to some, accepting it on brand preference suggests being without one's own opinion.

Authority figures like doctors and policemen often have credibility. Cialdini points out that people in general have a deep-seated sense of duty to all types of authority and have been taught that disobedience is wrong.[52] There are social rules as to what constitutes a credible authority and the quoting of such authorities, as in the case of a doctor on medical matters, can be an effective tactic in persuasion. Doubting the views of an authority on the issue is to deviate from a cultural given, so questioning appears unreasonable. As Cialdini says, information from an accepted authority is often seen as a valuable short-cut for deciding how to act as it saves time and cognitive energy. He also shows how vulnerable people are to the symbols of authority, thus an actor appears in an ad for caffeine-free Sanka brand coffee, still dressed as he was when playing the role of a doctor in a television series. Whatever types of clothing symbolize authority, they are put to the service of advertising. But how can celebrities who are not authorities be viewed as such by consumers? Partly through the halo effect but also because people want to imitate the people they admire. Psychologists point to what they call the *essentialist heuristic*: this is the rule of thumb whereby people act on the assumption, and believe others also act on the assumption, that when things look alike, they share deeper essences. *Hence if I dress and behave like my favourite movie celebrity, it will suggest to others similar essences.*

What is socially endorsed carries authority and credibility. As Cialdini explains, if a lot of people in our social milieu are doing the same thing, they must know something we do not. What he calls 'social proof' is common in advertising ('one million people can't be wrong', 'the most popular brand' and so on) and is exploited in everything from the use of canned laughter to salting the collection basket in church with one big note.

An *attractive source* is *liked*. Liking is not simply tied to physical good looks (though this counts) but involves a commonality of values and/or similar background or is the result of supportive interaction over time. Commonality of values, similar values, supportive interaction through time are, beyond physical good looks, the basis for finding another person pleasant to be with. American politicians stress their humble backgrounds (whenever possible) to be more attractive to the electorate. George Wallace's campaign biography stressed he was an 'ex-trucker married to a dime store clerk'. To the mass of people, it was an asset for Reagan to have gone to Eureka College – he could dismiss George Bush as a 'Yallie, preppy'. Even in nineteenth-century America, supporters of the aristocratic President Benjamin Harrison carried around miniature log cabins although he was actually the cousin of an English lord. Presidential candidate Dukakis presented himself as the son of Greek immigrants (true, but Dukakis senior had a medical degree from Harvard). When running for office, Pierre Dupont characterized himself as the 'descendant of immigrants', distracting attention from the fact that he was the scion of one of America's greatest industrial dynasties.

For attractiveness to come across, there must be a perceived potential for *sharing*, as this is the basis for getting on with someone. The persuasive appeal of an attractive source is that it is supportive of the audience's *self-image* or *self-esteem*. Acceptance of a message is tied to *identification* with the communication source. Hence if the communication source changes his or her mind, so does the receiver of the message. Spokespeople viewed as attractive personalities seem to possess an openness as 'if revealing all' (not surprising in that such people would appear disarming!), and having an ability both to understand themselves emotionally and to read the emotions of others. These abilities have come to be known as 'emotional intelligence' or 'emotional competence'. Those with emotional intelligence are aware both of their own feelings and of those of others and, as a consequence, are a 'pleasure to have around'.[53] One of the most unflattering things you can say of someone is that he or she is 'charmless'. A charming person was once defined as someone to whom you are saying 'yes' before he or she has made a request.

Advertisers hope that by identifying a brand with attractive celebrities, consumers will fantasize about being like them or feeling part of their in-group. All the consumer needs do is buy and display the product being advertised. A celebrity's credibility is increased if he or she appears objective, e.g. 'I had real doubts about the product at first but I just tried it once and all doubts were removed'. Yet the consumer typically knows it is all a 'con' and that the celebrity only uses the product because of having been paid to do so. In this sense, consumers become co-conspirators in their own self-deception. A celebrity may promote a style of behaviour as socially appropriate when previously it was socially taboo and, in this sense, can have a good or damaging effect on public behaviour. Showing European aristocratic women smoking cigarettes did much to encourage women in the United States to take up smoking after the First World War.

Why do celebrity endorsements work even when the audience knows that the celebrity is being paid to speak and probably has no other attachment to the product? Because an endorsement is an endorsement even when it does not reflect any deep commitment, as celebrities would not risk their reputation. It is also a co-production of an illusion, an invitation to share in an illusion with the celebrity.

Credibility and attractiveness are related. The attractiveness of a communication source can evoke the halo effect, meaning that attractive people have a sort of metaphorical halo round their heads which carries over into a belief in their credibility. On the other hand, there are people we classify as likeable rogues. The communication source need not be a person or a company but just the ad itself or even the product's packaging. And liking can be based on what something symbolizes rather than on any substantive properties. Using the same running shoes as an admired celebrity may have high symbolic meaning for the buyer.

Celebrities, as aspirational images, have potentially high credibility and attractiveness and, in adding something of their own persona to the brand, allow people to fantasize that if they use the product, some of the celebrity's persona will rub off onto them. The selection of the right celebrity (someone whose background, values and achievements the target audience can identify with) is critical. The late twentieth century made a cult of celebrity, bringing with it the commodification of celebrity and the phenomenon of manufactured celebrity. The Spice Girls did not have a pre-celebrity existence; the concept was worked out beforehand as a 'brand' with sub-brands (Posh Spice, Scary Spice, etc.) and hordes of girls were then simply auditioned. The inventor was a middle-aged accountant (who said accountants are incapable of understanding marketing?). The instant recognition provided by celebrity status is a great plus in persuasion. Celebrity endorsement bestows influence on the product in question. When Princess Diana was given a Dior bag by the wife of the French president and was seen to be endorsing the brand by carrying it with her, it led to a massive increase in demand for the bag.

Celebrities or spokespersons in an advertisement add more to their credibility if they disprove expectations. For example, anyone who is selling is expected to try the hard sell, so expectations will be disproved and credibility increased by not trying to sell too hard. We always assume that people have a self-interest in their own actions, so we are disposed to discount their persuasive appeals as self-serving. An extreme example would be a celebrity advocating a certain brand when he or she could not possibly be perceived as an expert.

Credibility and attractiveness do not just consist of what people say. Those who simply heard or read but did not watch the Kennedy–Nixon debate in 1960 concluded that Nixon had won. This was not the case with those who actually watched it. Rosser Reeves, one of the giants in advertising folklore, once tested a speech by General McArthur and found that hardly anyone remembered what he actually said though it was regarded as a great speech. Tone, appearance and gesture were critical. This is in line with findings on the psychology of interviews – the important thing is not what one says but the way one says it. Reeves went on to make the first advertisements in a US presidential election, the 'Eisenhower Answers America' series. Just saying something loudly (prosodics) or with laughter (paralinguistic) or with gesture (extralinguistic) can be just as relevant to persuasion as the words themselves. In print advertising, advertisers need to consider: (a) ambiance; (b) design; (c) use of white space; (d) significant images; (e) symbolic significance; (f) use of language; (g) type face; (h) functions of the product; (i) how the ad goes about the job of persuasion; (j) what roles it suggests we imitate.[54] Providing it ties in with the audience's concerns, emotion can be generated by any aspect of an ad's execution and this emotional arousal influences both attitude towards the ad and, as a spin-off, attitude towards the product itself.[55]

Colours are emotively symbolic. Thus, given a supporting context, red projects vitality, excitement, fear or tension while green projects calm and naturalness. A room in yellow and red colours projects a warm emotional mood while a concrete floor, plain wooden desk and bare light bulbs project a prison image.[56] Such symbolism tends to be culturally specific, however. Thus green is the colour symbolizing nationalism in Egypt. In Malaysia it represents jungle sickness.[57]

Ads with an emotional dimension strike a chord with the target audience by linking to their values. But the emotional images aroused should be congruent with the advertised product. For example, if an advertisement is implicitly declaring an allegiance to certain values, these should not appear to be an *illicit graft* on the brand being advertised. This was the problem, until very recently, with the Benetton institutional advertising which was tied to portraying offensive scenes and social strife.

The content/presentation of the message itself

All advertising carries a message and a tone. The content of the message can exploit any of the forms of argument or discourse set out in Chapter 2. These will not be repeated. Some of the well-established findings on other aspects of content can be summarized as follows. There is a latitude of acceptance of any message. Outside that latitude, consumers reject the message. A one-sided presentation appeals to the already converted but a two-sided presentation (yet leaning towards the advertiser's position) is better when not addressing the converted.

149

The advertising scene is a message-dense environment, so it is better to make conclusions clear. A liked message is more apt to be persuasive in an audio or visual medium. Surprisingly long messages, by suggesting substantive content, can be persuasive. David Ogilvy, an advertising legend, often used long messages, filling car ads with mechanical performance and other details. As already noted, a message that makes an audience *imagine* using and possessing the product can lead to *direct* self-persuasion. This is why many motor car ads do not just show a car but show it being driven in some idyllic setting, concentrating on the driver's facial reactions while implying social admiration. Those selling a house are advised not to show very personal things like family photographs as this can inhibit self-imagining or self-persuasion (talking oneself into it). Self-imagining occurs all the time in buying clothes as consumers 'get a kick' out of imagining how others will view them and how the new identity will feel when wearing or possessing this or that item of clothing. This is not to suggest that possessions are all-important in establishing one's sense of identity.[58] Self-identity must be rich enough to affect all the most important aspects of one's life.[59]

Consistency theory

People value the experience as well as the appearance of being consistent in social dealings. Appearing consistent in what we say and do projects an image of integrity which helps establish credibility. This applies to companies as well as individuals though insisting on consistency may on occasion go against the need for change. There are several models based on this consistency premise: the balance model, the congruity model and the cognitive dissonance model.

Balance model

According to the balance model, people seek a balance between their feelings (affects) and their beliefs (cognitions), since often something can be felt to be true but believed to be false. On the other hand, we may know things are true but feel they are false. If we are obliged to face up to this conflict, it can be emotionally discomforting. In persuasion we may need to bring the one into line with the other. Thus one ad showing a fox being ripped apart by hounds changed many people's beliefs (via the emotions aroused) to favour banning fox hunts. Beliefs when considering buying commonly take second place to feelings. You may not believe you are prepared to have a dog around the house but change on seeing the wistful look of that puppy. Persuasive appeals can draw attention to the inconsistency between professed feelings and beliefs in such a way that one is changed to favour the persuader. Thus advertising for insurance may remind its audiences that they feel deeply about their loved ones yet have not provided for them in the event of their death.

Congruity model

According to the congruity model, people seek to reconcile their attitude towards the source of a communication and towards things linked to the source so as to make them congruent. This is an additional explanation of why association is effective. It is a major reason for employing celebrities to promote a brand since, if the attitude towards the celebrity is very positive but the celebrity is associated with a brand with a negative image, it is hoped the negative image will change. It is also a reason for the importance attached to an audience liking an ad, as liking the ad helps in liking the brand. However, this is neither necessary nor sufficient, as demonstrated by comparative ads which are often effective even when disliked.

Cognitive dissonance/attribution model

Cognitive dissonance results when two inconsistent cognitions (beliefs) are held simultaneously or when there is a conflict between beliefs and actions. As with the other consistency 'theories', resolution of the conflict or inconsistency is regarded as a way to change attitudes. But inconsistency here differs from the logician's narrower concept whereby inconsistent beliefs imply logical contradiction. Instead, what matters is the idea that beliefs A and B (or belief A and behaviour B) are inconsistent if we would expect not both A and B but only A or B. Festinger claimed this state of inconsistency is uncomfortable and *motivates* people to reduce the conflict in the easiest way possible by changing one or both cognitions (beliefs).[60] When there is awareness of an inconsistency between behaviour and beliefs, consumers are emotionally uncomfortable. This occurs when the consumer buys a product and discovers later it could have been obtained more cheaply elsewhere. She can reduce the discomfort by depreciating the loss or enhancing the gain or others can reduce it by reassuring her on the wisdom of her choice. The critics of American Vietnam policy succeeded by exploiting the perceived gulf between belief and behaviour. Communications can deliberately arouse dissonance ('How can you believe in animal welfare when you agree with mink farms?') to facilitate persuasion.

Higgins classifies states of dissonance on the basis of the emotions that are aroused.[61] Inconsistency between self-image and ideal-image generates disappointment; that between self-image and what you *ought* to be generates guilt while inconsistency between self-image and what others think you should be also generates guilt. If we regard the discovery that we have made a poor purchase as giving rise to a sense of loss, that loss is more painful than a similar-sized gain. This is the thesis of Tversky and Kahneman who show that the pain of a given amount of loss is greater than the pleasure of the same size of gain.[62] The loss of 100 dollars or euros generates more pain than the pleasure of gaining that sum. In other words, emotional consequences differ between the two cases.

151

In criticism of consistency theories, it is pointed out that many beliefs are not firmly grounded: people are not always sure what they believe. This is one reason why polling can evoke very different results depending on how questions are worded. People can say one thing and do another. As a presidential candidate, President George W. Bush spoke convincingly about the need for the United States to exercise its power with humility, to reach out to allies and never be perceived as a bully. Condoleezza Rice contemptuously dismissed talk of 'nation building'. A change in circumstances can alter opinions. Although there is emotional pressure on everyone to be consistent in what they say and do, people may believe smoking is injurious to their health yet persist in doing it, or may claim to believe everyone is equal but act otherwise. With respect to cognitive dissonance, as Margalit says, we may hope we have bought well but are generally too experienced to really believe it; and we do not always even seek to reduce dissonance but may on occasion even seek to increase it, as when we positively invite insults.[63]

In an extension of the dissonance concept, *cultural* dissonance occurs when the basic perspectives of two interacting groups, like buyers and sellers, are not congruent. We argue that such dissonance, arising from non-congruent perspectives, is common and the resulting misunderstanding can be severe. Cultural dissonance occurs between the generations, particularly in times of cultural upheaval like the 1960s. Cultural dissonance can in fact be found among any two interacting groups whether business, ethnic, religious or national. Cultural dissonance makes it difficult to appreciate an ad meant for another culture. It is also causes problems for advertising agencies when they have to put across a proposal to a marketing director who is not in tune with the target audience's thinking.

Not-for-profit advertising often exploits favourable beliefs we have about ourselves as part of our self-image, e.g. 'I am generous to those less fortunate'. This can give rise to cognitive dissonance: 'This is how I see myself yet this is how I behave'. Unless inconsistency is brought to the attention of consumers, they, like people generally, tolerate much inconsistency in their beliefs by not bringing them to mind simultaneously. In fact, inconsistencies between beliefs and behaviour are legion. As long as the contradictory elements do not occur in the same context, people continue to subscribe to both. Many who claim to be Christian also believe in astrology, which dates back to a pre-Christian belief system. People may condemn the decline in family values but further that decline by divorcing. They worry about illegitimate children but accept extramarital sex; complain to others about pornography on TV but are happy to watch it and so on. Presumably, Father Charles Coughlin in the 1930s saw no problem in reconciling his hysterical anti-Semitism with the commandment to love thy neighbour or the parable of the Good Samaritan. What we call hypocrisy is often simply a failure to bring behaviour in line with professed beliefs which are compartmentalized separately in the mind. As regards conflicts in values, it is commonly pointed out that people support the principle of racial equality but not policies designed to realize it. This seeming inconsistency, however, may not arise from any clash between political ideology and policy preference: a person may support racial equality but believe that affirmative action is not the way to bring it about.[64]

The cognitive dissonance thesis has been difficult to test and *self-presentation* theory and *attribution theory* often act as substitute explanations.[65] Attribution theory argues that people attribute causes to others' behaviour. The *attribution error* is understating the influence of external factors on the actions of others. Thus it is not uncommon for minorities in society to be excluded from meaningful opportunities for advancement. In spite of this, their economic and social performance is assessed as if the society allowed them equal opportunity, and mediocre performance is attributed solely to their own poor efforts. On the other hand, the opposite of the attribution error results from simply assuming people's actions are outside the realm of individual responsibility.

The *self-serving error* lies in attributing personal success to oneself and personal failure to external factors like 'society'. The persuasive ad that attributes failure in love to the absence of a good after-shave is exploiting the self-serving error. Attributions tie in with the emotions. For example, Valins found that amplifying the sound of heartbeats affected young men's evaluation of slides of nude women: they attributed the amplified heartbeat to their own reaction, which made them believe they were more emotionally affected than was actually the case.[66]

The only emission this car produces.

Water. The sole by-product of this clean energy BMW. It uses liquid hydrogen instead of fossil fuels to produce an abundance of power, yet absolutely no greenhouse gases. Allowing you to enjoy the benefits of a BMW with a totally clear conscience.

The hydrogen powered engine will be available in future BMW models.

BMW Innovation

www.bmw
innovation.co.uk
Tel. 0800 325 600

The Ultimate
Driving Machine

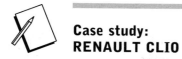

Case study:
RENAULT CLIO

Content of the advertising

Concept

This series ran in the British Isles for many years. It became a cult, with its set of illuminated tableaux depicting urban, and urbane, people who live in France: the car is a conduit to romance. The series thus comprises a formulaic concept, like a number of the other cases we have discussed in this book; a narrative momentum is created and, once the core idea has been established, it does not need the skills of a great copywriter to design epic copy on each occasion; the core concept is flexible and interesting enough to allow continuous refreshment. The immediate attributes sought for the Renault Clio are 'cheekiness and fun'. It is a non-conformist idea: 'the story-line follows the supposedly clandestine extra-curricular activities of a father (Papa) and his daughter Nicole, visiting her boyfriend. The Clio RT was featured in both instances as accomplice' (http:/advertising.metro.co.uk). One authority concluded that 'the right combination: of culture, lifestyle, a human face, and a twist in the plot has worked very well for Renault. It is a combination which few agencies managed to strike.'

The key contribution of the campaign was to broaden the age range of the purchasers of Renault. This was achieved by a genuinely differentiated product advertised in novel ways, and the impact of these advertisements was clearly demonstrable (see below).

Story

The advertisements have been described thus (www.jyanet.com):

> The first advertisement, without dialogue, showed Nicole in a spotted summer frock, slipping past Papa and driving away with the Clio for a rendezvous with her boyfriend. The second featured Nicole, even more chic in a black dress, and her new boyfriend taking Papa's Clio to a ball, now with Papa's consent. (Papa goes off on a romantic rendezvous, too.) A third saw Nicole and Papa on a skiing

Plate 5.2 *Reconciling cognitive dissonance: BMW*

Source: Courtesy of BMW

The only emission this car produces.

Water. The sole by-product of this clean energy BMW. It uses liquid hydrogen instead of fossil fuels to produce an abundance of power, yet absolutely no greenhouse gases. Allowing you to enjoy the benefits of a BMW with an absolutely clear conscience.

155

holiday, as research demanded they be together for a change. In every advertisement, there is a small twist, leaving questions unanswered. In 1994, with the new
generation Clio, Nicole grows up. Directed by Richard Loncraine and shot in
Provence, the TVCs continue le savon populaire. Instead of the typical car advertising gimmicks of macho postures and voice-overs ranting about the new driver's
side airbag, the 1994 blitz began with Nicole, now a sophisticated young woman,
on a shopping trip.

Thus the series featured two dramatis personae, 'Papa' and 'Nicole'. The basic idea
is that both have a lover in the neighbouring town. The question is always, who gets
to go in that car: Papa to his rendezvous (on one occasion he appears with a matronly
French lady), or Nicole to her boyfriend. It is a simple concept, a comedy of manners,
whose wit lies in the idea of mutual concealment. The scenes are all set in a southern
French town with its iron balconies, terracotta roofs and stucco walls, and the French
countryside. The journey is from the rural (family) to the town (amorous liaison) and
this sets the stage for a series of little stories. Papa and Nicole always meet up again
after their adventures, but there are of course plenty of surprises, for example they
might bump into each other in the town. The teaser is this, will each find out what
the other is up to? The Nicole–Papa campaign put people into the paratelic mode of
excitement and curiosity about where the romance was going without the vulgarity of
subsequent imagery (see below).

Exploitation of English Francophilia

The series did not employ negative images of France, such as its alleged chauvinism
or ethnocentricity, but rather played with a fantasy of France, France as Arcadia, a
perfect world of perpetual summer that is other than the world of its English viewers:
its brightness is implicitly contrasted with their greyness of climate, its rural and
small-town idiom with their suburbs, France's open space with their crowds. An
antithesis is established as the focus of English dreamers, a middle-class idealization
which targets the aspirational (manifest also in the English holidaymaker and purchaser
of property in France).

It was a benevolent caricature of the French; research revealed the affection with
which French culture is regarded by the British middle class. Thus Fiona Love of
Publicis, the company that produced the advertisements, claims that:

> extensive research carried out by Publicis revealed that there is a strong appreci-
> ation among the British public of the French way of life. They are regarded as
> enjoying a more relaxed, more rewarding lifestyle. With greater importance placed
> on culture and family values. The essence of this is that the French are perceived
> to enjoy a better and more desirable way of life.

(www.jyanet.com)

Nearly seven million Britons would rather live in France than any other country, apart from their own. Over two million Britons visit France every year and a book extolling the comatose pleasures of French provincial life, *A Year in Provence*, sold over 150,000 copies. But it is a certain image of France which Renault parades, an imaginary world where 'life is a long holiday'.

Exploitation of stereotypes

The mini-series works entirely through the agency of stereotype. It plays to English ideas about the French, and to a certain sense of inferiority that is cultural and aesthetic. Persuasive communications often seek to mobilize stereotypes, and few advertisements would succeed if they were required to offer them substantial challenge. Nicole is chic and vivacious, a classic daddy's girl, elegant yet naive. Papa is suaveness itself, the silver-haired mature Frenchman with perfectly cut clothing, exuding self-assurance and an easy paternalism. Both father and daughter are classically dressed, there is nothing modish about them and the idiom is patrician.

Although the serial's play with stereotypes of the French may seem self-parodic, it is no crass caricature. Significant here is the execution, with the recognition that Nicole should be realistic, all the characters appearing as authentic people. Nor might this have succeeded with a different set of actors, perhaps less personable, or less subtle.

The strategic marketing campaign

(Data and contextual detail for the following sections are available at http:/advertising.metro.co.uk, see below.)

Strategic objectives

In March 1991 Renault UK launched the Clio. The aim was to seek a premium position at the apex of the small car market and also to make the car attractive to older, as well as to its traditional younger, purchasers: no easy task, as this would mean rejecting the conventional marketing advice about focused segmentation.

The small car sector accounted for one quarter of new British car sales, and was therefore critical. The context of the introduction was an economic recession, increased congestion, an ageing population and a rise in two-car ownership. It was claimed that the product itself represented a quantum advance in styling, engineering, use of space and levels of luxury unique among small cars. The price reflected this difference as it was the second most expensive in the small car market, and thus the advertising objective was to justify this superior price by establishing a premium position. Renault badly needed a success in the UK, for in 1990 its total market share was at its lowest level for fifteen years.

Market research identified potential Renault Clio buyers as 'individualists' who placed a value on culture and style, and were aspirational with a desire to be different: this was a consumer defined by values and attitudes rather than age or class. Renault decided on a revolutionary break with their previous advertising style.

Tactics of the campaign

In anticipation of the launch teaser posters and commercials began to appear that featured a large metallic red egg ('Not just another Hatch'), followed on from launch day itself images of a mighty red Clio. This multimedia advertising blitz was followed by alternating television advertisements with magazine/newspaper pictures: 'in all, 66 per cent of the media spend in the first nine months of advertising activity was put on TV.'

Impact of the campaign

Market share

The campaign boosted Renault's portion of the small car market to 7.7 per cent. The market share of the total car market in the UK for Renault Clio was 1.82 per cent, that of its nearest competitor, the Peugeot-05, was 1.65 per cent. Clio was the market leader in the upmarket small car segment. In the first five weeks of the campaign, 52 per cent of Clios were bought to substitute for an existing Renault, but 44 per cent were revealed as 'conquest sales'.

Recall and awareness

Awareness levels rose to 56 per cent and then fell to 40 per cent, which is where they remained. Recall rates were excellent and the awareness index of seven was superior to the norm for car advertising; with one exception, these scores were better than in the preceding eight British car launches. Another measure of effectiveness is the extent to which advertising is remembered: the 'Millward–Brown baseline measure', establishes the point of recall after a campaign has ceased. The median here is 5–6 whereas Clio reached a very impressive nine. In 1994 *Marketing* magazine announced that these Renault advertisements were the most easily remembered, sustaining a 68 per cent prompted recall. Renault's Customer Link survey demonstrated that their television advertising gained the highest score for stimulating curiosity, and was the second most significant source of knowledge.

Likeability

The advertisements were regarded with affection: a study found 'a strong relationship to exist between the likeability of copy and its effectiveness'. In 1991 80 per cent of a sample 'positively endorsed' the advertisements while only 58 per cent did so for all the extant car commercials. Those surveyed admired the car for being 'stylish', 'for everyone', 'nippy' and 'small', and perceived it as attractive both to 'younger people with no commitments' and also to 'people over 40'. In 1995, Complete Car conducted a survey of half a million European drivers, who believed that Renault authored 'the most influential' advertising, and it emerged as 'the most persuasive advertiser' of cars in five countries. Even the dress worn by actress Estelle Skornik (Nicole) was reproduced at just under £40 by Selfridges.

New campaigns

But no series can last for ever, and this one is brought to a close by Nicole's dramatic non-wedding in Paris (an old boyfriend sabotages it and they escape *en Clio*). After this, Renault and their advertisers again pursued a radically new message. The new series featured a worldly, extrovert Parisian woman who drives the car and explains that 'It's size that matters'. Abrupt shifts in imagistic equity are surely problematic, and this overt crudeness challenges the meaning of the product, whose previous identity had been elaborated through a synthesis of youthful innocence and mature charm. The 'Nicole and Papa' stories offered various interpretations, both innocent and less innocent, but eschewed in-your-face sexuality. It is not surprising that they acquired a national following. This previous identity is entirely repudiated by a new earthiness that was attention getting but charmless.

By 2001 around 80,000 Clios were being sold every year in the United Kingdom. But, to their alarm, Renault were finding a gender imbalance in the customers for their car. Women buy three-quarters of small cars. They had been the primary target for the Clio. It was essential that the advertising appeal to them. Yet this brought problems of its own: 'Renault's long-running and memorable advertising campaigns for Clio have sparked one major problem – the car is seen as a motor for girls. It's even got a girl's name' (Julia Day, www.media.guardian). So a new campaign was launched, to persuade men that the Clio was for them. French World Cup footballer Thierry Henry was recruited to personify the new strategy. Renault's UK national advertising manager claimed that 'To many, Thierry represents a modern man who is skilled, intelligent and stylish and is therefore a perfect fit for us and for the Clio.' But of course the campaign could have the opposite effect – the footballer simply inspiring even more interest among women. As Julia Day commented in the *Guardian*, 'Henry is not only stylish, but Gallictastically gorgeous – and could reinforce Clio's reputation as a girl's car.' Yet this new campaign had a budget of £1 million, and the announced aim was to give the car a 'strong and masculine' side. Renault argued that 'the new campaign is primarily aimed at a younger, male audience and reflects the sporty versions of the Clio' (Julia Day). But intention cannot ordain reception and meaning is always negotiated, so whatever the intent, would more men really drive Clios?

159

Theoretic analysis: association and metaphor

If advertising is 'pouring meaning into the brand', what are these advertisements saying about the Renault Clio? All our case studies lend themselves to a number of possible theoretic approaches, and this is no exception. Certainly we could argue that they are working via associationism (links to prestige, values and valued images) in their pursuit of serial images – of status, people, etc. – which are very 'French' and will transfer to the car: 'from the foreigner's perception of French women as flirtatious and feminine, to the style that all French people are perceived unconsciously to possess. The style is carried through to their cars, research showing perceptions of French to include chic and flair' (www.jyanet.com). In one sense, this series might even be seen as exploiting ideas of the nation as a brand. Perhaps there was also an appeal to nostalgia implicit in these scenes.

But what is it declaring about the product? That the product is indeed intriguing – because there is an intrigue: young, witty, but also the traditional continuities at its heart – the mature engage in a micro-drama together with the immature. It is timeless: small town and rural France are observed with delight and it is rich in association. *But the real purpose of the advertising is metaphoric, and this campaign is proceeding via a metaphor for an automobile. The car in fact appears to become a metaphor for Frenchwomen, or vice versa: 'In the commercial Nicole serves to epitomise the generic small-car values of fun, nippiness, whilst Papa serves to broaden the age appeal of the car and reflect added refinement'* (www.metro.co.uk).

References

'Nicole? Papa?', CAP Online Features 1996, www.jyanet.com.
'Thierry Henry Replaces Nicole in Renault Clio T.V. Ads', www.anova.com.
Day, Julia, 'World Cup Bandwagon', www.media.guardian.co.uk, 23 May 2002.
Chandy, Caroline and Thursby-Pelham, Douglas, 'Renault Clio: Adding Value During a Recession', http:/advertising.metro.co.uk/newsinfo/downloads/Clio.pdg.

Case study:
GOLD BLEND

Gold Blend quickly became a legend through a protracted series of romantically engaged advertisements featuring two well-heeled neighbours, a man and a woman, residents of a smart block of flats. Essentially, the series was a soap opera, gaining narrative momentum from the mutual curiosity between this couple and their playful intrigue. Would they come together? Emotionally the series worked because it successfully captured the delight of romance with a stranger, and such interaction with a new personality generated potential for novelty. The series became a cult as it was performed in such an urbane way (the man, actor Tony Head, later became the teacher in the programme *Buffy the Vampire Slayer*). This advertising was effective at creating a brand identity that was witty, adult and mature, polished, upper-class; not a bad achievement for instant coffee. But the format, an unfolding story, was a master stroke. The story offered variety and avoided dull repetition.

The plots were trivial, involving chance meetings at dinner parties and the like, and the stories inched forward month by month: would they or wouldn't they get together, were they together, would they stay together? For example,

> the last episode showed sophisticated Sharon Maughan catching downstairs neigh-bour and 'on-off' lover Tony Head sharing a late night cuppa with a mystery woman. In the latest instalment, being unveiled on ITV around 8pm, Tony protests she was just an old friend. But Sharon walks off in a huff and the next scene shows her at a business meeting in Milan being charmed by a sharp-suited Italian.
>
> (D. Simpson, *Press Association News*, 10 August 1992)

The campaign was extraordinarily effective. The series began in November 1987 and within a year sales of Gold Blend had risen by 12 per cent. Over the next few years Nescafé was able to increase its sales by 60 per cent, creating a £100 million brand. Viewing figures reached fifteen million. By August 1992 consumption of Gold Blend had increased by an extra two million cups per day to ten million cups since the advertisements were first shown. Gold Blend became the second favourite instant coffee brand (D. Simpson, *Press Association News*, 10 August 1992).

And yet there is no inherent reason why that core advertising concept, a man and a woman neighbour with a mutual curiosity that became daily more intense, should have translated so effectively into cult status and massive increases in sales. The success of the series lay both in the tactical execution of the concept and in the talents of Maughan and Head; a sound but not brilliant idea, sensitively articulated. In the study of adver-tising we are perhaps apt to ignore the surface decoration of texts and the nuance, such as the raised eyebrow, which may be important in the construction of meaning and yet missed by the analyst. There was an aptness, a fitness about these actors for each other, and the charm of the series arose from perceptions of that suitability. Attractive (not pretty), they look as if they have lived. There is irony in their performance: self-conscious, self-parodic play acting. A sense of personal chemistry is created which could not have been easily achieved with a different set of actors; nor was it: the successor couple in the series failed, the magic was gone. It is this finely judged nuance which made the advertisements for a time a byword for sophistication.

But the effectiveness lay also in the conception of a man and a woman meeting as equals, for the woman is an independent professional and this made it a decidedly modern advertisement. Neither character carries any domestic responsibilities; they are free spirits. Both have their separate domains, and this is crucial: their living

161

together would end the story, with its dependence on individual powers being drawn towards each other by magnetic force.

The effect of these advertisements was to dignify a rather common product, instant coffee. The explanation for this effect lies fundamentally in the communication approach, since the focus is on two individuals who are both attractive and also credible, and, further, who became celebrities on account of these very qualities. Psychology of association, in particular the linkage of the product to position and prestige, may offer further insight (see Chapter 3). The two individuals exuded a social poise which few people really possess but many would like to; they were aspirational rather than normative images. Such people are certainly arbiters of taste and at some level we would like to identify with them. This product, Gold Blend, is also made to offer us the possibility of social involvement and thus of meeting our ideal partner through its agency; if it worked for them, why not for us?

References

Simpson, David, 'Trouble Brewing in the Coffee Opera', *Press Association News*, 10 August 1992, www.BetsyDa.com.
'Long Term Maintenance of a Classic Brand Name', www.thetimes100.co.uk.

KEY ASSERTIONS

■ If marketing management is to consider the widest range of persuasive tactics, persuasive appeals must not be confined to creating associations. There is a need to consider how information is processed by the consumer. In particular, there is a need to consider: (a) the individual receiver of the communication; (b) the communication/information source; (c) the content/presentation of the message.

■ If marketing management is to have an impact on its target audience, its first job is to get enough attention for the relevant concepts to be absorbed. After learning the concepts relevant to the product or offering, the target audience see the product differently and until this conceptual understanding is established, the consumer cannot develop a meaningful preference for the product. Learning new concepts is one way of changing perspectives.

■ If marketing management is developing an offering, anchor points, or the standards the consumer uses for comparison purposes, must be considered. Anchor points are important in influencing expectations.

■ If the marketing is communicating in any way, the extent of ego involvement must be gauged. The aim should be to avoid loss of face or humiliation. Advertising should enhance a consumer's self-esteem, not undermine it.

- If marketing management is to get its message across, repetition is important. Repetition induces familiarity and familiarity induces acceptance of the message.

- Providing a message is *roughly similar* to the beliefs and values held by the target audience, the *assimilation effect* will make them interpret it as closer to their own view than may really be the case. On the other hand, if the new message is in perceived conflict with the views of the target audience, the contrast effect will exaggerate the difference. Hence the advertising should try to cohere with the target audience's beliefs and values.

- If marketing management is to understand the target's shields against being persuaded, their social attachments (culture, reference groups, social class, emotionally grounded experiences), and individual perspectives (beliefs and values) must be identified, as these are very relevant to developing persuasive communications. The interpretation of an ad is tied to the culture, social experience and education of the target audience and these factors mould perspectives.

- If marketing management is putting across the case for its product, it presupposes the target audience have the 'right' perspective. People must be on the right wavelength to accept the message. If the audience have the same perspective as the seller, 'rational' arguments should be used since if we agree on assumptions, logic has a strong role to play. If not, the first task is to change the perspective of the target audience which may mean introducing new concepts. But, in general it is better to try to intensify a perspective than attempt to change it.

- If marketing management is concerned with changing perspectives, the focus has to be on indirect means of persuasion: rhetoric is needed, as a more direct approach will be strongly resisted. Rhetorical arguments are designed to induce a certain perspective from which they will be viewed favourably. Rhetoric is inseparable from all persuasion and great rhetoric is primarily metaphorical. The indirect approach to persuasion involves rhetoric with vivid imagery, using a good metaphor that sticks in the mind to challenge the existing perspective. Metaphors (e.g. 'the mind is a computer') challenge the existing perspective and arouse curiosity by defamiliarizing the familiar to reorient thinking. Metaphors affect how things are interpreted as they structure thinking and emotional reactions. The effectiveness of rhetoric, like the effectiveness of symbolism, is greater when there is uncertainty surrounding the buying decision.

cont.

163

- If marketing management's advertising communications are to be believed, they need to be credible. A statement can be true but not credible, or credible but not true. Credibility is tied to trustworthiness based usually on the firm's reputational capital and perceived technical expertise.

- If marketing management, as the source of a communication, does not seem to be forcing any view but presenting a perspective in a way that seems more like an offer of unity, affiliation or solidarity, the persuasiveness of the message will be enhanced. The use of dogmatic assertion is more likely to be effective to those without an opposing perspective.

- If marketing management is not faced with a strongly opposed perspective, redefining the situation in some way through advertising may be all that is required. Alternatively, asking questions can lower defences and channel the target audience's attention into re-examining their assumptions.

- If the communications of marketing management are to have impact, every attempt should be made to ensure the source (e.g. the message in the ad or the celebrity) of the message has credibility and attractiveness. When the cost for the consumer of gathering information is prohibitive, he or she will place much reliance on the credibility and attractiveness of the ad. A credible source is trusted and respected for the technical expertise displayed, so the message integrates with values and becomes internalized. On the other hand, an attractive source is liked, either because of commonality of background or supportive interaction through time, so the target audience identify with the source and want to accept the message. For attractiveness to come across there must be this potential for sharing. Credibility and attractiveness can form an interacting system in that each may influence the other.

- If marketing management is putting across a one-sided appeal, it is assumed the audience are already converted. If this is not so, a two-sided appeal, leaning towards the position advocated, is likely to have more impact.

- Lack of consistency between the target audience's feelings and beliefs or between the source of a communication and their attitude towards things linked to it or between beliefs and values/desires, can be exposed by marketing management to its advantage. Persuasive appeals can draw attention to the inconsistency in a way that favours the persuader.

- If marketing management accepts that motives need not be conscious, focus groups and unstructured interviews or protocols where people just talk 'off the top of their head' before, during and after buying can reveal both the conscious and some of the non-conscious factors that affected the purchase (see next chapter).

Chapter 6

Persuasive advertising appeals, 4

- Psychoanalytic psychology
- Zaltman Metaphor Elicitation Technique (ZMET)
- Psychology of the adaptive unconscious

This chapter elucidates the views of those who claim that the most effective persuasion taps into the unconscious mind. What is certainly true is the largely unappreciated influence of the unconscious mind on consumer behaviour. If it is true that (to revise Pascal) the unconscious has its 'reasons' which the conscious mind does not know, how are we to discover these 'reasons' that can influence behaviour? Freud thought the 'royal road' to the unconscious was through the analysis of dreams or, if this was not feasible, unstructured interviews. In applying psychoanalytic psychology to marketing, the method chosen was motivation research, preferably using projective techniques. A more exotic form of researching the unconscious, with roots in Freud, is found in the Zaltman Metaphor Elicitation Technique (ZMET). Finally there is the revised view of the unconscious, known as the *adaptive unconscious*.

The adaptive unconscious is far more pervasive than Freud's unconscious but the concept endorses the Freudian view about the dominant role the unconscious plays in people's lives. Those psychologists interested in the adaptive unconscious are adamant that the unconscious is not accessible to the conscious mind and so are less forthcoming about ways to influence the adaptive unconscious or have messages adapted to its dispositions. This does not mean these psychologists do not make large claims about the adaptive unconscious. They do, but they remain somewhat vague about the implications for changing behaviour. Because Freud was interested in neurotic behaviour, he sought changes in the unconscious by bringing repressed wishes (usually sexual) or fears out into the open where they could be dealt with. ZMET also rests on the assumption that the unconscious mind can be accessed and is interested in adapting the design of marketing offerings to the unconscious representations in the mind. Those interested in the adaptive unconscious do not disapprove of the use of projective techniques for researching the unconscious, but their approach in general is to take account of

165

findings and seek to 'educate' the adaptive unconscious through inducing a change in behaviour first.

THE PSYCHOANALYTIC APPROACH

Psychoanalytic psychology is associated with Sigmund Freud. Freud questioned the degree to which we understand the motives lying behind our actions and argued that people hide their real motives. For Freud, our unconscious motivators are the most basic motivators and he denied that these could be manipulated, as claimed by behaviourism, by rewards and punishments.

Psychoanalytic psychology is no longer regarded as a general psychology but as a psychology that focuses on unconscious inner conflicts as people strive towards achieving their goals. The unconscious is distinguished from the *subconscious* or what Freud called the 'preconscious' level, which is the level of mental life assumed to exist just below the threshold of consciousness. *Subliminal perception* is associated with this subconscious level.

Freudian psychology claims that the interplay of three systems of the mind causes behaviour, namely the *id* (the primitive urges of the flesh), the *superego* (social constraints/conscience) and the *ego* (the public and consciously known self). Psychoanalytic psychology can be interpreted as concerned with the effects of repressed desires (wants) and neurotic beliefs. The id could be viewed as repressed desires, and the superego as beliefs about social appropriateness and what constitutes moral behaviour, while the ego can be regarded as the decision-processing centre that checks and screens desires to ensure they fit some acceptable self-image. It is the job of the ego to reconcile the competing demands of the id and the superego. An *unconscious motive* in Freudian theory is one forbidden by the superego and not acknowledged by the conscious self.

Freudian psychology claims we can access the unconscious via slips of the tongue, depth interviewing and, most important, the analysis of dreams. In these ways, the relevant beliefs and desires can be discovered so that they can be confronted and exposed through rational argument, with the result that they lose their power over us. Dreams were considered the most important because they are places where socially unacceptable thoughts are most likely to occur, often in coded form. Freudian therapy assumes self-knowledge is possible since knowing about our desires and feelings is considered essential to the cure of neurosis. Freud, though, undermines our *trust* in self-knowledge since what we think are our real motives are not likely to be such. This is because the mind's eye does not have access to the unconscious, irrational part of the self. This lack of trust in self-knowledge is equally emphasized by psychologists studying the adaptive unconscious.

Defence mechanisms are the unconscious strategies of self-deception. For example, *rationalizations* protect the ego against the harsher aspects of reality.

166

Such rationalization is common in buying and can be a problem when asking consumers directly about their reasons for buying. This claim also finds support in studies of the adaptive unconscious.

There have been many deviations from Freud by his followers. Thus, Alfred Adler was convinced that the 'will to power' was as important as the sex drive in human motivation and believed that the frustration of the will to power gives rise to feelings of inadequacy and neurotic behaviour. Carl Jung formulated the concept of *archetypes* or inborn images held in common by all people, like the Hero, the Evil One, the Wise Old Man and so on. (Advertising sometimes seeks to link brands to such archetypes.)

In applying psychoanalytic psychology to marketing, the focus has been on identifying the *unconscious meanings* of a product which, once uncovered, reveal people's deepest motivations. The advertiser can then develop appeals that tap the buyer's deepest motivations. Freudian psychology holds that actions and things like goods and services can symbolize ('stand for') other things and, as a consequence, attract to themselves the emotions attached to what they symbolize. 'Rational' consciousness is enveloped by an irrational unconscious with rationality compromised.

Psychoanalytic psychology in marketing is associated with the advent of *motivation research* which focuses on the discovery of unconscious meanings attached to products. The discovery of these unconscious meanings allows advertisers to design appeals that tap the consumers' most basic motivations. The whole approach has its origins in Freud. Freud argued that there are *meanings* that are highly significant for human well-being that are obscured from immediate awareness. Predecessors of Freud regarded the unconscious as something ancillary to consciousness but Freud claimed just the opposite: the most important mental processes occur in the unconscious.[1] Freud conceptualized the unconscious as the storehouse of motivation: motivation enters into dreams and fantasies, slips of the tongue and neurotic symptoms. His *focus* was on the unconscious and 'irrational' elements in behaviour while his *method* of investigating the unconscious was through the interpretation of dreams and (only secondarily) through unstructured, free association interviews.

Motivation research and the name of Ernest Dichter are inseparable since his promotion of the technique in the 1950s.[2] Motivation research, whose heyday was in the 1950/60s, draws extensively on psychoanalytic psychology. Instead of a rational account of buying, motivation research seeks to reveal the 'real' buying impulses, urges, drives and feelings lying behind buying behaviour. For example, a motivation research study revealed that the 'real' reasons for the high percentage of repeat purchases of the same automobile were based on unconscious fears of automobiles as dangerous, powerful instruments, taking the form of fear of the unfamiliarity of a new make of car and fear of disloyalty to the

167

old car which had demonstrated its safety, as well as emotional attachment to the old car.

With motivation research it is common to use free association interviews where respondents give free rein to their thoughts to explore the symbolic meanings and hidden motives attached to buying a particular product. Alternatively, interviewers may use projective techniques or a structured approach in questioning followed by non-directive probes designed to elicit unconscious motives. In depth interviewing individuals are asked to recall their thoughts and actions in buying.

Projective techniques are commonly used in both interviews and focus groups. In the typical focus group about 3–10 participants or respondents assemble for an open-ended discussion of the product or brand. Projective techniques cover the inkblot test like the Rorschach test, sentence completion tests, graphic techniques like asking the respondent to draw a person or a house, and finally construction techniques like the Thematic Apperception Test (TAT). Projective techniques assume that the more ambiguous the stimulus, the greater the scope offered for respondents to project into their answers their real motivations and beliefs. The TAT technique is the one most commonly used, whereby the respondent constructs a story around some sketch or picture. The aim is to get respondents to talk freely and revealingly by asking them what is going on in the minds of the figures in the picture who (say) are about to consider buying a car or whatever product the researcher is interested in. Today focus groups routinely employ *projective techniques*. One classification of projective techniques is the following:

1 'association' techniques such as word association tests where the subject is presented with a word and asked to say immediately what it brings to mind;
2 'construction' techniques such as picture interpretations, where the respondent is asked to construct a story around a picture;
3 'completion' techniques such as sentence completion, where the subject is asked to complete a sentence(s) at high speed;
4 'expressive' techniques such as play therapy where the emphasis is on the way subjects express their emotions as they play.

A combination of focus groups, construction techniques and completion techniques are commonly used. For example, a bank interested in those taking out a mortgage gave each member of a focus group, composed of people seeking a mortgage, a drawing of two figures (a man and a woman) looking at advertisements for mortgage loans. Each respondent was asked to talk about what was going in the minds of the couple. At the same time they were asked to complete sentences such as the following: 'Buying a home, I worry most about . . .' and 'The worst thing about getting a home mortgage is . . .'

Dichter placed emphasis on the historical, social and contextual factors in buying and consumption behaviour but he is chiefly remembered today as tuning in to the sensual qualities of objects, e.g. the shape of a bar of soap in the hand.[3] He introduced the idea of products and brands having personalities and the importance of fantasy in consumer behaviour. David Ogilvy, in line with this, was to claim that it is not trivial product differences but the total personality of a brand that matters. His successful advertising involving the 'eye-patch' man for Hathaway shirts became the exemplar of this claim. It was Dichter who revived sales of the Betty Crocker cake mix by recommending an instruction to add eggs to the mix, so the housewife had a sense of creating the cake to assuage her 'guilt'.

The term 'motivation research' has almost fallen out of use but the ideas and approaches are still current. As we have already said, focus groups, together with projective techniques, are commonly used to uncover, if not unconscious motives in buying, then at least insights about buying. Advertisers have found many valid insights and useful metaphors from conducting such studies. For example, one study discovered that the pleasure in buying new consumer durables lies in their pristine condition and 'powers not weakened by use'. Another study offered the insight that habitual buying brings with it not only the avoidance of risk but also the comfort of 'predictable sameness' to balance the pressure of always seeking the novel. In *The Disciplines of Delight* Richards talks of the sameness in the habitual buy as pleasantly cohering with the fantasy of an endlessly plentiful maternal being who is neither weakened nor changed by repetitive demands and who never shocks by unwelcome surprise. This sort of metaphor enriches our thinking about buying. Similarly, brand loyalty becomes an affirmation of kinship and a demonstration of a bond to a powerful patriarch. For Wernick, the identities of major corporations, when attached to brands, evoke the fantasy of 'providing parents' who both nurture their offspring brands and look after those who buy them.[4] This again is a striking metaphor which captures some truth.

While the language of psychoanalytic psychology has spread into everyday use, among *psychiatrists* themselves, psychoanalytic psychology is in retreat with the growth in prestige of behavioural and psychopharmacological therapies. Anglo-American psychiatry has moved towards biomedical models of the mind where mental illness is regarded as a brain disorder with physical causes. While Freud's followers practise therapies based on verbal exchanges and interpretations of a patient's emotional past, bio-psychiatrists explore the medical histories of patients and their extended family, make laboratory tests and, most of all, prescribe pills. The rise of psychiatric pharmacotherapy is one of the most distinctive features of modern medicine.[5] Psychoanalysts have been excluded from psychopharmacology by both their basic perspective and their lack of knowledge about medication. However, among the numerous non-medically trained psychotherapists, Freudian techniques are still used, even if Freud's ideas receive a somewhat liberal interpretation.

169

Bio-psychiatrists are apt to treat Freud as unworthy of more than a passing glance to illustrate past error in the field. For many, Freud was just a fraud, his writings full of untestable theories and conceptual confusion, ignoring counterexamples, all amounting to chronic untruthfulness and aimed at parting credulous patients from their money. In a particularly damning book, Crews claims that Freud invented the data on which his major theories were based, that he lied about the outcome of treatments based on these theories and that he was simply a master of image management.[6] But to many people who read Freud, he is an interpreter of behaviour of the highest order and his insight about consciousness not being the major repository of what influences us is, through current interest in the adaptive unconscious, receiving more and more acceptance.[7]

Although the idea of the 'unconscious' is a legacy of Romanticism of the late eighteenth century, Freud developed the theory of the unconscious as a site of dynamic symbolic production. Freud's model or structure of the mind (the ego (conscious self) trying to balance the conflicting demands of the id (primitive and basic part of personality) and the superego (social conscience/integrity)) may be criticized but no other model has so far displaced it. Freud, contrary to common opinion, ceased to view unconscious fantasies as primarily aggressive or sexual, seeing them as also embracing a wide range of motives like the maintenance of self-esteem, security and so on. This is why motivation research was not just concerned with sexual connotations, as claimed. (One of the authors of this book who was a market research manager in the 1950s commissioned two motivation research studies: they were full of good marketing sense and certainly not confined to the sexual meanings of the company's products, contrary to current opinion.)

Psychoanalytic terminology and thinking are common in the humanities and in social science generally. Many social scientists find Freudian concepts such as inner conflicts, repression, wish-fulfilment and rationalization to be a matter of common experience and therefore demanding investigation. In response to the claim that the propositions of psychoanalytic psychology are not testable, many follow Freud in rejecting the utility of testing for establishing its value. They regard psychoanalysis not as a search for causes and effects but as a hermeneutical (interpretative) discipline, a search for a meaning in events.

While psychoanalysis itself remains controversial, the idea of unconscious forces affecting behaviour (buyer behaviour) has universal appeal. What can be said is that psychoanalytic explanations can 'make sense' and provide concepts we find useful. What has also come generally to be accepted is the idea of childhood experience affecting adult behaviour, sexuality as a pervasive drive and the idea of behaviour needing interpretation.[8] And many would accept that experience, as lived, is always a blend of fantasy, emotion, passion and imagination as well as hard rational calculation. If a psychology can only tell us what men and women respond to but not what they think or feel, or about the emotional conflicts they endure, then we have a dull and impoverished psychology.

170

Once we acknowledge that we are not always aware of our deepest needs and motivations (as we do not have access to the non-conscious processes that underlie many of our decisions), it follows that there will always be attempts to delve into the 'unconscious' mind. And, for those interested, Lear offers a very sympathetic account of Freud and a defence of non-doctrinaire forms of psychoanalysis.[9] He argues that the real attack on Freud is on the very idea that humans have unconscious motivation and that there is 'method in our madness' even when our actions appear weird and bizarre. A view initiated by Wittgenstein, the philosopher, is that psychoanalysis is essentially an interpretative system unlike the natural sciences which seek law-like generalizations. This is perhaps a useful way to approach psychoanalytic psychology.[10]

Ideas that have once made an impact and then suffer a decline tend to hibernate until a more favourable climate for their resurrection develops. Decline often comes about because we act as if ideas should exhibit the characteristics of scientific laws and be true or false. If an idea is shown to be wanting, progress demands it be discarded. But many ideas are contextually bound, like proverbs. It seems that, for every proverb, there is an equally defensible contradictory proverb ('too many cooks spoil the broth' versus 'many hands make light work'). Instead of just dismissing proverbs, and 'principles' in marketing and social science, we should just recognize that they are *objectively relative* in the sense that the appropriate application of the proverb or principle is relative to the context or situation but, nonetheless, can be objectively shown to be valid. None of us would have difficulty in recognizing a situation where the proverb 'too many cooks spoil the broth' should be applied and in distinguishing it from where the proverb 'many hands make light work' is appropriate.

ZALTMAN METAPHOR ELICITATION TECHNIQUE (ZMET): MOTIVATION RESEARCH UPDATED (?)

In this postmodern climate, it is not surprising to see a resurrection of Freudian influence. An example is Gerald Zaltman's ZMET.[11] Like Freudians, Zaltman claims people's deepest thoughts are non-conscious and it is these thoughts that account for their behaviour in the marketplace. For him, at least 95 per cent of the thinking that 'drives' behaviour occurs unconsciously and much of what we think of as conscious is really an after-the-fact construction (rationalization).[12] On this basis, he claims that consumers commonly buy products for reasons of which they are not conscious.

Basic for ZMET is the claim that unconscious thoughts are primarily visual. While thoughts must be represented in some way in the unconscious, it is by no means obvious that the process involves visual imagery. Since, as a matter of definition, we have no conscious access to the unconscious, claims about unconscious thought must inevitably be speculative. Even when we talk, it is a mystery

171

to all of us how, in speaking, things just come out. Zaltman assumes the unconscious is a hidden store of *visual metaphors* which influence behaviour.

Gibbs, a cognitive scientist, claims that much of our language is metaphorically structured, as is much of our cognition.[13] Gibbs argues that much of our conceptualization of experience is metaphorical and a great deal of our knowledge and thinking is constituted by metaphorical mappings from dissimilar sources and target domains. His work establishes the role of the metaphor in our thinking but it does not follow from this that our unconscious thoughts are visual. It is not even clear what evidence might be quoted to establish the validity of Zaltman's claim. ZMET, as a technique, relies, however, on this claim about visual images. Participants in studies collect pictures from magazines, catalogues or anywhere else that might capture their feelings about a product or brand; they then create a 'digital collage' with these images and record a short text about its meaning. The digital collage of images is a metaphor for the feelings and meanings evoked. In one study on Coca-Cola, Zaltman's team arrived at the conclusion that Coke evokes not just feelings of invigoration and sociability, as has been traditionally claimed, but 'feelings of calm, solicitude and relaxation as well'. He believes this finding distinguishes his method. If he is suggesting no other method would capture such a finding he is wrong. Those same feelings were also found in a study based on just listening to subjects 'talk off the top of their heads' before, during and after buying Coca-Cola. The analysis of the study referred to 'hedonic tone' or achieving inner harmony (a move away from tension), as reflected in such statements as 'After drinking I felt calm and relaxed'.[14]

Zaltman refers not to Freud but to the work of neuroscientists like Damasio as well as to semiotics as sources of his method. Although neuroscience does point to how much takes place at the non-conscious level, it does not license the claim that thought is visual while semiotics, defined as the study of all signs and the meanings they convey, is neutral on the matter. However, Zaltman does claim to be influenced by Carl Jung (1875–1961) who at one time was Freud's greatest disciple but parted from him over the Freudian focus on sexuality. Jung went on to develop analytical psychology and did a good deal of work on word association. Whatever ZMET turns out to be, its antecedents are tied more to Freud than to neuroscience. But ZMET cannot be regarded as a receiving-set tuned into the unconscious, capable of catching through its methods all relevant wavelengths emanating from consumer feelings. More fundamentally, we cannot infer from the consumer's actions either the conscious or unconscious feelings, wants and beliefs that enter into buying decisions. This is commonly forgotten elsewhere as well. In 1986 the FBI attended a public community dinner run by Palestinian students to celebrate Palestinian culture and politics. Although none of the FBI agents spoke a word of Arabic, this did not stop them making all sorts of dire inferences from the actions they observed, the 'tone' of the speeches, the music and the mood of the gathering. Fortunately, this type of nonsense was not accepted as evidence.[15]

Although consumers may act on feelings alone, following the likeability heuristic (just choosing on the basis of liking), they are apt to do some cognitive reflection about what they want, while the means they choose to satisfy that want depend on their beliefs. The ZMET consumer groups who did the collecting discussed the 'images during a two-hour private interview with a ZMET specialist' before going on to create 'a digital collage with their images and recorded a short text about its meaning'. The question arises as to what sort of training would make someone a specialist. It is not clear how anyone could be an expert in interpreting the data selected by the volunteer groups or how generalizing from such a non-random sample of data could be defended as a valid method for generalizing. In principle, interpretations of the images would be legion unless theoretical guidance is available, going well beyond simply dogmatic assertions about our deepest thoughts being unconscious and primarily visual. The so-called 'experts' imputed an interpretation based presumably on whatever ZMET suggested by way of theory. But whatever the interpretation of the studies, as with motivation research, inferences made depend crucially on the skills of the interpreter. Hacking makes a comment that is highly relevant:[16]

> To say that remembering is often of scenes, views, and feelings is not to imply that we remember in images or reproduce, internally, an image of a scene or an afterimage or interpretation of a feeling. We may do so, but we need not. Empirical psychology teaches that people are very different in the extent to which they (say they) visualize or form images.

But if Zaltman, a professor at the Harvard Business School, is ahead of the game, what are the implications? If Zaltman is right in thinking that the visual images in unconscious thought influence behaviour, it would suggest that advertising which draws on metaphor, particularly pictorial metaphor, will have less difficulty in getting the attention and interest of the target audience. Whatever the fact of the matter, ZMET does highlight the importance of visual metaphors in persuasion.

THE ADAPTIVE UNCONSCIOUS AND PERSUASION

Clinicians use the term 'consciousness' in three different senses: (a) our inner awareness of experiences; (b) our intentionally reacting to objects; and (c) knowledge of our conscious self.[17] In whatever way the term 'consciousness' is used, it contrasts with mental processes that happen outside awareness, that is in the unconscious. While the term 'consciousness' can have three *senses*, the term 'unconscious' has three distinct *meanings*: (a) that of being unconscious through disease or a brain injury; (b) that of being unconscious through being asleep; (c) that of being unconscious as the term is used in psychology, to mean that we are only aware of certain parts of our internal and external environment and are unconscious of the rest. As demonstrated by the electroencephalogram, these three states of unconsciousness are different organic states.[18]

Much that goes on in the human body, like breathing and blood circulation, occurs at the non-conscious level. While people acknowledge these non-conscious life-supporting mechanisms, they have difficulty in accepting that the non-conscious part of the mind, referred to as the unconscious mind, is other than a flawed library system or help-mate to the conscious mind.

Freud viewed the unconscious as having content that was once the content of consciousness: troubling memories and harmful fantasies, now repressed, yet still actively affecting conscious experience. The Freudian unconscious is guarded by a 'censor' which scans, interprets and screens the content of the memories for harmful material. Except for the less zealously guarded preconscious, this was Freud's concept of the unconscious and this is contrasted below with the more recent view of the *adaptive unconscious*.

Typical of a growing band of psychologists is Wilson, who claims the unconscious is at work in the higher-order mental processes of reasoning, making judgements, motivating and feeling, even in determining our personality.[19] Wilson's *Strangers to Ourselves: Discovering the Adaptive Unconscious* subscribes to the view that the unconscious is all-pervasive in human judgement, feelings, motives and behaviour; that we do not know ourselves very well mainly because much of what we would like to know about ourselves resides outside conscious awareness. If Wilson and others are right that the adaptive unconscious is a dominant force in thought and action, this limits the potential of introspection for self-understanding and also for understanding one's reasons for buying: no amount of introspection can cast light on the contents of an unconscious mind, not open to inspection.

IS THERE FREE WILL?

Wegner in his book *The Illusion of Conscious Will* goes so far as to suggest that whenever we explain our own actions as arising from conscious choice processes, we are practising *intention invention* because our actions emanate from countless causes of which we are unaware.[20] The trouble with this claim is that ex post facto we can never be sure about causes unless we are able to do a physical trace. If we focus on the neurological and physiological factors at work and split them up fine enough, there will always be causal chains and countless possible causes of a person's behaviour. We can never be sure we know the exact neurological/physiological causes of behaviour. This is why, in talking about (voluntary) actions, we talk about the reasons for action, leaving open the question of whether 'reasons' can be causes, and if so to what extent. That said, most philosophers today, according to Brown, a philosopher of science, hold that 'reasons are causes and reason explanations are causal explanations'.[21] And with notable exceptions, people are usually confident of knowing *the* reasons for their actions even if these are not the reasons made public. Bernard Williams, a distinguished philosopher, takes a different position, arguing that a person's motivational state (defined in terms of a person's beliefs and desires) should not be conceived as evidence for a person's conviction that it makes sense to act as he does.[22] For Williams, a person's motivational state does not cause his conviction but is *expressed* in that conviction, just as it is *expressed* in the action itself. Williams does not expand on this. Presumably, he is saying either that a person's conviction or action always characterizes a motivational state or that a person's conviction or action always communicates a motivational state. In either case, Williams is suggesting that there is a conceptual relationship between motivational state, conviction and action, rather than a causal relationship.

Wegner denies free choice or will, echoing classical conditioning theory. If he was correct, much of marketing would have to be reworked and rational choice theory, which assumes conscious rationality, discarded. The denial relies heavily on experiments where subjects press a button as they choose while simultaneously recording the time of their decision. Subjects take 0.2 seconds on average to press the button after choosing to do so. However, an electroencephalograph monitoring their brain waves indicates that the subjects' brains exhibited a spike of brain activity 0.3 seconds before they chose to press the button. It seems the unconscious chose to press the button before the conscious mind decided to go ahead. In other words the 'will' kicked in after the brain started preparation for action.

The problem is one of interpretation. Interpretation is tied to understanding the basis of the inference which in this case rests on the *method of agreement*. This canon argues that if AB precedes E, AC precedes E, AD precedes E, etc., then A, the spike of brain activity, being the one antecedent factor common in all instances, is causally connected to E, the decision to go ahead. The method of agreement depends on having a large number of instances that are different in all respects but one. It attempts to establish that A is a *sufficient condition* for E. If A is a sufficient condition for E, then if A occurs E always follows. Thus, if a sales manager employed a sales supervisor in a number of different regions and in each place labour turnover increased to a greater extent than elsewhere or previously, the manager might conclude the supervisor was to blame.

The difficulty lies in ensuring the agreement is in one respect only, since the method cannot distinguish between true cause and mere coexistence. We can never be sure, for example, that some additional factor was not at work in each sales region to which the supervisor was appointed. The Wegner experiment makes the assumption that *all* the relevant brain activity is being detected and

175

measured, a very big assumption. The relationship can be expressed as: antecedent variable (Z) (unconscious brain activity) *causes* the subject's decision (X), which, as a consequence, *causes* the dependent variable (Y) (pressing the button). Thus we have: *unconscious brain activity (Z)* $\rightarrow$ *subject's conscious decision (X)* $\rightarrow$ *pressing the button (Y)*. X, the conscious decision, which people typically assume to be an independent cause, takes the role of an intervening variable that intervenes between Z and Y; that is, Z operates via X to affect Y. It assumes that Z (the unconscious brain activity) is not a sufficient condition in itself to cause Y (pressing the button). If Z were in fact a sufficient condition for X, and X a sufficient condition for Y, then Z would be a sufficient condition for Y, which would make the postulating of X (subject's conscious decision) redundant. It is such reasoning that suggests consciousness X is an epiphenomenon, that is a by-product of neural processes which exert no influence in producing the subsequent behaviour Y. On these grounds, it is claimed that there is no freedom of choice or freedom of will.

Epiphenomenalism, as we have seen, is the doctrine that conscious mental phenomena are entirely caused by (physical) neurological phenomena in the brain but these conscious mental phenomena do not themselves have any effects, either physical or mental: consciousness is simply the side-effect of causal processes lying outside consciousness. On this basis, no *subjective* experience would have any significance for behaviour. Dreams are indisputably epiphenomena in that we assume these merely accompany biochemical and neurological events during sleep but have no causal efficacy. Behaviourism assumes epiphenomenalism in viewing consciousness as simply the epiphenomenal offshoot of bodily activity. Those in sociology who view social contextual factors as all-determining are adhering to an epiphenomenalist position. For example, we have the 'Strong Programme' in the sociology of knowledge which asserts that even the content of scientific theories is caused by social factors rather than scientific thinking.[23] These sociologists would have us believe that sociological inquiry is 'in a better position to deliver truth about science than science is to deliver truth about the world'.[24]

If we confine our research to the computer-like functions of the brain (which some cognitive psychologists do), there is support for epiphenomenalism. However, computer-like functions are not what distinguishes humans. As Modell says, *subjective* human experience must be part of any scientific explanation of how the mind works.[25] He rejects the idea that mental functioning can be equated with some form of computation as the *construction of meaning* is not the same as information processing.

As an alternative interpretation, if we assume that Z (unconscious brain activity) is an antecedent variable that operates through X (subject's conscious decision) to produce Y (pressing the button), it may be that Z's association with X is one of *arousing* the conscious mind and inputting data. It could be that, when subjects are thinking about pressing buttons, the unconscious mind goes into gear with the conscious mind then pressing the accelerator. But the fact that activity in the brain precedes any conscious decision does not show that, once the conscious mind is activated, it has no causal control over behaviour or is not in a position to change whatever is received from the unconscious, making the action taken dependent on the conscious mind. This is not to suggest X, the intervening conscious decision, is always necessary for activating behaviour since people can act without reflection. In other words, a person may go along with the positive or negative feeling aroused by Z. On the other hand, the initial disposition to go along with Z might be blocked by the intervention of X ('On second thoughts I don't think I will'). We often catch ourselves on 'automatic pilot', having to 'collect our wits' to stop us using, say, the car key to get into the house.

While we are willing to accept that the various roles we adopt in life such as parent, supervisor or consumer influence what we do, we nonetheless feel we are not bound to do what the desires of adaptive unconscious would have us do, since we feel we could have done otherwise. We are like chess players writ large, bound by the rules of chess but choosing our own individual tactics within the rules.[26]

Does the adaptive unconscious dominate?

Wilson's book *Strangers to Ourselves* makes claims for the dominance of the unconscious. He uses the word 'modern' to label what he has to say, giving the impression that he is describing current, accepted orthodoxy. Wilson ignores serious dissenters like John Searle who claims that all bona fide mental states are conscious mental states.[27] For Searle, there are no unconscious mental states but simply non-conscious neural states and processes. Searle rejects the idea that the unconscious acts on 'rules' that are inaccessible in principle to consciousness.

Wilson and Nisbett are pioneers in promoting and researching the claim about the pervasive power of the unconscious in thought and action.[28] Wilson defines the unconscious as a mental process that is inaccessible to consciousness but impacts on judgements, feelings and behaviour. This definition is theory-loaded as it reflects a theoretical position which others like Searle would not accept. In any case there is vagueness about the word 'inaccessible'. It is true that I cannot remember something that has been forgotten just because I want to do so. In this sense unconscious memory is inaccessible. But many memories we try to recall we usually do recall, unless age or illness has reduced the ability. There are also tactics that help us extract 'lost' memories. But just as important is the way a memory is recalled. As Margalit points out, moral emotions largely motivate us through the *way* they are remembered since it is this that energizes the memory.[29]

Although denying that the conscious mind is an epiphenomenon, Wilson endorses Wegner and Wheatley who argue that the experience of a conscious will is often an illusion.[30] The use of the words 'experience' and 'often' makes this statement hard to pin down. We have a sense not of 'experiencing' free will but only of 'exercising' free will, and we feel free to do that anytime unless addicted. We can also imagine satisfying our desire for instant gratification while having the desire not to have this desire. Is this a case of not having free will? Wegner and Wheatley argue that, because a thought is followed by an action in line with the thought, it does not demonstrate that the thought is the cause of the action. The relationship between thought and action can be spurious since both thought and action may result from antecedent happenings in the adaptive unconscious. This is indeed a logical possibility but it ignores how thoughts can be deliberated and concepts manipulated in the conscious mind to arrive at new thoughts and decisions. This is not to deny that we may at times do whatever first comes to mind. Wilson's own position, he claims, is between the two extremes of consciousness-as-the-chief-executive and consciousness-as-epiphe-nomenal-press-secretary. Any reader who has read much mental philosophy will have a sense of déjà vu as psychologists come to grips with this issue.[31] Wilson usefully contrasts the adaptive unconscious with consciousness.

First, the adaptive unconscious consists of multiple systems in the form of a collection of modules that perform independent functions at the non-conscious level. On the other hand, consciousness is a single, solitary mental system, not a collection of different modules. Unless people suffer from multiple personality syndrome, they possess only one conscious self. Wilson does not quote any evidence for this statement. Although it is not in the province of psychology to supply the evidence, the physiological evidence should have been given. The evidence in fact is not unequivocal. In his book *Of Two Minds: the Revolutionary Science of Dual-Brain Psychology*,[32] Schiffer claims we do in fact have two minds or two consciousnesses, not just one brain that is split, each consciousness having a different degree of maturity and each associated with the left or the right brain. Schiffer demonstrates his thesis with experiments, some of which we can carry out on ourselves, for example, showing we can experience different moods by closing off one conscious mind as opposed to the other.

Second, Wilson argues that the adaptive unconscious is an on-line detector of patterns in the environment, acting as quickly as possible to signal whether something is good or bad. Among others, Damasio's work supports the claim that everything we encounter is evaluated as good or bad within a quarter of a second.[33] We often react emotionally before there is time to consciously interpret and evaluate incoming material. Wilson contrasts this immediate unconscious reaction with the role of consciousness as an 'after-the-fact-checker'.

Third, the adaptive unconscious focuses on the here and now whereas the long view requires the involvement of consciousness to do the mental simulation involved in planning. Is Wilson being consistent here? If the focus of the adaptive unconscious is on the here and now, how does Wilson reconcile this with his statements about the adaptive unconscious being involved in planning and goal setting? Planning as a process is *par excellence* a process of looking ahead to see what needs to be done. It is so much a part of the human condition that human beings can be defined as planning agents looking beyond the here and now.

Fourth, the unconscious undertakes automatic (fast, unintentional) processes as opposed to the controlled (slow/intentional) processing occurring in consciousness. This claim is consistent with Damasio but is it consistent with the extravagant claims Wilson makes about the role of the unconscious? Is it consistent with Wilson's claim that the adaptive unconscious 'plays a major executive role in our mental lives. It gathers information, interprets and evaluates it, and sets goals in motion, quickly and efficiently'?[34] It is difficult to evaluate Wilson's claims since there is a pervasive vagueness about the *referential* meaning (what exactly it refers to) of most of the terms used to express his thesis, as if these concepts were all unproblematic.

Fifth, Wilson argues that the unconscious tends to rigidity in bending information to fit preconceptions, making it next to impossible to realize that our preconceptions are wrong. The study he quotes to support this is well known. It is a study where students were arbitrarily classified on an IQ basis. Subsequent teacher behaviour and assessments of the students became a self-fulfilling prophecy cohering with the IQ scores arbitrarily given. This study would seem to indicate that the teacher's prior preconceptions about the students could be completely uprooted by information from a credible source, regardless of contrary observable evidence. But this study can also be interpreted as supportive of the claim that preconceptions need not lead to biasing the interpretation of new information to cohere with preconceptions, but that preconceptions can be uprooted by changing expectations through new information.

Sixth, non-conscious skills such as implicit learning can appear before children have acquired the ability to reason at the conscious level. It is probably true that we can learn 'how' skills before we can learn 'why' in terms of explanation. This is true not just in the case of children.

Seventh, it is claimed that the unconscious is more sensitive to negative information while consciousness is more sensitive to positive information. There is evidence that positive and negative information is processed in different parts of the brain. It may be that negative information is more likely to involve the emotional centres of the brain, such as the amygdala, than is positive information. This may explain the separate processing.

The adaptive unconscious and personality

Wilson argues that it makes little sense to talk about a 'single' self as the adaptive unconscious and the conscious self have different patterns of responding to the social world. There are two selves. On this basis, he rejects the idea of our having just a single personality while arguing that the prediction of behaviour on the basis of current personality measures is further stymied by the influence of the social situation in shaping people's behaviour, independent of personality. For Wilson, the failure of personality measures to predict behaviour (and this has been generally true in marketing and in advertising appealing to certain personality types) is tied to our having both an adaptive self and a conscious self. The unconscious self impacts more on our uncontrolled, veiled responses, whereas the consciously constructed self influences our deliberative, explicit responses. As Wilson says, someone's 'self-theory' that she is shy and introverted can be at odds with her adaptive unconscious which over time may have become quite extroverted. Personality is more likely to reside in the adaptive unconscious. Personality, under the control of the adaptive unconscious, is more likely to explain and predict spontaneous, quick 'impulse buys'. In contrast, the deliberated decision to go ahead and purchase a particular house is more likely to fall under the control of conscious self-attributed motives. This suggests that while purchases made under the control of the adaptive unconscious are likely to be justified by rationalizations, the reasons given for deliberated purchases are more likely to encompass 'real' reasons.

Wilson explicitly rejects the doctrine of epiphenomenalism, that consciousness is simply an incidental effect of neural processes and not a cause of thought or action. Yet the impression he gives is that the unconscious mind is all-dominant. For instance, he uses the metaphor of the snowball as representing the conscious mind with the massive iceberg of the adaptive unconscious hidden from view. This is analogous to talking about 99 per cent of our DNA being shared with the apes as if each percentage were of equal significance and as if DNA were everything when it cannot do anything on its own. Similarly, the wording of the assertions made by Wilson creates the impression that the adaptive unconscious is the key force in all behaviour. Yet no one has laid out the full range of thoughts and actions in a way that would allow us to talk confidently about what is likely to be responsible for what. The studies quoted, the usual experiments on college students, do not severely test Wilson's assertions since other interpretations of the studies are possible and need to be explored. The few neurological experiments quoted are more impressive but less relevant to the wider claims made.

It is true that not all actions are deliberated. Many choices more resemble 'picking behaviour' than deliberated actions. In picking behaviour, we have reason to make a choice but no particular reason to make a specific choice.[35] Just as a consumer, when faced with a shelf of detergents, may simply pick at random, being indifferent to any distinctions between them, so people may on occasion just act as the mood takes them. It is doubtful whether such behaviour can be ascribed to a submission to the adaptive unconscious; it may be more a conscious decision not to make the effort needed to make a more reasoned choice.

The Freudian versus the adaptive unconscious

Before Freud, the unconscious was viewed as something ancillary to consciousness. Freud claimed it was just the opposite in that the most important mental processes occur in the unconscious.[36] Wilson shares this opinion. He speaks of 'the adaptive unconscious' in order to emphasize that non-conscious thinking is an evolutionary adaptation and also to distinguish it from Freud's unconscious which he regards as too limited – too limited even though he claims that Freud's greatest insight was to recognize the pervasiveness of non-conscious thinking. What then justifies talk about Freud's limited view? Wilson, like some other psychologists, sees a far more vast unconscious system, different from that imagined by Freud. He does not deny that there may be dynamic forces keeping unpleasant thoughts out of awareness as in Freud's concept of repression. But Freud believed that access to the unconscious was possible. Wilson claims the unconscious mind is closed to consciousness: a black box, while he hints that there are ways of discovery like projective techniques. But where Wilson and Freud differ most is in the actual functions attributed to the unconscious. Wilson credits the unconscious with functions most of us would regard as the exclusive province of the conscious mind:

1   sizing up the world and warning of dangers. The ability to bypass the conscious so as to assess the environment quickly can on occasion be a matter of survival. This has the support of neuroscientists. Both Damasio[37] and LeDoux[38] demonstrate that the initial appraisal of things that are tied to our values or core concerns is non-conscious, and may be at variance with the more reflective (conscious) appraisal that occurs subsequently;

2   learning unconsciously. Although we think in terms of consciously making an effort to learn, a good deal of learning is unconscious. The traditional view of *conditioning* was that it occurred unconsciously but it is now more or less accepted that operant conditioning is unlikely to occur without conscious awareness, making the label 'operant conditioning' no longer appropriate.[39] *Incidental* learning is a candidate for unconscious learning when it occurs without reward, effort or purpose, as can result, say, from watching ads on television. There is also learning from *imitating* others. This can be a matter of consciously copying, as viewers might copy some celebrity on TV; or it can be unconscious learning when the imitation is

181

an after-effect of watching. Wilson points to studies that show subjects non-consciously learning rules that would be very difficult to learn consciously. It is also true that we can learn unconsciously to like something that has become familiar. Thus repeated exposure to a brand or an ad for a brand leads to familiarity and with familiarity comes increased liking that occurs at the unconscious level;

3 setting goals. Wilson quotes Bargh *et al.* who argue that events in the environment can give rise to goals and give direction to behaviour, all outside consciousness.[40] There is no doubt that we can find ourselves strongly disposed to move in a certain direction. However, because unconscious forces press us in a certain direction, are we justified in claiming this is setting goals and giving direction to behaviour? The setting of goals is a purposeful activity that can only be done deliberately, that is consciously. It is a category mistake to place an unconscious activity within a category that belongs to conscious activity – unless we are speaking metaphorically which Wilson does not appear to be doing;

4 interpreting and evaluating. We can instantaneously interpret and evaluate incoming information. People have *chronic ways* of interpreting and evaluating situations and Wilson claims these interpretations and evaluations are the ones likely to be acted upon. This does happen as we are creatures of habit but the question arises as to its incidence. After all, we have 'gut' reactions that are not acted upon because the conscious mind comes into play to assess the wisdom of the impulse. It may be, however, that we are prepared to go along with most unconscious assessments because most are inconsequential. Wilson argues that in our reactions to others, first impressions emanating from unconscious evaluations are likely to dominate as this 'gut feel' is not in competition with rival conscious assessments at the time. This is an important point as it can lead to bias, say, in interviews and similar situations like selecting a service provider. Wilson, like other psychologists, uses the metaphor of the 'immune system', saying our psychological immune system uses a 'feel good' criterion when it comes to interpreting and evaluating information. This psychological immune system is applied to rationalize, discount and limit all sorts of trauma. People have *chronic ways* of interpreting and evaluating situations and Wilson claims these are the ones likely to be acted upon. People tend to bias their interpretations to enhance a sense of well-being and this bias is built into the adaptive unconscious. It may also be built into the conscious mind since people also *consciously* interpret and evaluate in the way that most promotes their ego, viewpoint and preferences. We are commonly unaware of these biases and we cannot just decide to eliminate them;

5 generating feelings. Wilson claims that the adaptive unconscious not only selects what to consider, and interprets and evaluates it, but also 'feels'.[41] It is not quite clear what this means since we have no access to the unconscious to know whether it feels or not. If this is a shorthand for saying the adaptive unconscious generates feelings, it can be accepted;

6 initiating action. Wilson illustrates how the unconscious can initiate action by quoting the well-known case reported by Claparède.[42] Each time Claparède, a physician, visited a woman with amnesia, she was unable to recall seeing him before and he had to reintroduce himself. On one occasion he concealed a pin in his hand which pricked her when they shook hands and this led her to withdraw her hand quickly. Next time he visited the woman she still did not recognize him but refused to shake his hand. This case is used to demonstrate how information can come from the unconscious, resulting in action being taken without any conscious awareness of what was happening. Another demonstration (not quoted by Wilson) of how the unconscious can control action without conscious awareness is found in attempts to get workers to break their old skills so that improved methods can be adopted. Mowrer showed that making a worker carry out the old skill in a conscious and deliberate way was a method of eliminating it as workers found it difficult to remember what to do.[43] Men who wear bow ties and tie them themselves find the task difficult when asked to tie one slowly for others to follow. A skill that has been delegated to unconscious control can be lost on consciousness.

Wilson acknowledges that the adaptive unconscious captures much of the received wisdom on the unconscious: (a) lower-order mental processes occur outside consciousness; (b) non-conscious information processing can occur while the conscious mind is dealing with something else; (c) the unconscious can make much thinking habitual; (d) the unconscious uses stereotypes to categorize and evaluate people and this can lead to prejudiced judgements; (e) the unconscious can produce feelings and preferences of which people are unaware; (f) central parts of our personalities remain hidden in the non-conscious self, so we do not have access to aspects of who we are. Wilson argues that basic processes of perception, memory and language comprehension are in the unconscious and cannot be accessed by the conscious mind, not because this would be anxiety provoking as Freud believed, but simply because they are not accessible to conscious awareness. Judgements, feelings, motives and so on occur outside conscious awareness for reasons of efficiency, not because of repression which was Freud's view.

Although Wilson's view of the unconscious as not consisting of any single entity leads him to reject the view of mind as a single 'homunculus', the absence of any explanation of how the unconscious carries out these processes raises the

183

spectre of Gilbert Ryle's mocking rejection of the distinction between 'mind' and 'matter', and the description of such Cartesian dualism as the dogma of 'the Ghost in the Machine'.[44]

How the adaptive unconscious 'decides' priorities

How does the adaptive unconscious 'decide' what is important (and what is not) so as to allow priorities to be determined, e.g. whether even to look at an ad. Wilson draws on the concept of 'accessibility', that is whether information in the memory can be activated or energized. This, in turn, depends on: (a) self-relevance of the information; (b) how recently the information has been entertained; (c) how often the information had been used in the past since usage facilitates recall. Whatever concerns us is likely to be accessible in that it will be self-relevant and will have been thought about both recently and often in the past. Anything that seriously concerns us is the key factor in emotion genera-tion[45] so the adaptive unconscious is likely to be sensitive to emotional matters and give them accessibility. This suggests the adaptive unconscious will decide on ground that is emotionally anchored.

Our adaptive unconscious harbours not only stereotypes but also representa-tions of specific people who, for better or worse, have influenced our lives. Thus if a person, for example, has a fond memory of a parent, he or she will have a positive reaction to those who are like that parent and vice versa. There may be a 'generalized' stereotype of a baby, mother, father, brother or friend which may equally evoke positive reactions.

Motives reflect values. Wilson suggests that the motives or goals that are most important in life and are embedded in the adaptive unconscious are the desires for affiliation (friendship, intimacy, mutual understanding), achievement (to do something better than has been done before) and power (concern for having a strong impact on others). These are the three 'need categories' of human motives developed by McClelland and popularized in the 1960/70s in texts on organi-zational behaviour.[46] McClelland assumed these motives were learned (as opposed to being inborn), perhaps through early conditioning, and that just one of them would dominate in any one individual, even if situational factors might operate to modify the reaction. Although the idea of *unconscious* conditioning is now being challenged, it is surely reasonable to assume that some conditioning is uncon-scious. (Students in experiments may be aware of being conditioned but such awareness is less likely among others.) Wilson does not discuss conditioning but it is reasonable to assume that it can be one way of influencing the unconscious. We think this is so.

While McClelland has been criticized for assuming just one dominant motive, the major criticism has revolved around the method (projective techniques, namely the TAT or Thematic Apperception Test) used to find which motive dominates. In the TAT the subject is given a number of black and white pictures of various settings, each capable of being interpreted in many ways. The subject is asked to tell a story about each picture. These stories are analysed for the 'themes' introduced and these are assumed to tap the subject's deep needs/ motives. Wilson shows no qualms about the test's validity but argues that the TAT assesses motives captured in the adaptive unconscious, whereas self-report measures assess self-attributed motives or people's conscious theories about their needs. These may differ from their non-conscious needs. Thus Wilson seems to agree with those using projective techniques that this is one way in which the content of the unconscious might be leaked even if the conscious mind cannot directly access the unconscious.

If the adaptive unconscious dominates, brand ads should be associated (where possible or appropriate) with having an increased impact on others, achieving more than has been done before, or getting on better with others. All this suggests investigating which motive is most likely to be dominant (affiliation, achievement or power) in our target audience and using ad appeals that cater to such motives while at the same time paying some attention to the motives which are self-attributed in answers to questionnaires. If there is no one dominant motive, advertisers might appeal at various times to each of the three motives. McClelland regarded his list of motives as learned, not innate like the motives to satisfy biological and safety needs, and different societies are likely to emphasize one rather than another. Other motives, too, may be innate. For example, the motives that attract people to religion seem to have more to do with innate motives such as the desire for immortality, the horror of oblivion, and the wish to move away from isolation and loneliness to a supportive group of similar mind.

For Wilson the adaptive unconscious interprets and judges in a way that reinforces a view of reality that gives most pleasure; that is, the criterion at work in interpretation is a 'feel good' criterion. What ads are likely to make the consumer feel good? The adaptive unconscious focuses on instant gratification which suggests offering in the ad something here and now to give pleasure. But this cannot be the whole story since people need to be realistic even if it does not make them feel good: it would be silly for the adaptive unconscious to interpret the growl of a wild lion nearby as a sign of liking. Wilson talks later in *Strangers to Ourselves* of promoting personal well-being. This seems more apt. He argues that people promote their sense of well-being by assessments that exaggerate their superiority to others. This implies that the adaptive unconscious is open to ads that reinforce the target audience's sense of well-being and superiority. (A unifying appeal to the nation about its superiority vis-à-vis opposing nations is a well-known propaganda device for enlisting support for narrow nationalism.) This desire to feel good about ourselves can be in conflict with the need for accuracy, and Wilson admits that accuracy tends to be sacrificed if self-deception helps to maintain a positive view of ourselves and to be optimistic about the future.

185

Wilson claims that some aspects of the self-concept are located in the adaptive unconscious and other aspects in consciousness. As a consequence, conflict may arise between unconscious motives and conscious motives, leading to inconsistency in behaviour and less emotional well-being.

In *The Illusion of Conscious Will* Wegner points out that when a neurologist causes a limb to jerk, the patient often says he meant to move that limb and invents reasons why this was so. Such post hoc invented explanations are termed 'confabulations' and are common in such circumstances. Pascal (1623–62) illustrates this by pointing out that if someone arrives at a belief in God by choosing to be conditioned into it because he fears there is even a small risk that there may be a hell, he will also come to believe that it was the wisdom and benevolence of God that set him on the road to believing. People naturally seek a rational explanation of behaviour which appears non-rational. But does this mean that confabulations are the norm? People 'need' to feel they are in control of what they do and invent reasons to satisfy that need but accepting that this is so does not give any licence for the claim that, *in general*, people's reasons for their behaviour are inventions. It is difficult to see how people could survive if self-explanations of behaviour were generally confabulations.

Wilson supports Wegner by drawing on neurological studies involving split brain patients, carried out by Gazzaniga and LeDoux, to illustrate how we make up reasons for our behaviour when access to the real reasons is not available.[47] Gazzaniga and LeDoux argue that all of us are disposed to confabulate explanations, since the conscious verbal self (left hemisphere) often does not know why we do what we do and thus creates the explanation that makes most sense. Wilson endorses the 'hunch' of Gazzaniga and LeDoux that people often give explanations of their behaviour without realizing these are confabulations: 'that our conscious selves often do not know the causes of our responses and thus have to confabulate reasons'.[48] The term 'confabulation' in psychology refers to making up details or an unconscious act in which falsification serves as a defence mechanism. In particular, we are likely to confuse cause with non-causal antecedent, as in using a placebo. Given Wilson's claim that much, or even most, behaviour is initiated by unconscious motives and unconscious understandings of the world and occurs without conscious monitoring, it follows that the reasons given for our behaviour may be largely fabrications. More specifically, given that many judgements, emotions, thoughts and behaviours are produced by the adaptive unconscious and people do not have access to the unconscious, their conscious selves make up reasons for why they responded as they did.

The normal criticisms of marketing research pale by comparison with this attack that says the answers to questions about reasons for buying and so on are commonly meaningless rationalizations. Since Gazzaniga and LeDoux acknowledged their hypothesis was mere speculation, Wilson has to back his claim. He does this by quoting a study conducted by him and Nisbett[49] where the students in an experiment agreed that noise had lessened their enjoyment of a film when other evidence suggested it had not. This study is not convincing, not just because it is so far removed from being representative, but because the group subject to the noise were likely in the circumstances to have felt obligated initially to rate enjoyment high but were in fact affected by the noise which they acknowledged later. Without being a participant it is hard to identify what contextual pressures were at work that are relevant to giving socially appropriate answers. But even assuming unconscious imperatives trigger behaviour without awareness, reasons given for that behaviour need not be confabulated. Like Sherlock Holmes, people employ abduction to reason back from the context and memory to reason back to the best explanation. Wilson quotes George Kelly with approval. Yet it was George Kelly who viewed man as acting like a scientist:

> Might not the individual man, each in his own personal way, assume more of the stature of a scientist, ever seeking to predict and control the course of events with which he is involved? Would he not have his theories, test his hypotheses, and weigh his experimental evidence?[50]

On the basis of the evidence quoted by Wilson, it cannot be claimed that most reasons people give for their actions are confabulations. If they were, the implications for social trust would be immense.

To what extent do dispositional pressures from the adaptive unconscious bypass the conscious so as to evade evaluation and revision? Wilson simply says that the adaptive unconscious is responsible for a 'good deal' of our behaviour while agreeing that people also possess a conscious self that directs behaviour, 'at least sometimes'.[51] As this sentence suggests, there is a reluctance to credit much behaviour to the conscious mind. Words like 'a good deal' suggest the adaptive unconscious predominates while 'at least sometimes' suggests consciousness has a minimal role. In terms of the evidence quoted (and that quoted by others elsewhere) this is not in the least justified. Wilson later backs off to some extent, saying that there may be relatively few cases in which a response is only the output of the adaptive unconscious or only the output of the conscious. If this is so, do they work in tandem or sequentially, with the conscious mind taking inputs from the unconscious to evaluate, reject or incorporate? Wilson is silent on this question. He plays with epiphenomenalism when he says that it may be unconscious 'intention' that causes both the conscious thought and action. If this were so, conscious thought would simply be an epiphenomenon. In terms of Wilson's thesis and to use his own words, he has a 'chronically accessible trait' to see only the adaptive unconscious at work: *Strangers to Ourselves* is heavy on claims but weak on justification.

Wilson speculates that despite the vast amount of information people have, he 'suspects' their explanations of their responses to be no more accurate than those of a complete stranger who lives in the same culture would be. Without first documenting the possible range of responses this cannot be justified. In any case much depends on what we mean by 'cause', a concept that Wilson seems to think is unproblematic.

If reasons for action are causes, then strangers would find it next to impossible to deduce both motives and beliefs (reasons) from action alone. If we are talking about contextual influences, the stranger may be as good as the individual but this (Humean) sense of cause is only appropriate where cause X and effect Y are contiguous in time and place. On the other hand, if we are taking account of both contextual factors and knowledge of a person's personality to *simulate* the total situation, it may well be that strangers are good at explaining responses. But Wilson's hypothesis may amount to no more than that his own adaptive unconscious is offering a safe harbour for epiphenomenalism which pops up whenever there is doubt about the intervention of the active, conscious mind. Perhaps Fodor is right when he says that practically all experimental psychologists continue to be behaviourists of one kind or other but have just ceased to notice that they are.[52]

Wilson endorses the idea of our having unconscious feelings that contradict conscious feelings. He quotes as an example that I may say, 'I love my horse' when in fact I may hate it. There is a confusion here. When I say 'I love my horse' I am simply expressing a belief which may or may not be true. On the other hand, love is an emotion. Having 'emotions' can mean: (a) having a latent disposition to have certain types of experience, like having a latent disposition to love someone; or (b) having the experiences themselves. When we love a horse, the experience is not something ongoing but something that is aroused on certain occasions. In other words, we are not constantly conscious of what we love. Hence we fall back, when asked, on our beliefs which may at the time have no felt emotion to draw on, so we draw on default beliefs for an answer. Emotional feelings are aroused by highly negative or positive appraisals of some action, event or attribute and we do not undertake such appraisals all the time in front of a loved one.

Wilson argues that the adaptive unconscious might produce feelings independently of people's conscious thoughts about their feelings. He draws on *self-perception theory* which asserts that people's beliefs and attitudes are commonly determined by observation of their own behaviour: just as we judge the feelings of others from observing their behaviour, we also infer our own attitudes from self-observation. Wilson cites a well-known experiment in which the experimental group was injected with epinephrine which produces physiological arousal in the sympathetic nervous system. This experimental group seemed to be the most amused by the film in the experiment as they laughed and smiled the most while watching it. When the experimenters asked participants to rate how funny the film was and how much they enjoyed it, the responses of the experimental group were no different from that of the control groups. Wilson's interpretation of this experiment was that the adaptive unconscious inferred the film was funny because they laughed a lot but, when actually asked how funny the film was, people based their responses on their personal theories about their liking for this type of film: 'the adaptive unconscious felt one way whereas people's conscious selves feel differently'.[53] Again, we can dispute this interpretation. Did the student participants in the experimental group naively believe they were simply injected with a vitamin compound? If someone finds himself laughing at a film, will his adaptive unconscious, of necessity, attribute it to the film being funny or is he simply in a good mood and so predisposed to laugh in order to experience a sense of sharing with the people around? Self-perception theory is meant to explain how we might change attitudes or beliefs by first changing behaviour rather than the other way round. Hence it suggests that advertising might focus on getting members of the target audience to act in a way that favours the brand, like writing for a sample, taking a test drive and so on.

Affective forecasting

In reaching a buying decision, consumers commonly have expectations about the emotional consequences of doing this rather than that: we arrive at a belief that one brand rather than another or one product rather than another will give us pleasure. This happens all the time in, say, buying a car. Psychologists discuss this topic under the heading of 'affective forecasting'. Wilson draws on the evidence in psychology to suggest that we all tend to overestimate both the intensity and the duration of future emotional hurt or joy. This means that the pleasure we anticipate before a purchase can differ from that experienced when the product is bought. We can even 'miswant': we may dream of a special holiday and find we miss the routines of everyday life. Affective forecasting has 'durability biases', a tendency to overestimate the duration of positive or negative reactions to events in the future. This overestimating serves the function of motivating consumers to take action.

In buying, the pleasure from a purchase tends to be less than expected. In the same way, people cannot dwell on a loss or disappointment for ever. This is all true. Nonetheless, any deep loss or disappointment has a habit of giving rise to recurrent recalls of the emotion: certain losses or disappointments leave emotional scars, lasting longer than physical ones. This is because losses and disappointments have a strong emotional impact (e.g. being denied an expected promotion), and greater staying power than corresponding gains (e.g. achieving the promotion).[54] Any humiliation suffered can plague us, to be relived throughout life, so it is not clear what is meant by saying the emotion will not last as long as expected. It is often harder to forget than it is to remember. Just as we feel a loss more than an equivalent gain, the staying power of a loss emotion is longer than that arising from some corresponding gain. This is not to deny that we typically over-estimate the duration of both joy and grief but simply to say it is not some scientific law.

If the adaptive unconscious has preferences which cannot be accessed directly, consumers cannot undertake introspection to discover all the attributes wanted at the unconscious level and their weightings for relative importance. Wilson thus dismisses models such as the multiattribute model on the ground that people are not fully aware of their preferences in advance. On these grounds, consumers should recognize that their reasons for buying may not fully capture *the* reasons at work so they can be misled by following any procedure that lists the attributes sought and weights them for importance to arrive at the relative scores for the alternatives considered. Wilson quotes Goethe (1749–1832) with approval: 'He who deliberates lengthily will not always choose the best.'

Wilson 'tests' Goethe's hunch in a study of people engaged in choosing a work of art. Those who analysed why they liked or disliked each of the five art posters seemed to lose sight of which one they really liked best. We agree with Wilson in his criticism of models like the multiattribute model but this study is poor evidence for dismissal, since, when liking is the sole criterion for preference, there is no further purpose for preference beyond the feelings evoked. If asked to provide reasons, consumers can do no more than state the type of enjoyment expected, e.g. 'I found the picture beautiful', an answer that does not tell the questioner why they like what they like.

Intuition

Wilson distinguishes between informed and uninformed gut feelings. The trick, he argues, is to gather enough information to develop an informed gut feeling and then refrain from analysing it too much. (This is in fact what consumers usually do.) Wilson claims we should let our informed adaptive unconscious undertake the job of forming reliable feelings and then trust those feelings, even if we cannot explain them entirely. This allows the adaptive unconscious to make a stable, informed evaluation rather than an ill-informed one. This is quite an endorsement of those who advocate following intuition or gut feeling when making decisions. But there is evidence that the claim does have some validity.

Intuition invades the conscious mind with an 'unreasoned' answer which need not necessarily be short on rationality. Gigerenzer *et al.* demonstrate how fast decision making can be as accurate as strategies that try to use all the information available.[55] Klein shows that experienced workers, even when under extreme pressure, produce action plans that are rational. They do this by drawing on experience to identify familiar patterns in the problems with which they are faced.[56] At the conscious level, the workers run a quick mental simulation to confirm that the intuitive plan is a good one. Typically, with experienced workers, it is. This seems strange unless we accept that much thinking happens not in the conscious mind but out of sight, in the unconscious. Thinking involving interpretation, evaluation and suggested action can occur not only in the conscious mind but also in the unconscious. There is thus dual processing: conscious and non-conscious.

While interpretation, evaluation and action evoke our notion of purely conscious rational thinking, in fact the conscious mind also indulges in undirected fantasy and imaginative thinking, harnessing fantasy and memory to create plans and ideas.[57] Does the unconscious also do these things? Wilson would probably answer in the affirmative. In any case, intuition works well on occasion since it can be based on a great deal of experience, but as this is not always so it needs a reality check as to desirability, feasibility and commercial viability, rather than automatic acceptance. Myers marshals the relevant research and concludes that intuition can help us empathize with others and perform rote tasks like driving, but it can also be perilously wrong.[58]

Is Wilson being consistent when he talks about the adaptive unconscious making stable, informed evaluations? After all, is this not the same adaptive unconscious that focuses on the here and now and biases interpretations and evaluations? If this is so, why should gathering all the relevant information lead to a stable, informed evaluation? Also is this not the same adaptive unconscious that commonly (not just occasionally) bypasses the conscious mind in inducing behaviour? If this is so, how can the conscious mind insist on gathering all the relevant information?

THE IMPORTANCE OF CONSIDERING THE CONSCIOUS

Many psychologists, like Wilson, make claims for the amount of work done by the unconscious. However, the point is never how much work is done but the nature of the work done; quantity is not the issue but significance. Philosophers and psychologists who focus on consciousness are drawn to talking about thought experiments which involve manipulating concepts in the mind. Conceptual understanding, and even completely new understandings, are achieved through thought experiments. The imagination conjures up images, and contemplates and fantasizes about delights not yet experienced. Wilson ignores these elements of thinking though they need to be acknowledged if we are to improve our understanding of the respective roles of the conscious and the unconscious. Conscious thinking cannot be ignored. In watching an ad we can progress from finding it pleasant to think along the lines that it suggests, to thinking how pleasant it would be to possess the brand advertised, to actually choosing that brand. It is through simulations in the conscious mind that innovative thinking evolves.

Because Wilson fails to establish the qualitative differences between the conscious and the unconscious, everything associated with the conscious is free to be classed as also

191

belonging to the unconscious; only common sense restrains Wilson from the view that the conscious is a non-causal entity, to be eliminated altogether. Whatever input is received from the unconscious by the conscious, it can be reasoned about, leading to new wants and beliefs, leading to intentional action. Not surprisingly, Wilson makes no mention of decision making in the sense of a deliberative conscious processing of the pros and cons of choosing one option rather than another.

While by no means fully endorsing self-perception theory, Wilson argues that there are occasions when what we feel is by no means clear. Then we act like observers and decipher feelings and attitudes from observing our own behaviour. He regards observing our own behaviour as a good strategy if it reveals feelings of which we were previously unaware, and a poor strategy if it results in the fabrication of feelings. He claims that most experiments on self-perception theory typically result in fabrication, with people misunderstanding the real reason for their behaviour and making mistaken inferences about their feelings. Nonetheless, he argues that if we want to change the inclinations of the adaptive unconscious, we should induce a behaviour change first. Changing our behaviour to fall in line with our conscious conceptions of ourselves is a way to bring about changes in the adaptive unconscious. In other words, we should follow the adage of being true to ourselves in all our actions. People should commit themselves to a coherent self-narrative and this will come to correspond to their adaptive unconscious. This involves the belief that consciously changing behaviour in line with one's concept of oneself will bring in line the adaptive unconscious. This would suggest that in appealing to some generalized ideal self-image of its target audience advertising may enlist not only the conscious mind but the unconscious as well.

We have mainly focused on Wilson's book *Strangers to Ourselves* because it is the most recent one to bring together the work on the adaptive unconscious. While the current interest in the unconscious is welcome, there are good reasons for believing that the claims now being made are going too far. Wilson fails to distinguish between assertions which have backing and assertions that merely reflect his own speculations based on his commitment in psychology to the notion of a dominant unconscious.

KEY ASSERTIONS

Freudian approach

- If advertisers aim at identifying the unconscious meanings that are attached to products so as to exploit the implied motives in these meanings, the use of projective techniques (particularly construction techniques like the Thematic Apperception Test) using focus groups may be recommended since these remain the main means of uncovering unconscious motives in buying. Other approaches include depth interviewing or even a structured approach to questioning followed by non-directive probes designed to elicit unconscious motives. Unstructured interviews where respondents just talk off the 'top of their head' can also be revealing.

■ Advertisers should recognize that their brands need to stand for something in the mind of the consumer and thus they need to ensure that their brands stand for values endorsed by the target audience.

ZMET approach

■ If advertisers recognize that much of our conceptualization of experience is metaphorical and a great deal of our knowledge and thinking is constituted by metaphorical mappings from dissimilar sources and target domains, persuasive appeals couched in metaphorical language should be used. If the unconscious is a hidden store of visual metaphors, these might be identified to understand the consumer's perspective and orientation towards a particular brand. It is being claimed that ZMET, as a technique, is one way to do this for the design of product offerings and persuasive appeals.

The adaptive unconscious

■ If advertisers accept that the adaptive unconscious produces feelings and preferences that affect subsequent choices, they will appreciate the need to find out about them.

■ If advertisers recognize that target audiences immediately and unconsciously appraise a message as something of interest (good) or of no interest (bad/poor), they will ensure that their ads resonate with the target audience as advocating something that will enrich their lives.

■ If advertisers accept that the adaptive unconscious focuses on the here and now, then any message that promises instant gratification will have appeal.

■ If a company has an offering that meets some key concern of its target audience, advertisers should design persuasive appeals that can be honest in saying how far it meets that key concern as the target audience will bend the message to fit their desires.

■ If advertisers aim at undermining competition, negative messages about competitors are likely to be persuasive as, at the very least, they create doubts and indecisiveness.

cont.

- If advertisers encounter negative 'rumours' about their company or brands, it is essential that they be immediately attacked. Otherwise they will be believed through constant repetition.

- If advertisers are to understand the orientation of the adaptive unconscious, what consumers within their market segment do 'impulsively' is a guide.

- To understand the consumer, advertisers must recognize the incidental learning that results from watching films and TV and then influences customer behaviour.

- If seeking to tune their messages to their target audience, advertisers should try to identify how members of their target segment generally tend to interpret and evaluate ads for brands in their segment.

- If advertisers are to affect the accessibility of their persuasive messages for their target audience, they must ensure their persuasive messages: (a) have self-relevance for their target audience; (b) are advertised enough to ensure the message has been recently entertained; (c) are easily recalled by a facilitating slogan or whatever. In fact any message that deals with key concerns of the target audience will resonate emotionally and ensure accessibility.

- Advertisers who are intent on taking account of unconscious motives should focus on affiliation (getting on better with others), achievement (achieving more than has been done before) and power (having an impact on others) since these are likely to be the motives learned in life. This suggests appealing to these motives in advertisements while paying attention to those that have been self-attributed in answers to questionnaires. If there is no one dominant motive, advertisers might appeal to the different motives at various times.

- If advertisers are intent on taking account of unconscious motives, they should take account of the need to make the audience feel good about themselves, and should think in terms of persuasive appeals that uphold personal well-being, and help the target audience be optimistic.

- If advertisers recognize that persuasion is self-persuasion, then persuasive appeals that manage to get members of the target audience to be involved with the product (e.g. send for sample, pull off a strip in a magazine, take a test drive and so on) will impact on both the conscious and unconscious mind in a way that favours the advertiser.

- If advertisers want to change the inclinations of the adaptive unconscious, the aim should be to suggest members of the target audience be true to themselves and act according to some ideal self-image. In any case, achieving a change in behaviour does have an impact on unconscious dispositions.

- If persuasive appeals are to continue to have credibility, they should not explicitly promise too much since the joy of possession is not long lasting while disappointment can leave emotional scars.
- If advertisers use emotionally toned persuasive messages, consumers are more likely to go along with the message as this is what their gut feel and intuition would suggest.

Notes

1   WHAT FACILITATES PERSUASION AND WHAT INHIBITS IT?

1   *The Economist* (2002) 'High Hopes in Adland', 7 December, pp. 59–60.
2   Ives, Nat (2003) 'As an alternative to pop-up ads, marketers are trying to create useful Web sites to draw viewers', *The New York Times*, 11 February, p. C8.
3   *The Economist* (2003) 'Heave ho, TiVo!', 8–14 February, p. 60.
4   Quart, Alissa (2003) *Branded: the Buying and Selling of Teenagers*, New York: Perseus.
5   Scheibe, Karl E. (2000) *The Drama of Everyday Life*, Cambridge, MA: Harvard University Press, p. 102.
6   Watts, Duncan (2003) *Six Degrees: the Science of a Connected Age*, New York: W.W. Norton.
7   Foster, Richard (1986) *Innovation*, New York: Summit Books.
8   O'Shaughnessy, John (1995) *Competitive Marketing: a Strategic Approach*, London: Routledge, p. 324.
9   Frank, Jerome D. (1974) *Persuasion and Healing*, New York: Schocken Books.
10 Bhagwati, Jagdish (2002) *Free Trade Today*, Princeton, NJ: Princeton University Press.
11 Kohn, M.L. (1969) *Class and Conformity: a Study in Values*, Homewood, IL: Dorsey, p. 3.
12 Phillips, Kevin (2002) *Wealth and Democracy: a Political History of the American Rich*, New York: Broadway Books.
13 Douglas, Mary (1996) *Thought Styles: Critical Essays on Good Taste*, London: Sage Publications.
14 Scheibe, Karl E. (2000) *The Drama of Everyday Life*, Cambridge, MA: Harvard University Press, p. 102.
15 Quoted in Alvarez, Lizette (2003) 'Consumers in Europe Resist Gene-Altered Foods', *The New York Times International*, 11 February. p. A3.
16 Kammen, Michael (1978) *A Season of Youth: the American Revolution and the Historical Imagination*, New York: Alfred A. Knopf.
17 Hacking, Ian (1995) *Rewriting the Soul: Multiple Personality and the Sciences of Memory*, Princeton, NJ: Princeton University Press, p. 13.
18 Park, Robert L. (2001) *Voodoo Science: the Road from Foolishness to Fraud*, New York: Oxford University Press.
19 Gratzer, Walter (2001) *The Undergrowth of Science: Delusion, Self-deception and Human Frailty*, Oxford: Oxford University Press.

20 Kelly, G.A. (1955) *The Psychology of Personal Constructs*, Vol. 2: *Clinical Diagnosis and Psychotherapy*, New York: W.W. Norton.
21 Boyer, Pascal (2001) *Religion Explained: the Human Instincts that Fashion Gods, Sprits and Ancestors*, London: Heinemann.
22 Kuhn, Deanna (1991) *The Skills of Argument*, New York: Cambridge University Press.
23 Scheibe, *The Drama of Everyday Life*.
24 Ibid, p. 45; Goffman, E. (1969) *The Presentation of Self in Everyday Life*, Garden City, NY: Doubleday Anchor.
25 McGuire, William J. (2000) *Constructing Social Psychology: Creative and Critical Processes*, New York: Cambridge University Press.
26 Flyvbjerg, Bent (2003) *Making Social Science Matter*, Cambridge: Cambridge University Press.
27 Deutsch, David (1997) *The Fabric of Reality*, London: Penguin Books, pp. 65–66.
28 Toulmin, Stephen (2001) *Return to Reason*, Cambridge, MA: Harvard University Press.
29 O'Shaughnessy, *Competitive Marketing: a Strategic Approach*, Chapter 12.
30 Wollheim, Richard (1999) *On the Emotions*, New Haven, CT: Yale University Press.

2 RATIONALITY, SYMBOLISM AND EMOTION IN PERSUASION

1 Blaxter, M. (1990) *Health and Lifestyles*, London: Tavistock and Routledge.
2 Margalit, Avishai (2002) *The Ethics of Memory*, Cambridge, MA: Harvard University Press, p. 129.
3 Smith, Murray (2003) 'Darwin and the Directors: Film, Emotion and the Face in the Age of Evolution', *The Times Literary Supplement*, 7 February, pp. 13–15.
4 Holbrook, Morris B. and O'Shaughnessy, John (1984) 'The Role of Emotion in Advertising', *Journal of Psychology and Marketing*, (2) (May): 45–64.
5 Olney, Thomas J., Holbrook, Morris B. and Batra, Rajeev (1991) 'Consumer Responses to Advertising: the Effects of Ad Content, Emotions and Attitudes Toward the Ad on Viewing Time'. *Journal of Consumer Research*, 17 (March): 440–453.
6 Batra, Rajeev and Ray, Michael (1986) 'Affective Responses Medicating the Acceptance of Advertising', *Journal of Consumer Research*, 13 (September): 234–249.
7 Edell, Julie A. and Burke, Marian C. (1987) 'The Power of Feelings in Understanding Advertising Effects', *Journal of Consumer Research*, 14 (December): 421–433.
8 Friestad, Marian and Thorson, Esther (1993) 'Remembering Ads: the Effects of Encoding Strategies, Retrieval Cues and Emotional Responses. *Journal of Consumer Psychology*, 2 (January): 1–23.
9 Markus, Hazel and Kitayama, Shinobu (1991) 'The Cultural Construction of Self and Emotion: Implications for Social Behavior', In *Emotion and Culture: Empirical Studies of Mutual Influence*, Shinobu Kitayam and Hazel Markus (eds). Washington, DC: American Psychological Association, Chapter 4.
10 Aaker, Jennifer L. and Williams, Patti (1998) 'Empathy versus Pride: the Influence of Emotional Appeals across Cultures', *Journal of Consumer Research*, 25 (December): 241–261.

11 Schwartz, Tony (1973) *The Responsive Chord*, New York: Basic Books.
12 Fairclough, Norman (1999) *New Labour, New Language?*, London: Routledge.
13 Dewey, Clive (1998) Book Review, *The Times Literary Supplement*, 17 April, pp. 9–10.
14 Novick, Peter (1988) *The Noble Dream: the 'Objectivity Question' and the American Historical Profession*, Cambridge: Cambridge University Press, p.14.
15 Gibbs, Raymond W. (1994) *The Poetics of the Mind*, Cambridge: Cambridge University Press.
16 Eysenck, Hans J. (1998) *Intelligence*, New Brunswick: Transaction.
17 Simmons, Annette (2000) *The Story Factor: Secrets of Influence from the Art of Storytelling*, New York: Perseus Publishing.
18 Parker, Patricia (1990) 'Metaphor and Catachresis', in John Bender and David E. Wellberg (eds) *The Ends of Rhetoric*, Stanford, CA: Stanford University Press.
19 Pennington, N. and Hastie, R. (1993) 'A Theory of Explanation-based Decision Making', in C. Klein, J. Orasanu, R. Calderwood and C.E. Zsambok (eds) *Decision Making in Action: Models and Methods*, Norwood, NJ: Ablex, pp. 188–201.
20 Damasio, Antonio R. (1994) *Descartes' Error: Emotion, Reason and the Human Brain*, New York: A Grosset/Putnam Book.
21 Tajfel, H. (1981) *Human Groups and Social Categories*, Cambridge: Cambridge University Press.
22 Murphy, Gregory L. (2003) *The Big Book of Concepts*, Cambridge, MA: MIT Press.
23 Warnock, Mary (1998) *An Intelligent Person's Guide to Ethics*, London: Duckworth.
24 Singer, Peter (1979) *Practical Ethics*, Cambridge: Cambridge University Press.
25 Rokeach, Milton (1973) *The Nature of Human Values*, New York: Free Press.
26 MacIntyre, Alasdair (1981) *After Virtue: a Study in Moral Theory*, London: Duckworth.
27 Langer, S.K. (1957) *Philosophy in a New Key*, Cambridge, MA: Harvard University Press.
28 Greenspan, P.S. (1995) *Practical Guilt*, New York: Oxford University Press.
29 Jhally, Sut (1990) *The Codes of Advertising: Fetishism and the Political Economy in the Consumer Society*, New York: Routledge.
30 Obituary of Walter Landor, *The Economist*, 24 June 1995.
31 Goffman, Erving (1959) *Presentation of Self in Everyday Life*, New York: Anchor.
32 Albert, Katherine A. (1996) *Get a Good Night's Sleep*, New York: Simon & Schuster.
33 Levere, Jane L. and Stellin, Susan (2002) 'Business Fliers' Loyalty May Be United Asset', *New York Times*, 10 December, p. C6.
34 Burke, Kenneth (1970) *A Grammar of Motives*, Berkeley: University of California Press.
35 Kuhn, Deanna (1991) *The Skills of Argument*, New York: Cambridge University Press.
36 Ramachandran, V.S. (with Sandra Blakeslee) (1988) *Phantoms in the Brain: Human Nature and the Architecture of the Mind*, London: Fourth Estate.
37 Warner, Michael (ed.) (1999) *American Sermons: the Pilgrims to Martin Luther King Jr*, New York: The Library of America.

38   Coleman, Simon and Watson, Helen (1992) *An Introduction to Anthropology*, London: Tiger Books International, pp. 50–51.

39   Meyer, Michel (1994) *Rhetoric, Language, and Reason*, Philadelphia, The Pennsylvania State University Press.

40   Gilbert, Michael A. (1995) 'Coalescent Argumentation', *Argumentation*, 9: 837–852.

41   Quine, W.V.O. (1953) 'Two Dogmas of Empiricism', in *From a Logical Point of View*, Cambridge, MA: Harvard University Press.

42   Peppers, Don, Rogers, Martha and Dorf, Bob (1999) 'Is Your Company Ready for One-to-One Marketing?', *Harvard Business Review*, January–February: pp. 151–160.

43   Evans, Dylan (2001) *Emotion*, Oxford: Oxford University Press.

44   Myerson, George (1994) *Rhetoric, Reason and Society: Reason as Dialogue*, New York: Sage Publications.

45   Foucault, Michel (1972) *The Archaeology of Knowledge* (trans. A.M. Sheridan Smith), New York: Pantheon.

3   PERSUASIVE ADVERTISING APPEALS, 1

1   Margalit, Avishai (2002) *The Ethics of Memory*, Cambridge, MA: Harvard University Press.

2   *The Economist* (2003) 'As Potent as its Moniker', 18 January, p. 65.

3   Leary, Mark R. (1995) *Self-Presentation: Impression Management and Interpersonal Behavior*, Madison, WI: Brown & Benchmark.

4   Williams, Bernard (2002) *Truth and Truthfulness*, Princeton, NJ: Princeton University Press, p. 203.

5   Elliott, Stuart (2002) 'Sears, Riding Wave of Nostalgia, Emphasizes Heritage in Campaign', *The New York Times*, 23 August, p. 4.

6   Lauro, Patricia Winters (2003) 'Rheingold Hopes to Rekindle the Romance Between the Beer and New York City'. *The New York Times*, 12 February, p. C8.

7   Rozin, Paul, Millman, L. and Nemeroff, C. (1986) 'Operation of the Laws of Sympathetic Magic in Disgust and Other Domains', *Journal of Personality and Social Psychology*, 50: 703–712.

8   Ives, Nat (2002) 'The Odd Embrace of Marketing and Anti-establishment Music', *The New York Times*, 6 November, p. C3.

9   Anderson, S.M. and Glassman, N.S. (1996) 'Responding to Significant Others When They Are Not There. Effects on Interpersonal Inference, Motivation, and Affect', in R.M. Sorrentino and E.T. Higgins (eds) *Handbook of Motivation and Cognition*, Vol. 3, New York: Guilford Press, pp. 262–321.

10   Damasio, Antonio (1994) *Descartes' Error: Emotion, Reason and the Human Brain*, New York: A Grosset/Putnam Book.

11   Quoted in the introduction by the editor Seymour Chatman (1996) *Benjamin Graham: the Memoirs of the Dean of Wall Street*, New York: McGraw-Hill.

12   Simonson, Itamar (1993) 'Get Closer to Your Customers by Understanding How They Make Choices', *California Management Review*, Summer: pp. 68–84.

13   Montgomery, H. (1989) 'From Cognition to Action: the Search for Dominance in Decision Making', in H. Montgomery and O. Svenson (eds) *Process and Structure in Human Decision Making*, Chichester: Wiley.

14 Lewicka, Maria (1997) 'Is Hate Wiser than Love', in Bob Ranyard, W. Ray Crozier and Philip E. Tetlock (eds) *Decision Making; Cognitive Models and Explanations*, London: Routledge.

15 Beach, L.R. (1993) 'Broadening the Definition of Decision Making: the Role of Prechoice Screening of Options' *Psychological Science*, 4: 215–220.

16 Kim, W. Chan and Mauborgne, Renée (1999) 'Coffee Blended with Emotion', *Financial Times*, 20 May.

17 Rozhon, Tracie (2003) 'A Bored Shopper's Lament: Seen a Store, Seen Them All', *The New York Times*, 4 January, p. B1.

18 Scheibe, Karl E. (2000) *The Drama of Everyday Life*, Cambridge, MA: Harvard University Press, p. 152.

19 Mayhew, Leon H. (1997) *The New Public*, Cambridge: Cambridge University Press.

20 Goldman, Robert and Papson, Steven (1996) *Sign Wars: the Cluttered Landscape of Advertising*, New York: Guilford Press.

21 Bornstein, R.F. (1989) 'Exposure and Affect: Overview and Meta-analysis of Research, 1968–1987', *Psychological Bulletin*, 106: 265–289.

22 Kunst-Wilson, W.R. and Zajonc, R.B. (1980) 'Affective Discrimination of Stimuli that Cannot Be Recognized', *Science*, 207: 557–558.

23 Homans, George C. (1950) *The Human Group*, New York: Harcourt, Brace & World.

24 Leymore, V.L. (1975) *The Hidden Myth*, New York: Basic Books.

25 Collins, Jim (1990) *Uncommon Cultures: Popular Culture and Post-Modernism*, London and New York: Routledge.

26 Sandall, Roger (2002) *The Culture Cult*, Oxford: Westview.

27 See, for example, O'Shaughnesssy, John (1995) *Competitive Marketing: a Strategic Approach*, New York and London: Routledge pp. 205–209.

28 Solomon, Michael R. (1999) 'The value of status and the status of value', in Morris Holbrook (ed.) *Consumer Value*, New York: Routledge.

29 O'Shaughnessy, *Competitive Marketing*.

30 Douglas, Mary (1996) *Thought Styles: Critical Essays in Good Taste*, New York: Sage Publications.

31 Douglas, Mary and Isherwood, Baron (1979) *The World of Goods*, New York: Basic Books.

32 Richardson, Paul (2003) *Indulgence: Around the World in Search of Chocolate*, Boston: Little, Brown.

33 Dittmar, Helga (1992) *The Social Psychology of Personal Possessions: to Have Is to Be*, New York: St Martin's Press.

34 Flanagan, Owen (1996) *Self-expressions: Mind, Morals and the Meaning of Life*, New York: Oxford University Press.

35 Maalouf, Amin (2001) *In the Name of Identity* (trans. Barbara Bray), New York: Arcade Publishing.

36 Berger, Arthur Asa (1991) *Media Analysis Techniques*, Newbury Park, CA: Sage Publications.

37 Riesman, D. (1950) *The Lonely Crowd: a Study of the Changing American Character*, New Haven, CT: Yale University Press.

38 Lukas, Paul (1999) 'Tippecanoe and Tylenol Too!' *Fortune*, 1 February.

39 Kleinberg, Stanley S. (1991) *Politics and Philosophy*, Oxford: Blackwell, pp. 9, 21.

40 Shanks, J. Merrill and Miller, Warren E. (1985) 'Policy Direction and Perform-ance Evaluation', paper given at the American Political Science Association annual meeting.

41 Wildavsky, Aaron and Dake, Karl (1990) 'Theories of Risk Perception: Who Fear What and Why?', *Dadalus, Risk*, 119 (4): 41–60.

42 Levitin, Teresa E. and Miller, Warren E. (1979) 'Ideological Interpretations of Presidential Elections', *American Political Science Review*, 73: 751–771.

43 Sniderman, Paul M., Brody, Richard A. and Tetlock, Philip E. (1991) *Reasoning and Choice: Explorations in Political Psychology*, New York: Cambridge University Press.

44 Rawls, J. (1972) *A Theory of Justice*, New York: Oxford University Press, pp. 48–51.

45 Miller, Jonathan (2002) 'The United Kingdom Is Being Divided', *Washington Post National Weekly Edition*, 26 October.

46 Ryan, Nick (2003) *Homeland: Into a World of Hate*, Edinburgh: Mainstream.

47 Margalit, *The Ethics of Memory*.

48 Sennett, Richard (2003) *Respect in a World of Inequality*, New York: Norton.

49 Mayhew, *The New Public*.

50 Lupia, Arthur (1994) 'Shortcuts Versus Encyclopedias: Information and Voting Behavior in California Insurance Reform Elections', *American Political Science Review*, 88: 63–76.

51 Pratkanis, Anthony and Aronson, Elliot (1991) *Age of Propaganda: the Everyday Use and Abuse of Persuasion*, New York: W.H. Freeman.

52 Davis, Natalie Zemon (2000) *The Gift in Sixteenth-century France*, Madison: University of Wisconsin Press.

4   PERSUASIVE ADVERTISING APPEALS, 2

1 Apter, Michael J. (1989) *Reversal Theory*, New York and London: Routledge.

2 Harré, Rom (1997) 'Social Life as Rule-governed Patterns of Joint Action', in Craig McGarty and S. Alexander Haslam (eds) *The Message of Social Psychology*, Oxford: Blackwell.

3 Thayer, Robert E. (1996) *The Origin of Everyday Moods: Managing Energy, Tension, and Stress*, New York: Oxford University Press.

4 Keller, Punam Anand, Lipkus, Isaac M. and Rimer, Barbara K. (2003) 'Affect, Framing, and Persuasion', *Journal of Marketing Research*, XL (February): 54–64.

5 *The Economist* (2002) 'Mood Swings and Downswings', 14 September, p. 70.

6 Mackie, Diane and Worth, Leila (1989) 'Processing Deficits and the Mediation of Positive Affect on Persuasion', *Journal of Personality and Social Psychology*, 57: 27–40.

7 Heidegger, Martin (1962) *Being and Time* (trans. John Macquarrie and Edward Robinson), Oxford: Blackwell.

8 Allen, C.T. and Janiszewski, C.A. (1989) 'Assessing the Role of Contingency Awareness in Attitudinal Conditioning with Implications for Advertising Research', *Journal of Marketing Research*, 26 (February): 30–43.

9 Skinner, B.F. (1953) *Science and Human Behavior*, New York: Free Press.

10 Foxall, Gordon R. (1990) *Consumer Psychology in Behavioral Perspective*, London: Routledge.

11 Foxall, Gordon R. (2003) Unpublished manuscript.

12 Pinker, Stephen (1994) *The Language Instinct*, New York: William Morrow.

13 Dretske, Fred (1988) *Explaining Behavior: Reason in a World of Causes*, Cambridge, MA: MIT Press.

14 Garcia, John and Koelling, Robert (1966) 'Relation of Cue to Consequences in Avoidance Learning', *Psychonomic Science*, 4: 123–134.

15 Humphrey, N. (1983) *Consciousness Regained*, New York: Oxford University Press.

16 Malcolm, Norman (1977) *Thought and Knowledge*, Ithaca, NY: Cornell University Press.

17 Elster, Jon (1989) *Nuts and Bolts for the Social Sciences*, Cambridge: Cambridge University Press.

18 Hilgard, E. and Marquis, D. (1961) *Conditioning and Learning*, New York: Appleton-Century-Crofts.

19 Foxall, Gordon R. (1987) 'Radical Behaviorism and Consumer Research: Theoretical Promise and Empirical Problems', *International Journal of Research in Marketing*, 4: 111–129.

20 Foxall, *Consumer Psychology in Behavioral Perspective*.

21 Dennett, Daniel C. (1986) *Brainstorms: Philosophical Essays on Mind and Psychology*, Cambridge, MA: MIT Press.

22 Goldman, A.I. (1970) *A Theory of Human Action*, Princeton, NJ: Princeton University Press.

23 Rosenberg, Alexander (1988) *Philosophy of Social Science*, Boulder, CO: Westview Press.

24 Blum, Deborah (2002) *Love at Goon Park: Harry Harlow and the Science of Affection*, Cambridge, MA: Perseus Publishing.

25 Hull, C. (1943) *Principles of Behavior*, New York: Appleton-Century-Crofts.

26 Harlow, H.F. (1953) 'Mice, Monkeys, Men and Motives', *Psychological Review*, 60: 23–32.

27 Hebb, D.O. (1955) 'Drives and the C.N.S. (Conceptual Nervous System)', *Psychological Review*, 62: 243–254.

28 Robinson, Daniel N. (1985) *Philosophy of Psychology*, New York: Columbia University Press.

29 Dretske, *Explaining Behavior: Reason in a World of Causes*.

30 Foxall, *Consumer Psychology in Behavioral Perspective*.

31 Tolman, E.C. (1925) 'Purpose and Cognition: the Determiners of Animal Learning', *Psychological Review*, 32: 285–297; Tolman, E.C. (1948) 'Cognitive Maps in Rats and Man', *Psychological Review*, 55: 189–208.

32 Lattin, James M. and Bucklin, Randolph E. (1989) 'Reference Effects of Price and Promotion on Brand Choice Behavior'. *Journal of Marketing Research*, 26 (August): 299–310.

33 Brody, Nathan (1983) *Human Motivation: Commentary on Goal-Directed Action*, New York: Academic Press.

5 PERSUASIVE ADVERTISING APPEALS, 3

1 Lyons, William (2001) *Matters of the Mind*, Edinburgh: Edinburgh University Press.

2 Hovland, C.I., Janis, I.L. and Kelly, H.H. (1953) *Communication and Persuasion*, New Haven, CT: Yale University Press.

3 Colley, Russell H. (1961) *Defining Advertising Goals for Measured Advertising Results*, New York: Association of National Advertisers.

4 Zajonc, R.B. (1980) 'Feeling and Thinking: Preferences Need No Inferences', *American Psychologist*, 35: 151–175.

5 Damasio, Antonio R. (1994) *Descartes' Error: Emotion, Reason and the Human Brain*, New York: A Grosset/Putnam Book.

6 LeDoux, Joseph (1997) *The Emotional Brain*, New York: Simon & Schuster.

7 Goleman, Daniel (1995) *Emotional Intelligence*, New York: Bantam Books.

8 Ray, Michael L. (1982) *Advertising and Communication Management*, Englewood Cliffs, NJ: Prentice Hall.

9 Petty, Richard, and Cacioppo, John (1986) *Communication and Persuasion: Central and Peripheral Routes to Attitude Change*, New York: Springer-Verlag.

10 Berlin, Isaiah (1993) *The Magus of the North: J.G. Hamann and the Origins of Irrationalism*, London: John Murray.

11 Barthes, Roland (1997) *The Eiffel Tower and Other Mythologies* (trans. by Richard Howard), Berkeley: University of California Press.

12 Moore, R. Laurence (1994) *Selling God*, New York: Oxford University Press.

13 Galanter, Marc (1989) *Cults*, New York: Oxford University Press.

14 Neitz, Mary Jo (1987) *Charisma and Community*, New Brunswick, NJ: Transaction Publishers.

15 Polanyi, Michael and Prosch, Harry (1975) *Meaning*, Chicago: University of Chicago Press.

16 Ramachandran, V.S. (with Sandra Blakeslee) (1988) *Phantoms in the Brain: Human Nature and the Architecture of the Mind*, London: Fourth Estate.

17 Petty, R.E., Cacioppo, J.T. and Goldman, R. (1981) 'Personal Involvement as a Determinant of Argument-based Persuasion', *Journal of Personality and Social Psychology*, 41: 847–855.

18 Vyse, Stuart A. (1997) *Believing in Magic: the Psychology of Superstition*, New York: Oxford University Press.

19 Simon, Herbert A. (1983) *Reason in Human Affairs*, Stanford, CA: Stanford University Press.

20 Sutherland, Stuart (1992) *Irrationality: the Enemy Within*, London: Constable.

21 Kline, P. and Barrett, P. (1983) 'The Factors in Personality Questionnaires Among Normal Subjects', *Advances in Behavioral Research and Therapy*, 5: 141–202.

22 Sperber, Dan and Wilson, Deirdre (1990) 'Rhetoric and Relevance', in John Bender and David E. Wellbery (eds) *The Ends of Rhetoric*, Stanford, CA: Stanford University Press, pp. 140–155.

23 Thompson, Michael (1979) *Rubbish Theory*, London: Oxford University Press.

24 Hovland, C.J., Harvey, O.J. and Sherif, M. (1957) 'Assimilation and Contrast Effects in Reaction to Communication and Attitude Change', *Journal of Abnormal and Social Psychology*, 55: 244–252.

25 Haack, Susan (1998) *Manifesto of a Passionate Moderate*, Chicago: University of Chicago Press, p. 18.

26 Proctor, Robert N. (1995) *Cancer Wars: How Politics Shapes What We Know and Don't Know About Cancer*, New York: Basic Books.

27 Fursenko, A. and Naftali, T. (1997) *One Hell of a Gamble*, New York: J. Murray.

28 Smart, J.J.C. (1984) *Ethics, Persuasion and Truth*, London: Routledge & Kegan Paul, p. 132.

29 Richards, I.A. (1935) *Science and Poetry*, London: Kegan Paul, Trench and Trubner, p. 29.

30 Kleinberg, Stanley S. (1991) *Politics and Philosophy*, Oxford: Blackwell.

31 Perelman, C. (1982) *The Realm of Rhetoric*, Notre Dame, IL: University of Notre Dame Press.

32 Vickers, Brian (1988) *In Defence of Rhetoric*, Oxford: Clarendon Press.

33 Holland, R.F. (1980) *Against Empiricism*, Totowa, NJ: Barnes & Noble.

34 Warnke, G. (1987) *Gadamer: Hermeneutics, Tradition and Reason*, Stanford, CA: Stanford University Press.

35 *The Economist* (1988) 6 June, p. 65.

36 Fogelin, Robert (1988) *Figuratively Speaking*, New Haven, CT: Yale University Press.

37 Klein, Gary (1998) *Sources of Power: How People Make Decisions*, Cambridge, MA: MIT Press.

38 Gibbs, R.W. (1994) *The Poetics of the Mind: Figurative Thought, Language, and Understanding*, Cambridge: Cambridge University Press.

39 Brown, Stephen (1995) *Postmodern Marketing*, London: Routledge.

40 Hobson, R.F. (1985) *Forms of Feeling: the Heart of Psychotherapy*, New York: Methuen.

41 Stebbing, L. Susan (1937) *Philosophy and the Physicists*, New York: Penguin Books.

42 Haack, *Manifesto of a Passionate Moderate*.

43 Lakoff, George and Johnson, Mark (1998) *The Embodied Mind and its Challenge in Western Thought*, New York: Basic Books.

44 Kapner, Suzanne (2002) 'French Bank Uses Bugs to Sell Itself', *The New York Times: World Business*, 5 June, p. W1.

45 McLuhan, Marshall (1963) *Understanding Media: the Extensions of Man*, New York: Signet Books.

46 McCloskey, Donald N. (1990) *If You're So Smart: the Narrative of Economic Expertise*, Chicago: University of Chicago Press.

47 Mason, Jeff (1989) *Philosophical Rhetoric*, London: Routledge.

48 Ibid., p. 29.

49 Austin, J.L. (1962) *How to Do Things with Words*, Oxford: Oxford University Press.

50 Harré, Rom (1997) 'Social Life as Rule-governed Patterns of Joint Action', in Craig McGarty and S. Alexander Haslam (eds) *The Message of Social Psychology*, Oxford: Blackwell.

51 Mayhew, Leon H. (1997) *The New Public*, Cambridge: Cambridge University Press, p. 65.

52 Cialdini, Robert B. (1993) *Influence: the Psychology of Persuasion*, New York: William Morrow.

53 Salovey, P. and Mayer, J.D. (1990) 'Emotional Intelligence', *Imagination, Cognition and Personality*, 9: 185–211.

54 Berger, Arthur Asa (1991) *Media Analysis Techniques*, Newbury Park, CA: Sage.

55 Holbrook, Morris B. and Batra, Rajeev (1986) 'Assessing the Role of Emotion as Mediators of Consumer Responses to Advertising', Research Working Paper No. 86 AV-10, Columbia University.

56 Argyle, Michael (1994) *The Psychology of Interpersonal Behaviour*, London: Penguin Books.

57 Burke, Marian Chapman, and Edell, Julie A. (1989) 'The Impact of Feelings on Ad-Based Affect and Cognition', *Journal of Marketing Research*, 26 (February): 69–83.

58 Dittmar, Helga (1992) *The Social Psychology of Material Possessions*, Hemel Hempstead: Harvester Wheatsheaf.

59 Williams, Bernard (2002) *Truth and Truthfulness*, Princeton, NJ: Princeton University Press.

60 Festinger, Leon (1957) *A Theory of Cognitive Dissonance,* Stanford, CA: Stanford University Press.

61 Higgins, E.T. (1987) 'Self-discrepancy: a Theory Relating Self to Affect', *Psychological Review*, 94: 319–334.

62 Tversky, A. and Kahneman, D. (1986) 'Rational Choice and the Framing of Decisions', in 'The Behavioral Foundations of Economic Theory', R.M. Hogarth and Melvin W. Reder (eds), *The Journal of Business*, 59(4), Part 2 (October): S251–S278.

63 Margalit, Avishai (2002) *The Ethics of Memory*, Cambridge, MA: Harvard University Press, p. 124.

64 Sniderman, Paul M., Brody, Richard A. and Tetlock, Philip E. (1991) *Reasoning and Choice: Explorations in Political Psychology*, Cambridge: Cambridge University Press.

65 Leary, Mark (1995) *Self-Presentation: Impression Management and Interpersonal Behavior*, Madison, WI: Brown & Benchmark.

66 Valins, S. (1966) 'Cognitive Effect of False Heart-rate Feedback' *Journal of Personality and Social Psychology*, 4: 400–408.

6   PERSUASIVE ADVERTISING APPEALS, 4

1   Person, Ethel S. (1996) *The Force of Fantasy*, New York: HarperCollins.

2   Dichter, Ernest (1960) *The Strategy of Desire*, London: Boardman.

3   Richards, Barry (1994) *The Disciplines of Delight: the Psychoanalysis of Popular Culture*, London: Free Association Books.

4   Wernick, A. (1991) *Promotional Culture*, London: Sage.

5   Healy, David (1998) *The Antidepressant Era*, Cambridge, MA: Harvard University Press.

6   Crews, Frederick (ed.) (1998) *Unauthorized Freud*, New York: Viking.

7   Elliott, Anthony (ed.) (1998) *Freud 2000*, Oxford: Polity.

8   Beloff, John (1973) *Psychological Sciences*, London: Crosby, Lockwood, Staples.

9   Lear, Jonathan (1988) *Open Minded*, Cambridge, MA: Harvard University Press.

10 Rycroft, Charles (1995) *A Critical Dictionary of Psychoanalysis*, London: Penguin.

11 Eakin, Emily (2002) 'Penetrating the Mind by Metaphor', *The New York Times*, 23 February, Arts & Ideas section.

12 Useem, Jerry (2003) 'This Man Can Read your Mind', *Fortune*, 20 (January): 48.

13 Gibbs, Raymond W. (1994) *The Poetics of the Mind: Figurative Thought, Language, and Understanding*, Cambridge: Cambridge University Press.

14 O'Shaughnessy, John and Holbrook, Morris B. (1988) 'Understanding Consumer Behaviour: the Linguistic Turn in Marketing Research', *Journal of the Market Research Society*, 30(2): 197–223 (quote from p. 215).

15 Cole, David (2002) 'Misdirected Snooping Doesn't Stop Terror', *The New York Times*, 4 June, p. 23.

16 Hacking, Ian (1995) *Rewriting the Soul: Multiple Personality and the Sciences of Memory*, Princeton, NJ: Princeton University Press. p. 252.

17 Sims, Andrew (1995) *Symptoms of the Mind: an Introduction to Descriptive Psychopathology*, London: W.B. Saunders Company, p. 24.

18 Ibid.

19 Wilson, Timothy D. (2002) *Strangers to Ourselves: Discovering the Adaptive Unconscious*, Cambridge, MA: The Belknap Press of Harvard University Press.

20 Wegner, Daniel (2002) *The Illusion of Conscious Will*, Cambridge, MA: MIT Press.

21 Brown, James Robert (2001) *Who Rules in Science*, Cambridge, MA: Harvard University Press, p. 152.

22 Williams, Bernard (2002) *Truth and Truthfulness*, Princeton, NJ: Princeton University Press.

23 Bloor, David (1983) *Wittgenstein: a Social Theory of Knowledge*, New York: Columbia University Press.

24 Williams, *Truth and Truthfulness*, p. 3.

25 Modell, Arnold H. (2003) *Imagination and the Meaningful Brain*, Cambridge, MA: MIT Press.

26 Peters, R.S. [1958] (1969) *The Concept of Motivation*, London: Routledge & Kegan Paul.

27 Searle, John (1992) *The Rediscovery of Mind*, Cambridge, MA: MIT Press.

28 See, for example, Nisbett, R.E. and Wilson, T.D. (1977) 'Telling More than We Know: Verbal Reports on Mental Processes', *Psychological Review*, 84: 231–259.

29 Margalit, Avishai (2002) *The Ethics of Memory*, Cambridge MA: Harvard University Press.

30 Wegner, D.M. and Wheatley, T. (1999) 'Apparent Mental Causation: Sources of the Experience of Will', *American Psychologist*, 54: 480–492.

31 See epiphenomenalism in: *A Companion to the Philosophy of Mind*, ed. Samuel Guttenplan, Oxford: Blackwell.

32 Schiffer, Fredric (1998) *Of Two Minds: the Revolutionary Science of Dual-Brain Psychology*, New York: The Free Press.

33 Damasio, Antonio (1994) *Descartes' Error: Emotion, Reason and the Human Brain*, New York: A Grosset/Putnam Book.

34 Ibid, p. 35.

35 Margalit, *The Ethics of Memory*.

36 Person, *The Force of Fantasy*.

37 Damasio, *Descartes' Error: Emotion, Reason and the Human Brain*.

38 LeDoux, Joseph (1997) *The Emotional Brain*, New York: Simon & Schuster.

39 Brewer, W.F. (1974) 'There Is No Convincing Evidence for Operant or Classical Conditioning in Adult Humans', in W.B. Weimer and D.S. Palermo (eds) *Cognition and the Symbolic Processes*, Hillsdale, NJ: Erlbaum, pp. 1–42.

40 Bargh, J.A., Gollwitzer, P.M., Chai, A.L., Barndollar, K. and Trotschel, R. (2001) 'The Automated Will: Nonconscious Activation and Pursuit of Behavior Goals', *Journal of Personality and Social Psychology*, 81: 1014–1027.

41 Wilson, *Strangers to Ourselves*, p. 31.

42 Claparède, E. [1911] (1951) 'Recognition and "me-ness"', in D. Rapaport (ed.) *Organization and Pathology of Thought*, New York: Columbia University Press, pp. 58–75.

43 Mowrer, O.H. (1960) *Learning Theory and Behavior*, New York: Wiley.

44 Ryle, Gilbert (1949) *The Concept of Mind*, New York: Barnes and Noble Books, p. 15.

45 O'Shaughnessy, John and O'Shaughnessy, Nicholas (2003) *The Marketing Power of Emotion*, New York: Oxford University Press.

46 McClelland, D.C. (1961) *The Achieving Society*, New York: Van Nostrand.

47 Gazzaniga, M.S. and LeDoux, J.E. (1978) *The Integrated Mind*, New York: Plenum.

48 Wilson, *Strangers to Ourselves*, p. 99.

49 Nisbett and Wilson, 'Telling More Than We Know'.

50 Kelly, George [1955] (1965) *A Theory of Personality*, New York: W.W. Norton, p. 5.

51 Wilson, *Strangers to Ourselves*, p. 106.

52 Fodor, Jerry (2003) 'Is It a Bird? Problems with Old and New Approaches to the Theory of Concepts', *The Times Literary Supplement*, 17 January, p. 4.

53 Wilson, *Strangers to Ourselves*, p. 132.

54 Frijda, Nico H. (1988) 'The Laws of Emotion', *American Psychologist*, 43(5) (May): 348–358.

55 Gigerenzer, Gerd, Todd, Peter M. and the ABC Research Group (1999) 'Fast and Frugal Heuristics: the Adaptive Toolbox', in *Simple Heuristics that Make Us Smart*, Oxford: Oxford University Press, pp. 3–34.

56 Klein, Gary (2003) *Intuition at Work. Why Developing Gut Instincts Will Make You Better at What You Do*, New York: Doubleday.

57 Fish, F. (1967) *Clinical Psychopathology*, Bristol: John Wright.

58 Myers, David G. (2002) *Intuition: Its Powers and Perils*, New Haven, CT: Yale University Press.

Index

academics 29
acceptance 133
achievement: adaptive unconscious desire for
    184, 194; goals 95, 117
action-orientation 69, 70
adaptive unconscious 165–6, 170, 173–4,
    177–91, 192, 193–5
Adler, Alfred 167
affect 123, 124, 125, 127, 130, 150; *see also*
    emotions
affective forecasting 189–90
affiliation: adaptive unconscious desire for 184,
    194; offer of 23, 41, 43, 81–2, 91, 144, 164
age 10, 13
Agnew, Spiro 139
Albert, Katherine A. 40
Allen, C.T. 101
Amazon.com 3
ambiguity 97, 99, 117
American Idol 1
American Medical Association 34
analogy 33–4, 52, 139
analytic definitions 34–5
anchor points 133, 162
anecdotes 31–2, 52
animal behaviour 107–8, 109
animal rights 36, 43
Annan, Kofi 35
anthropology 43, 57
anxiety 18, 93, 95, 96–7, 116, 117
apperception 32; *see also* Thematic
    Apperception Test
Apple Macintosh 144
Apter, Michael J. 93, 96, 98
archetypes 167

Aristotle 42, 44, 45–6, 55, 76, 82
arousal: reversal theory 93–6, 116; sensory
    deprivation 110–11
assimilation effect 132, 163
association 55, 57–63, 90, 99; classical
    conditioning 101; Death cigarettes 116;
    Gold Blend advertisements 162; Mecca Cola
    89; prestige/status 83; solidarity 63, 80–3;
    values 63, 64–8; word association
    techniques 168
associationism 55, 86, 101, 160
Aston Martin 1
attention 131, 162
attitudes: brand conceptions 37; definition 18;
    elaboration likelihood model of persuasion
    126; hierarchy of effects 124
attractiveness 8, 145, 147–9, 164
attribution theory 153
Austin, J.L. 143
authenticity: descriptive words 32; nostalgia
    59; Stella Artois commercials 50
authority 146

backwater isolation 73, 75
balance model 150
bargains 111, 112, 118
Bargh, J.A. 182
Barthes, Roland 127
Battleship Potemkin 66
Bayer 57
Beatles, The 60
Bechterev, Vladimir M. 102
Beck's 97
behaviourism 30, 99–114, 117–19;
    associations 55, 63; epiphenomenalism 176;

Fodor 188; Freud contrast 166; operant conditioning 15, 44, 100, 102–12, 113, 114, 181; Pavlovian (classical) conditioning 100–1, 102, 105, 112, 175, 176; purposive 112, 113, 114; relational 112, 113–14; Tolman 100, 112–14

beliefs 5, 8–9, 10, 25; adaptive unconscious 188; assimilation/contrast effects 132–3, 163; attitudes measurement 18; balance model 150; brand conceptions 37; cognitive dissonance 151–3; cultural preferences 78; emotions influence on 27, 30; Freudian psychology 166; group norms 11; inconsistency 152, 164; influence definition 6; perspectives 14, 19, 23, 43, 138; persuasive communications 132, 163; principle-orientation 70; rubbish theory 131; self-perception theory 188, 189; social conformity 12; systems 42; *see also* attitudes; perspectives; values

Benetton 149
Bentham, Jeremy 19
Berger, Arthur Asa 76
Bhagwati, Jagdish 11
bias 182
billboards 1
Blair, Tony 29
BMW 1, 154, 155
BNP Paribas 142
Body Shop, The 64–5
Bombardier 56
boredom 66, 93, 95, 99, 116, 117
Borges, Jorge Luis 139
Bower, Marvin 11–12
box metaphor 19
Boyer, Pascal 18
BP (British Petroleum) 60
brain hemispheres 42
brand: affiliation 82; anchor points 133; association 57, 58–61, 62, 90, 99; conditioning 101, 117–18; congruity model 151; consistency 66; excitement arousal 116; familiarity 40, 63, 67, 90, 182; favourable feelings towards 126; halo effect 62; image 39–40, 44, 53, 59–60, 63, 66–7, 90; loyalty 6, 40, 76, 169; names 57, 58; new products 52; perception 37; personality 39, 169; reinforcement 103, 105, 110, 118, 119; sense-meaning 37; signs 37; social

norms 65; solidarity 91; switching 118; symbolic meaning 5, 38–40, 53, 90; values 64, 193; *see also* case studies; products
Breck 59
Bricker, John 35
Bright, John 140
British Petroleum (BP) 60
Brosnan, Pierce 84
Brown, James Robert 175
Brown, Stephen 140
Brylcreem 59
Bucklin, Randolph E. 113
Burger King 76
Burke, Kenneth 41
Bush, George 9, 147
Bush, George W. 30, 63, 81, 152

cable internet access 11
Cacioppo, John 126, 127, 128, 129
Cadell, Patrick 72–3
Calvin Klein 59
Campbell's 76, 87
capitalism 36, 140
cars 39
Cartesian dualism 184
case studies: Death Cigarettes 114–16; Gold Blend 160–2; Mecca Cola 88–9; Oxo family 86–7; Renault Clio 155–60; Stella Artois 48–52
categorization 34
celebrities 6, 11, 61, 146, 147–8, 151
central routes to persuasion 101, 126–7, 130
chaining 104
Charlie 34
Chartism 45
Chiquita Brands 60
chocolate 72
Chrysler 31
Churchill, Winston 137
Cialdini, Robert B. 146
Cicero 33
cinema 41
Claparède, E. 183
class *see* social class
classical (Pavlovian) conditioning 100–1, 102, 105, 112, 175, 176
classification 34, 52
Clinton, Bill 72, 76, 142
Club Med 74–5
co-production 37, 135, 148

Coca-Cola 39, 66, 88, 172
coercion 7, 8, 9, 23, 81
cognition: cognitive dissonance 151–3; hierarchy of effects 123, 124, 125; processes 31, 55, 106
cognitive energy 60, 98
cognitive psychology 15, 99, 112, 121–30; apperception 32; elaboration likelihood model of persuasion 121, 126–30; expectations 113; hierarchy of effects 121, 123–6; rational decision making 93
cognitive synergy 98, 117
coherence theory of truth 42
Colley, Russell H. 123
colours 149
communication: persuasive 121, 130–50; word-of-mouth 4, 12, 57–8
comparative advertising 72, 151
comparisons 33, 52
competition 1, 5, 193
competitive advantage: brand image 53; comparative advertising 72; need for 65; product parallelism 4
'completion' techniques 168
conation 123, 124, 125
conditioning 63, 99–114; drive reduction theory 110, 113; operant 15, 44, 100, 102–12, 113, 114, 181; Pavlovian (classical) 100–1, 102, 105, 112, 175, 176; unconscious 184
confabulation 186, 187
confidence 96, 117
conformity 12, 126
congruity model 151
connotations 34, 37–8, 52, 58
consciousness 167, 173–4, 176, 178–9, 180–3, 187, 191–2
consciousness-raising 25, 27
conservatism 31, 73–4, 87
consistency: basic values 77; brand associations 66, 67; consistency theory 89, 116, 121, 150–3; persuasive communications 164
'construction' techniques 168
consumerism 12
consumers: advice 146; affective forecasting 189–90; anchor points 133, 162; attitudes 18; behaviourism 15, 118; brand associations 58, 62; brand loyalty 40; confidence 96, 117; expectations 111, 113,

133, 162, 189; implicit favourite model 62; labelling with common characteristics 34; likeability heuristic 60; Mary Douglas thesis 71–80; 'picking behaviour' 181; product costs 119; product descriptions 5; rationalization 167; reference groups 10, 11; reinforcement 104, 105, 118; self-image 20; social class 12–13; telic/paratelic modes 96, 97, 98–9; trust 6; unconscious feelings 171, 172, 173; VALS 2 classification 68–71; Zaltman Metaphor Elicitation Technique 171, 172, 173; see also target audiences
context 20, 21, 24
contiguity 55, 58, 61, 100, 112, 113; see also Pavlovian conditioning
contrast effect 132, 133, 163
corporate image 60
Coughlin, Charles 152
country image 61
Coward, Noel 135
creativity 102
credibility 8, 79, 195; brand image 39; celebrities 147; communication source 45, 128, 129, 145–6, 148–9, 164; consistency 150; scientific 41
Crews, Frederick 170
critical advantage 4, 65
Cuban missile crisis 134
cult of celebrity 148
cultural dissonance 152
cultural myths 141–2
cultural preferences 77, 78
cultural theory 71, 75–7
cultural values 9, 67–8, 78
culture: cultural drift 43; as external shield 8, 9–10, 23; Mary Douglas thesis 71, 73, 75–6, 77; persuasive communication 132, 163
Cunningham, B.J. 114–16
curiosity 29, 66, 119

Dake, Karl 77
Damasio, Antonio R. 62, 124, 172, 178, 179, 181
Davis, Natalie Zemon 82–3
Day, Julia 159
Death Cigarettes 68, 88, 114–16
deceit 6

decision making: cognitive psychology 93; dominance structuring 62–3; fast 190; reason/emotion mix 45; social factors 130; symbolic logic 41–2; values 64; Wilson 192
decoding 135, 139
defence mechanisms 42, 166–7
definition 34–6, 52
Dell 61
Dennett, Daniel C. 109
denotation 38
description 7, 32–3, 52
destination marketing 97, 117
Deutsch, David 20–1
Diana, Princess of Wales 72, 148
Dichter, Ernest 167, 169
Dickens, Charles 141
Die Another Day 1
Diesel 68
differentiation: product 68; social 13; subcultures 68
digital video recorders 1
Dilthey, Wilhelm 5
Dior 148
discriminative stimuli 103–4, 108, 109, 118
Disraeli, Benjamin 41–2, 143
'dissident enclaves' 73, 74–5
distraction 132
Dittmar, Helga 73
dominance structuring 62–3
Douglas, Jeff 80
Douglas, Mary 68, 71–80, 81, 83, 88, 91, 116
dreams 165, 166, 167, 176
Dretske, F. 111
drive reduction theory 110–11, 113
drugs: anti-drug advertising 37, 130; drug companies 57; hard 35; recreational 32; reference groups 37
Dukakis, Michael 147
Dupont, Pierre 147

EAB *see* experimental analysis of behaviour
economics 21, 142
effect, law of 102, 107, 109–10
egalitarianism 73, 74–5, 76, 79
Egg Banking 4
ego 133–4, 162–3, 166, 170; *see also* self
elaboration likelihood model of persuasion 121, 126–30
Eli Lilly 57

elitism 76, 137
Elster, Jon 108
embarrassment 134
EMC 140
emotional intelligence 147
emotions 25, 27–30; adaptive unconscious 184, 188; affective forecasting 189–90; attribution theory 153; consumer expectations 111; decision making 45; description 32; elaboration likelihood model of persuasion 127; emotionally grounded experiences 8, 9, 14, 23, 132, 163; hate 72; hierarchy of effects 124; intuition 195; marketing messages 52; metaphors 139; music 40–1; negative associations 60, 118; *pathos* 46; personality characteristics 129–30; reversal theory 63, 93–9; self-esteem 71; significant meaning 38; symbolic meaning 39, 40; values 9, 19, 27, 30, 36–7, 53, 64–5, 149; *see also* affect
encoding 135, 139
Energizer 79
energy: cognitive 98; mood states 96–7, 117
Enlightenment 127
Enron 31
Epictetus 7–8
epiphenomenalism 102, 176, 178, 180, 187, 188
episodic advertising 104, 118
Esprit 79
essentialist heuristic 146
Estée Lauder 65
ethnicity 10, 13, 19
ethos 45–6
Europe: comparative advertising 72; genetically modified foods 14; values 64
evaluative language 7
evangelists 129
excitement 63, 93, 95, 99, 116
existentialism 108
expectations: anchor points 133, 162; celebrity advertising 148; consumers 111, 113, 133, 162, 189; Tolman's behaviourism 100, 112–14
experimental analysis of behaviour (EAB) 102
experimental psychology 55, 188
exposure effect, repeated 3, 63, 67, 91, 118, 182
'expressive' techniques 168

external shields 8, 9–14, 23
extroversion 129
Eysenck, Hans J. 30

fair trade 11
faith 127, 145
familiarity 40, 63, 67, 90, 131, 163, 182
family 10, 86–7
Federal Communication Commission 11
'feel good' criterion 185, 194
Festinger, Leon 151
Flanagan, Owen 73
Fluoride Free 79
Flyvbjerg, Bent 20
focus groups 164, 168, 169, 192–3
Fodor, Jerry 188
folk psychology 110
Ford 59, 122, 123
Foster, Richard 4
Foucault, Michel 46
Foxall, Gordon R. 102, 103, 109
framing 34
France 61, 82, 156–7
Frank, Jerome D. 7
free association interviews 164, 167, 168
free will 175, 176, 178
frequent flyer programmes 114
Freud, Sigmund 106, 134, 165; adaptive
    unconscious 174, 181; psychiatry 169–70;
    repression 31, 55, 181, 183; unconscious
    motivation 166–7, 171
frustration 97

Gadamer, H.G. 138
Galanter, Marc 127
Garcia, John 107
Gazzaniga, M.S. 186
gender 10, 13, 19, 159; see also women
genealogy 32
genetically modified foods 10, 14, 34, 137
Germany 15, 61
Gestalt psychology 61–2, 63
Gibbs, Raymond W. 30, 172
gift-giving 82–3, 134
Gigerenzer, Gerd 190
Gilbert, Michael A. 44
Gladstone, William 42, 143
GlaxoSmithKline 57
goals: achievement 95, 117; setting 182

Goebbels, Joseph 41
Goethe, Johann Wolfgang von 190
Goffman, Erving 19, 39
Gold Blend 160–2
Goldman, A.I. 109–10
Goldman, Rachel 128
Goldman, Robert 66
Goleman, Daniel 124
goodwill 1, 6
Gorgias 138
Graham, Benjamin 62
Graham, Billy 127
'granfalloon' technique 34, 82, 91
Gratzer, Walter 16
Great Britain: Anglophobia 15–16; Indian
    troops 34; see also United Kingdom
green values 65, 74
Greenspan, P.S. 38
groups: affirmation 8; membership 81, 128;
    norms 11, 12; solidarity 80–3, 91; see also
    reference groups

Haack, Susan 132
Hacking, Ian 16, 173
halo effect 62, 63, 148
Harlow, Harry 110
Harré, Rom 95, 143
Harrison, Benjamin 147
Hastie, R. 31
hate groups 80
health food 34
Hebb, D.O. 110
Heidegger, Martin 99
Heineken 1
Helena Rubinstein 38
Helms, Jesse 139
Henry, Thierry 159
hierarchy: conservative social structure 73–4;
    prestige 83, 91; social class 13
hierarchy of effects 121, 123–6, 131
Higgins, E.T. 151
Hilgard, E. 108
Hitler, Adolf 35, 140, 141
Hobbes, Thomas 139
holidays 97, 117
Homans, George C. 67
homeostasis 110
Hovland, Carl 123, 132
Hugo Boss 60

Hull, C. 110, 111, 113
humour 132
Humphrey, N. 107–8
hypocrisy 152

id 166, 170
ideal types 77
identity: corporations 169; group membership
   81; Mary Douglas thesis 73, 76; Muslim
   88–9; products 39; reference groups 10;
   self-identity 73, 150; social 10, 39, 90
ideology 76, 77, 140, 153
illocutionary speech acts 143, 144
image: brand 39–40, 44, 53, 59–60, 63,
   66–7, 90; corporate 60
imitation 104, 181–2
implicit favourite model 62, 90
incidental learning 181, 194
income inequalities 13
India 34
individualism 37, 73, 74, 76
inequalities of income 13
Infiniti 79
influence 6, 23
information: accessibility 184; credibility 129,
   145–6, 148–9; positive/negative 179;
   preconceptions 179; validity 127
informational conformity 12, 126
instant gratification 111, 118, 178, 185,
   193
instrumental learning 103
internal shields 8, 14–20, 23
Internet 1–3, 136, 146
interpretation 32, 131, 135–6, 173, 182
interviews 164, 167, 168, 193
introversion 129–30
intuition 190–1, 195
involvement 125
Iococca, Lee 31
Isuzu 79
Italy 61
ITT 60

Jaguar 39
Janiszewski, C.A. 101
Japan 61
Johnson, Mark 142
journalism 37
Jung, Carl 167, 172

Kahneman, D. 151
Kammen, Michael 15
Kant, Immanuel 127
Kelly, George A. 17, 187
Kennedy, John F. 134, 149
Khrushchev, Nikita S. 134
Kim, W. Chan 64–5
King, Martin Luther 138, 145
Klein, Gary 139, 190
Koelling, Robert 107
Kohn, Melvin 13
Kraft 3
Kuhn, Deanna 18, 42
Kuhn, Thomas 44, 138

Lacoste 30
Laffer curve 138
Lakoff, George 142
Langer, Suzanne 37–8
language: evaluative 7; new concepts 136;
   perlocutionary speech act 143–4; self-
   knowledge 106; subcultures 53, 67–8, 90;
   vernacular 41; words 11, 29, 32, 52, 136,
   137; *see also* metaphors
latent learning 112
Lattin, James M. 113
Law, Andrew Bonar 43
law of effect 102, 107, 109–10
law of social impact 129
Lear, Jonathan 171
learning: behaviourism 104, 105, 108;
   conditioned 101, 104; implicit 179;
   incidental 181, 194; instrumental 103;
   latent 112; new concepts 136, 162;
   reinforcement 114; theories of 55, 121,
   123–6; unconscious 181–2
Leary, Mark R. 58
LeDoux, Joseph 124, 181, 186
Lenin, Vladimir Ilyich 41
Lévi-Strauss, Claude 67
Levitin, Teresa A. 78
Lewicka, Maria 63
Lewis, Oscar 43
Lexus 1, 39
Leymore, V.L. 67
lifestyle 67, 68, 91; marketing 69; Mary
   Douglas thesis 71, 73, 74, 75; VALS 2
   system 68–71
likeability heuristic 60, 124, 158–9, 173

Lippmann, Walter 138
literature 135–6
Living Omnimedia 61
Locke, John 139
locutionary speech acts 143
logic 41–2, 46, 137, 163
logo 62, 67
logos 46
Love, Fiona 156
loyalty 6, 40, 76, 169
Lupia, Arthur 81
luxury shopping 97–8

Maalouf, Amin 73
McClelland, D.C. 184, 185
McCloskey, Donald N. 142
McDonald's 22, 38
McGuire, William 20
MacIntyre, Alasdair 37
McKinsey 4, 11–12
McLuhan, Marshall 142
magic 128
Malcolm, Norman 108
Malinowski, Bronislaw 128
Mao Tse Tung 17
Margalit, Avishai 27, 57, 80–1, 152, 177
market growth 4–5
market research 156–7, 158
marketing: adaptive unconscious 165;
  attitudes measurement 18; behaviourism
  112, 114; brand image 90; destination 97,
  117; emotional appeals 52; expectations
  113; lifestyle 69; metaphors 140;
  one-to-one 45; perspectives 53;
  psychoanalytic psychology 167; Renault
  Clio campaign 157–8; self-persuasion 27;
  target audience 23
Marlboro 10, 115
Marquis, D. 108
Mars, Gerald 77
Mars, Valerie 77
Mason, Jeff 143, 144
material reward 7, 8
Mathlouthi, Tawfik 80, 88
Mauborgne, Renée 64–5
Mauss, Marcel 82
Maxwell House 72
Mayhew, Leon H. 66, 81, 82, 83, 145
Mazda 55

meaning: brand associations 58–9;
  encoding/decoding 135; sense-meaning
  37–8, 57, 58; symbolic 5, 38, 39, 40, 53,
  90; unconscious 167
Mecca Cola 80, 88–9, 116
Medicare 137
Medtronic 3
memory 80–1, 177
Mercedes-Benz 27, 34, 38
message content 149–50
message repetition 131–2, 163
metaphors: changing perspectives 30;
  persuasive communication 139–42, 143,
  144, 145, 160, 163; Zaltman Metaphor
  Elicitation Technique 172, 173, 193
Meyer, Michel 44
Midas 79
middle classes 13
Middle East 80, 88, 89
Miller Brewing 3–4
Miller, Warren E. 78
Milosevic, Slobodan 16
Modell, Arnold H. 176
Molson 80
Monsanto 14
Montgomery, H. 62–3
moods 95, 96–7, 117, 132
Moore, Laurence 127
moral principles 35, 36
motivation: adaptive unconscious 184–5;
  brand conceptions 37; conviction/action
  relationship 175; emotions influence on 27;
  operant conditioning 107; research 165,
  167–8, 169, 170; reversal theory 93, 95;
  self-esteem 71; unconscious 113, 164,
  166–7, 171, 184–6, 192–3, 194
Mowrer, O.H. 183
music 40–1, 60
Muslim identity 88–9
Muslim Up 88
My Big Fat Greek Wedding 57–8
Myers, David G. 191

names 57, 58
narratives 31–2
natural rights 35, 36
negative advertising 79, 193
negative associations 58, 60–1, 63, 90
negative reference groups 11, 38

negative reinforcement 103, 114, 118
Neitz, Mary Jo 127
Nescafé Gold Blend 160–2
Nestlé 104
networks 12
neuroscience 172, 181
neuroticism 130
Nietzsche, F.W. 17
Nike 58, 60, 79
Nisbett, R.E. 177, 186–7
Nissan 17
Nixon, Richard 139, 149
norms: anti-smoking 130; cultural 68; group
    11, 12; informational validity 127; social
    10, 36, 45, 63, 65, 83, 127; subcultures
    68
nostalgia 40, 59, 87
not-for-profit advertising 33, 152
novelty: curiosity for 29, 66, 119; lack of 65;
    reversal theory 116; 'shock' advertising 4;
    word-of-mouth communication 58; see also
    creativity

obsessionality 130
Ogilvy, David 150, 169
Oliver Sweeney 2, 94
Omega 1, 84
one-to-one marketing 45
operant conditioning 15, 44, 100, 102–12,
    113, 114, 181
Oxo family 86–7

P&G 72
Panerai 85
Papson, Steven 66
paradigms 44, 138
paratelic mode 95–9, 116–17
Park, Robert L. 16
partial reinforcement 111–12, 118
Pascal, Blaise 165, 186
pathos 46
Pavlovian (classical) conditioning 100–1, 102,
    105, 112, 175
peer group affirmation 8
Pennington, N. 31
Pepsi 68
perception: brands 37, 59; consumer
    perspectives 17; emotional reactions 32;
    informational validity 127; restructuring

136–7; of risk 125, 145; subliminal 166; see
    also self-perception theory
Perelman, Chaim 138
performance utterances 143
peripheral routes to persuasion 101, 126–7,
    130
perlocutionary speech acts 143–4
personal construct theory 17–18
personal identity 73, 76
personality: adaptive unconscious 180; brand
    39, 169; inventories 129–30
perspectives 8–9, 14–20, 25, 43–5, 55;
    marketing 53; persuasive communications
    132, 162, 163; relevance 136–7; rhetoric
    137, 138; see also beliefs; values
perspectivism 20
persuasive communication approach 121,
    130–50
persuasive definition 35
Petty, Richard 126, 127, 128, 129
Pfizer 57
phenomenology 93
Philip Morris 144
photographs 33
physicalism 101
'picking behaviour' 180–1
pictures 33, 40, 52
Pilkington Glass 46, 47
Plato 123, 138, 143
Polanyi, Michael 127–8
political advertising 28, 138, 149
politicians 7, 31, 73, 134, 147
politics: art of political agitation 36; brand
    loyalty relationship 76; election posters
    139; emotive language 32–3; Mecca Cola
    88, 89; negative advertising 79; political
    cultures 76; public interest 81; rhetoric
    129; rights 36; US political advertising 28,
    138, 149; voting behaviour 77, 81
Pop, Iggy 60
Pope, Alexander 43
populism 73
Porsche 79
positive reference groups 11
positivism 20, 101
postmodernism 37, 46, 126
poverty 33, 81
power 57, 184, 194
preconceptions 179

prediction 7, 20–1
preferences 77, 78, 132, 190
prejudice 29, 183
presentation 66, 149–50
prestige 38, 57, 63, 83, 91, 160, 162
prices 5, 39, 62, 113
Priestley, J.B. 41
primacy of affect 124
principle-orientation 69–70
print advertising 149
Proctor, Robert N. 133
product placement 1
products: association 57, 60; convergence
    4–5; costs 119; differentiation 68;
    parallelism 4, 5; radiation 5; reinforcement
    114; social identity 39; see also brand; case
    studies
projective techniques 165, 168, 181, 184,
    185, 192
propaganda 19, 32, 135, 136, 185
Prosch, Harry 127–8
protection frames 96, 97
protest 71–2, 73, 79, 80, 88, 91, 116
psychiatry 169–70
psychoanalytic psychology 165, 166–71,
    192–3; see also Freud
psychographics 68–71
psychology: apperception 32; associationism
    55, 101; experimental 55, 188; folk 110;
    Gestalt 61–2, 63; persuasive approaches 21;
    psychoanalytic 165, 166–71, 192–3;
    tripartite system of the mind 123; see also
    behaviourism; cognitive psychology
psychotherapy 16
psychoticism 130
Publicis 156
purposive behaviourism 112, 113, 114

qualitative approaches 45
quantitative approaches 45
questions 144–5, 164
Quine, W.V.O. 44–5

R&D (research & development) 4
racial discrimination 10
racial equality 153
radiation 5
Ramachandran, V.S. 42, 128
rational choice theory 25, 32, 130, 175

rationality: cultural preferences 78; elaboration
    likelihood model of persuasion 127;
    integration with emotional appeals 25, 45;
    logic 42; logos 46; psychoanalytic psychology
    167; social norms 36; see also reason
rationalization 166–7, 171, 180, 186
Rawls, John 78
Ray, Michael L. 125
Reagan, Ronald 31, 41, 66, 77, 137, 138,
    140, 147
reason 37, 42, 45, 108, 127; see also rationality
reciprocity 1–3, 82–3, 134
Redfield, Robert 43
Reeves, Rosser 149
reference groups 8, 9, 10–12, 23; drug-taking
    37; persuasive communication 132, 163;
    status-orientation 69; see also groups
reflective equilibrium 78
reframing 28, 52
reinforcement 63, 102–5, 113–14, 118–19; as
    change agent 15; critiques of operant
    conditioning 107, 108, 109, 110; partial
    111–12, 118
rejection 133
relational behaviourism 112, 113–14
relationship marketing 45
relaxation 63, 93, 95, 116, 117
religion: belief systems 42; coercion 9;
    conversions 127; evangelists 129; motives
    185; subcultures 10
Renault Clio 155–60
repeated exposure effect see exposure effect,
    repeated
repetition of message 131–2, 163
reputation 45, 145, 146, 148
reputational capital 6, 61, 146, 164
research & development see R&D
response: associations 55; generalization 105,
    118; operant conditioning 102–3, 105, 106,
    107, 108, 109; Pavlovian conditioning
    100–1, 102; relational behaviourism 114
reversal theory 63, 93–9, 116–17
rewards 7, 8, 103, 109, 114, 119
Rheingold Brewing Company 59
rhetoric 137–44, 163; Aristotle 42, 45–6;
    indirect persuasion 137; postmodernist
    claims 126; of presentation 66; TV
    evangelists 129; war propaganda 32
Rice, Condoleezza 152

Richards, Barry 169
Richards, I.A. 135–6
Riesman, D. 76
rights 35–6
risk: minimization 133; perceived 125, 145
Robinson, Daniel N. 111
Rokeach, Milton 36
Rolls-Royce 38
Roosevelt, Franklin D. 33, 140, 144
Rosenberg, Alexander 110
Royal Caribbean 60
Rozin, Paul 59
rubbish theory 131
Ryle, Gilbert 184

Said, Edward 29
St. Joseph 59
sales promotions 126
Sartre, Jean-Paul 31
satiation 97, 111
Scheibe, Karl E. 19, 66
Schiffer, Fredric 178
Schwartz, Tony 28
Scientology 128
Scotland 79
Sea & Ski 59
Searle, John 177
Sears 59
Second World War 34, 41
segmentation 13
self 166, 180; *see also* ego
self-confidence 18, 19, 20, 23, 39, 96
self-esteem: attractive sources 147;
    enhancement 163; group solidarity 91; high
    susceptibility to persuasion 18; VALS 2
    classification 71; values 19, 20, 23
self-identity 73, 150
self-image: adaptive unconscious 192, 194;
    attractive sources 147; cognitive dissonance
    151, 152; Freudian psychology 166;
    perlocutionary speech act 144; values
    19–20, 23
self-orientation 69–71
self-parody 135, 161
self-perception theory 188–9, 192
self-persuasion 27, 134–5, 150, 194
self-presentation theory 153
self-serving error 153
semiotics 172

Sennett, Richard 81
sense-meaning 37–8, 57, 58
sensory impressions 121
serial advertising 104
sermons 43
services 98–9
sex 59
sexuality 170
shaping 105
shared memory 80–1
'shock' advertising 3–4, 6
shopping 97–8
signs 37–8
Silk Cut 26
Simmons, Annette 31
Simon, Herbert 129
Simonson, Itamar 62
Simpson, D. 161
Simpson, O.J. 144
sincerity 6, 50
Singer, Peter 36
Skinner, B.F. 99–100, 102, 104–6, 107,
    108–9, 114
slogans 39
Smart, J.J.C. 134–5
Smith, Murray 28
smoking 25–7, 114–16, 130, 148, 152
Sniderman, Paul M. 78
social attachments 8, 9–14, 15, 19, 23, 55;
    informational validity 127; persuasive
    communication 132, 163; target audience
    perspective 44
social class 8, 9, 12–14, 23; persuasive
    communication 132, 163; self-image 19;
    subcultures 10; *see also* status
social conformity 12, 126
social constructionism 143
social differentiation 13
social groups 12, 78; *see also* reference groups
social identity 10, 39, 90
social impact, law of 129
social norms 10, 36, 45, 63, 65, 83, 127
social proof 146–7
social relationships 39, 82
social science: context 20–1, 24; discredited
    theories 131–2; Freudian influence 170;
    metaphors 140; perspectives 43, 138;
    quantitative approaches 45; researchers 43;
    sensitizing concepts 21, 24, 136

social trends 86, 87
socialism 36
socialization 114
sociology 176
Socrates 10, 42, 143
solidarity: associations 63, 80–3; Bombardier
    advertisement 56; brand representation 91;
    emotional appeals 45; marketing
    communications 164; Mecca Cola 89
Solomon, Michael R. 69
source expertise 128, 164
speciesism 36
Spencer, Lady Diana, Princess of Wales 72,
    148
Sperber, Dan 130
Spice Girls, The 148
spin 28, 137
sports sponsorship 1
Stanford Research Institute (SRI) 69
statistical evidence 30, 52
status 13, 38, 57, 83; see also prestige
status-orientation 69, 70
Stebbing, Susan 141
Stella Artois 48–52
stereotypes 157, 183, 184
Stewart, Martha 61
stimuli: associations 55; discriminative 103–4,
    108, 109, 118; generalization 105; operant
    conditioning 103–4, 105, 106, 108, 109,
    113; Pavlovian conditioning 100–1, 102,
    117–18; primacy of affect 124; relational
    behaviourism 112, 113–14; visual 61
stories 31–2, 52
structural phenomenology 93
subconscious 166
subcultures 10, 37, 53, 67–8, 90
subliminal perception 166
superego 166, 170
superstition 105, 128
Sutherland, Stuart 129
symbolism: colours 149; Freudian psychology
    167; logic 41; Mecca Cola 88, 89; meta-
    phors 141, 145; repeated exposure 67; social
    bonds 57; Stella Artois commercials 51–2;
    symbolic meaning 5, 38, 39, 40, 53, 90
symbols 38, 40, 53, 57, 64; cultural
    opposition 68; political advertising 139;
    rhetoric of presentation 66; valued 90
synergy 98, 117

tabulae rasae 17
target audiences: adaptive unconscious 193,
    194; beliefs 132–3, 164; elaboration
    likelihood model of persuasion 126;
    emotions 28; external/internal shields 8–9;
    hierarchy of effects model 123;
    identification with 41; informational
    credibility 129, 164; marketing 23;
    perspectives 15, 44, 53, 136–7, 162, 163;
    self-perception theory 189; self-persuasion
    27; 'shock' ads 4; solidarity 81; subcultures
    67; symbols 40; television advertising 3;
    values 37; see also consumers
TAT see Thematic Apperception Test
technology: product convergence 4–5;
    R&D 4
teenagers 3, 98
television advertising: Gold Blend 160–2;
    Oxo family 87–8; Renault Clio 155–60;
    Stella Artois 48–52; threats to 1;
    unprofitability 3
telic mode 95–9, 116–17
tension 96–7, 117
terminology 29
terrorism 134–5
Thayer, Robert E. 96
Thematic Apperception Test (TAT) 168,
    184–5, 192
thinking 121, 123
Thompson, J. Walter 100
Thompson, Michael 131–2
thought networks 55
Times Literary Supplement, The 29
TiVo 1, 3
Tolman, E.C. 100, 112–14
Toulmin, Stephen 21
Toyota 30
transformational advertising 134
trust 6, 23, 146, 164
truth 6, 42, 128, 150
Tversky, A. 151

uncertainty: attraction of 66; brand image 53;
    confusion over values 77; groups 128;
    nostalgic appeals 59; rhetoric 145, 163;
    symbolic logic 41
unconscious: adaptive 165–6, 170, 173–4,
    177–91, 192, 193–5; brain activity 175–7;
    dual processing 191; Freudian 165, 166–7,

170, 171, 174, 181–3; motivation 113,
164, 166–7, 171, 184–6, 192–3, 194;
Zaltman Metaphor Elicitation Technique
171–2, 173
United Airlines 40
United Fruit 60
United Kingdom: income inequalities 13;
middle classes 13; *see also* Great Britain
United Nations 35
United States: Anglophobia 15–16; anti-
smoking campaign 130; brand familiarity
63; Bush speech 152; class divisions 13;
comparative advertising 72; country image
61; fair trade 11; genetically modified foods
14; German view of 15; hatred against 80,
88; income inequalities 13; Khomeini
description of 141; lack of solidarity 81;
Medicare 137; political advertising 138,
149; politicians 147; psychographics 70;
right-wing groups 80, 140; values 37, 64,
138; Vietnam War 33, 151
Universal Declaration of Human Rights 35

Valins, S. 153
VALS (Values and Lifestyles) 2 system 68–71
value systems 19, 64
values 5, 8–9, 19–20; American 37, 64, 138;
assimilation/contrast effects 163; association
63, 64–8, 90; attractiveness 147; brand
193; conflict in 152–3; consistency 77; core
44; cultural 9, 67–8, 78; egalitarianism 75;
elaboration likelihood model of persuasion
127; emotions 27, 30, 36–7, 53, 64–5,
149; influence definition 6; lifestyle 91;
Mary Douglas thesis 71; perspectives 14,
23, 43; persuasive communications 132,
163; psychographics 68–71; rationality 45;
social class 13; VALS 2 system 68–71; *see
also* attitudes; beliefs; perspectives
verbalization 121
Viagra 57, 58
Vickers, Brian 138

videos 1
Vietnam War 33, 151
visibility 3, 4, 8, 129
visual evidence 33, 52
visual metaphors 142, 172, 173, 193
voodoo science 16
voting behaviour 77

Wal-Mart 105
Wallace, George 147
war 32, 141
Warnock, Mary 36
Watson, J.B. 99, 100–1, 105, 108
Weber, Max 132
websites 1–3
Wegner, Daniel 174, 175, 178, 186
Wernick, A. 169
Wheatley, T. 178
Wildavsky, Aaron 76, 77
will to power 167
Williams, Bernard 175
Wilson, Deirdre 130
Wilson, Timothy D. 174, 177–83, 184,
185–92
Windex 39
Wittgenstein, Ludwig 171
women: domestic division of labour 73–4;
'liberated' 34; rights 36; *see also* gender
Woolton, Lord 41
word-of-mouth communication 4, 12, 57–8
words 11, 29, 32, 52, 136, 137
Wrangler 60

Zajonc, R.B. 67, 124
Zaltman, Gerald 171–3
Zaltman Metaphor Elicitation Technique
(ZMET) 165, 171–3, 193
Zamzam Cola 80, 89
ZMET *see* Zaltman Metaphor Elicitation
Technique
Zoellick, Robert B. 14
Zyman, Sergio 66